WEIGHT WATCHERS®
International Cookbook

Introduction by
JEAN NIDETCH

A PLUME BOOK
NEW AMERICAN LIBRARY
TIMES MIRROR
NEW YORK AND SCARBOROUGH, ONTARIO

Acknowledgments

The task of creating this book, selecting and testing the recipes, amassing and organizing the information dealing with the foods of the various countries, and of preparing and supervising the color photography was accomplished by many people who deserve special thanks. We gratefully express our appreciation to our dedicated staff, our publisher, and Nedda C. Anders and her staff for their tireless efforts in editing this cookbook.

FELICE LIPPERT
Vice-President—
Director of Food Research
Weight Watchers International

Copyright © 1977 by Weight Watchers International, Inc.

Library of Congress Catalog Card Number: 80-80067

PLUME TRADEMARK REG. U.S. PAT. OFF. AND FOREIGN COUNTRIES
REGISTERED TRADEMARK—MARCA REGISTRADA
HECHO EN BRATTLEBORO, VERMONT

SIGNET, SIGNET CLASSICS, MENTOR, PLUME, MERIDIAN and NAL BOOKS are published in the United States by The New American Library, Inc., 1633 Broadway, New York, New York 10019, in Canada by The New American Library of Canada, Limited, 81 Mack Avenue, Scarborough, Ontario M1L 1M8.

First Plume Printing, March, 1980

1 2 3 4 5 6 7 8 9

PRINTED IN THE UNITED STATES OF AMERICA

Contents

Introduction

What a joy it is for me to introduce this book to you! In traveling around the world to Weight Watchers classes, I've often had the pleasure of tasting the food specialties of different countries, prepared for me by members and friends familiar with our Food Plan. And just as often, I've wished I could share those delicious dishes with our many friends at home. Now my wish has come true.

Here is a gourmet taste-tour of the world's most scrumptious dishes, prepared our style. We've adapted the famous specialties of China, France, Italy, India, Mexico, Spain, and many other countries: 24 delicious cuisines! Enjoy savory soups, piquant appetizers, exotic entrees, unusual vegetables and salads, an array of fabulous desserts, and a host of "extras" you can snack on (in moderation!) without your waistline giving you away.

The dishes have come from a variety of sources. Nedda Anders and Felice Lippert have created and adapted many exciting recipes. Others were created or adapted by Weight Watchers chefs and home economists. Many other wonderful ideas came from our friends, both in this country and abroad. Whatever its source, almost every one of the recipes has been tested in Weight Watchers kitchens. This means that *you* can duplicate each mouth-watering dish in *your* kitchen.

You should find our recipe directions easy to follow, even if you haven't spent much time cooking, or have never cooked in our special style. The inspiring color photographs show that our foods look as delectable as they taste!

These splendid dishes from the world's great cuisines fit into our basic Food Plan. Therefore, the book may be used by Weight Watchers members. However, its value is not just for members, but for anyone who wishes to lose—or maintain—weight. In all cases, it is essential to realize that these exciting dishes are only part of an overall eating plan. They should be consumed with an awareness of the total amount of food appropriate for the day, and with a vigilant eye on portion control!

If you love good food . . . if you want to expand your culinary repertoire, without expanding your waistline . . . if you would like a collection of fabulous recipes done in our style . . . this is a book you should have.

And now, dear reader, I hope you will join us as we feast our way around the world.

Jean Nidetch

General Information

1. In any recipe for more than one serving, it is important to mix the ingredients well and, when serving, *to divide the mixture evenly*, so that each portion is the same size.

2. For those following the Weight Watchers Food Program, certain recipes will provide only part of a lunch or dinner. These recipes must be supplemented as required and have been marked with an asterisk.

3. Meat must be well trimmed, with all visible fat removed.

4. We use fruit fresh, frozen or canned with no sugar added. The canned fruit may be packed in its own juice or in a juice blend, or in water or packed with artificial sweetener.

5. The herbs used in these recipes are dried unless otherwise indicated.

6. Nonstick pans make it possible for you to cook without fat. Use pans manufactured with a nonstick surface, or spray an ordinary pan with a release agent, following directions on the aerosol can. Release agents with less than 2 calories per spray are acceptable.

7. In any recipe calling for bouillon or stock, you may use homemade chicken or homemade beef stock (see recipes below). To make bouillon, you may use instant broth and seasoning mixes, instant bouillon or bouillon cubes.

HOMEMADE CHICKEN STOCK

2 chicken carcasses	3 parsley sprigs
2 quarts water	1 garlic clove, crushed
1 rib celery with leaves, sliced	1 bay leaf
1 medium carrot, sliced	¼ teaspoon thyme
6 peppercorns	Salt to taste

Combine all ingredients in a kettle. Bring to a boil; lower heat. Simmer for 1½ hours. Strain to remove solids. Chill in refrigerator. When fat congeals on surface, skim off and discard. Divide into ¾-cup portions. Makes about 1 quart.

HOMEMADE BEEF STOCK

3	pounds beef bones	½ bunch parsley stems
2	ribs celery with leaves, cut up	10 peppercorns, crushed
4	ounces onion, quartered	2 cloves
2	medium carrots, sliced	1 bay leaf
4	quarts water	
2	canned medium tomatoes, chopped	

Place bones on a rack in a roasting pan. Place celery, onion and carrots in another pan. Roast both bones and vegetables for ½ hour or until browned, turning bones once. Place bones and vegetables in a kettle with remaining ingredients. Bring to a boil; lower heat. Simmer for 3 hours. Strain, discard solids. Chill in refrigerator. When fat congeals on surface, skim and discard. Divide into ¾-cup portions. Makes about 2 quarts.

In any recipe calling for Whipped Topping, use the recipe below.

WHIPPED TOPPING

¼ cup water	¼ teaspoon vanilla extract
1½ teaspoons unflavored gelatin	¼ cup chilled evaporated
Artificial sweetener to equal	skimmed milk
2 tablespoons sugar	

In small pan sprinkle gelatin over water; heat slowly stirring until gelatin dissolves. Pour into small mixing bowl; add artificial sweetener and vanilla; cool. Add chilled milk; beat at high speed until very thick. Cover and refrigerate. Makes 4 servings.

Your Microwave Oven

Many of our recipes can be done in your microwave oven. You will have to experiment with your unit and follow manufacturer's advice for timing, since there is no one standard that applies to all, but generally, you should allow about ¼ of the cooking time. That is, if our recipe suggests 16 minutes, allow 4 minutes in your microwave oven (or slightly less, since it's wiser to undercook than overcook). Please also note that our roasting procedures for beef, ham, lamb and pork require the use of a rack, so that you can lift cooked meat out of the fat which drains off into the pan. A plastic rack is available for use in the microwave oven.

Our kitchens tested a number of basic foods and have the following timing tips for you:

Baked apple (1 medium): Set in custard cup, cook 3 minutes; let stand several minutes. Makes 1 serving.

Baked fish fillets (1 pound): Cook 7 minutes; let stand several minutes. Makes 2 servings.

Baked potato (1 3-ounce): Make crosswise cut, cook 4 minutes; let stand 2 to 3 minutes. Makes 1 serving.

Roast beef (1 pound boneless): On plastic rack set in baking dish, cook 4 minutes; turn, cook 4 minutes more; let stand 10 to 15 minutes. Makes 2 servings.

Hamburger patty (6-ounce, 4-inch diameter): Coat with browning sauce. Place on plastic rack set in baking dish. Cover with paper towel. Cook 2 minutes; turn patty, cook 1 minute. Makes 1 serving.

Roast chicken (4 to 4½ pounds): On plastic rack set in baking dish, breast-side down, cook 7 minutes; turn breast-side up, cook 7 minutes, turn dish, cook another 7 minutes. Let stand 10 to 15 minutes. Remove skin. Weigh portions. Makes 6 servings.

Roast pork (1 pound): Rolled. On plastic rack set in baking dish, cook 6 minutes. Turn roast, cook 6 minutes more. Turn roast, cook 4 minutes. Let stand 10 to 15 minutes. Makes 2 servings.

Acorn Squash (1¼ pounds): Pierce skin in several places. Cook 4 to 6 minutes. Scoop out pulp and weigh 8 ounces. Makes 2 servings.

Slow Cookers

If you enjoy using this appliance, there's no reason why you can't adapt many of our recipes to its use. We're giving you a headstart on your own experiments with the following guidelines from our kitchen. See index for the recipes:

Chicken Marengo: Cook chicken, stock, herbs and spices on low for 6 to 7 hours. Add vegetables and extract and cook covered on high 30 to 40 minutes or until tomatoes are tender.

Chicken Cacciatore: After browning the chicken in skillet, cook with remaining ingredients in slow cooker covered on low 6 to 8 hours.

Navy Bean Soup: Multiply to serve 4. Combine all ingredients and cook covered on low 8 to 10 hours.

New England Baked Lima Beans: Divide recipe in half, to serve 4. Cook covered on low 8 to 10 hours.

Deviled Chicken Legs: Follow recipe but bake in slow cooker covered on low for 8 hours.

Apricot Brown Betty: Multiply to serve 16 (smaller amounts impractical). Combine apricots and bread in slow cooker. Top with mixture of remaining ingredients. Toss, cover, cook on high for 2½ hours.

Homemade Chicken Stock: In slow cooker, combine all ingredients, cover and cook on low for 12 hours. Strain and proceed as in basic recipe.

About Saccharin

The use of artificial sweeteners on the Weight Watchers Food Program has always been optional. Natural sweetness is available in the form of fruits, which we do permit on our eating plan. Your use of saccharin is completely optional, and we believe that the decision about using it should be made by you and your physician. If you decide against this product, we hope you'll enjoy the more than 600 saccharin-free recipes included in this book.

Africa

Cyril Connolly, the famous critic and author, once punned that a midday meal in South Africa consists mainly of the "cold table" which, he added, "covers a multitude of tins." The Dutch and British who settled here do indeed use lots of canned goods to provide a taste of homeland cooking but, in general, the food of this continent is far from dull. North African cuisine is pungent with peppers of every kind, from small red hot to large sweet green or red. Herbs and spices such as cinnamon, coriander, cumin, mint and thyme, a legacy of the Saracen invaders who swarmed across the deserts centuries ago from Syria and Arabia, are favorite seasonings. A typical tripe stew of Central Africa—made almost exactly the same way by the blacks of the West Indies—is hot and zesty with okra and thyme. So our collection of treats from Africa—rather than being bland and canned—is savory with spicery . . . a spiffy beginning for your slim-gourmet's tour of the world of international cooking.

MINTED TUNA PASTE*

A North African appetizer, it could become a complete luncheon entrée. For each serving, add 3 ounces cooked dried white beans seasoned with chili pepper, and ½ cup spinach (steamed in chicken or beef bouillon and well drained). Another variation: omit the bread and pile the paste into slender cupped endive leaves. Serve chilled.

8 ounces canned, drained tuna or other cooked fish, flaked
4 teaspoons vegetable oil
1½ teaspoons chopped fresh mint leaves
½ teaspoon nutmeg
½ teaspoon (or more to taste) Worcestershire or lemon juice
4 slices enriched white bread

Mash together all ingredients except bread to make a paste. Serve on bread. Makes 4 servings.

CONGO CHICKEN AND OKRA (Fetri Detsi)

4 boned and skinned chicken breasts, 6 to 8 ounces each
4 ounces onion, chopped
1 teaspoon salt
2 medium tomatoes, peeled
2 to 4 hot green chili peppers, seeded, or ½ teaspoon crushed red pepper
2-inch slice fresh ginger root
4 cups water
12 ounces fresh or frozen okra, sliced
¼ cup tomato paste
2 cups cooked enriched rice (optional)

Place chicken and onion in a heavy saucepan or Dutch oven. Sprinkle with salt. Using the fine blade of a grinder, chop tomato, chili peppers and ginger (or chop very fine in blender, food processor fitted with steel blade, or by hand). Add mixture to chicken. Pour in water and bring to a boil. Reduce heat and simmer, covered, for about 20 minutes or until chicken is barely tender. Add okra. Stir in tomato paste. Continue simmering, uncovered, until chicken and okra are tender. Place each breast on an individual dinner plate. Divide vegetable and liquid evenly and pour over chicken breast. Serve over ½ cup rice if desired. Makes 4 servings.

MEAT AND POTATOES, BOER STYLE (Bobotie)

8 ounces cooked ground beef
4 ounces onion, chopped
1 teaspoon curry powder
2 medium apricots, peeled, pitted and chopped
1 medium tomato, peeled and chopped
2 slices enriched white bread, made into crumbs
½ cup evaporated skimmed milk
Salt and pepper to taste
1 bay leaf
½ cup tomato puree
1 packet instant beef broth and seasoning mix
Browning sauce (optional)
1 teaspoon chopped fresh parsley

Place beef in a mixing bowl; lightly brown onions in a nonstick pan and add to beef with curry powder, apricots, tomato, bread and milk. Mix well. Season to taste. Shape into a loaf, place bay leaf on top and wrap in aluminum foil. Bake in 375° F. oven for 35 minutes or until firm. Heat tomato puree; add broth mix and browning sauce as desired. Divide loaf equally and serve half of the sauce over each portion. Sprinkle with parsley. Makes 2 servings.

TRIPE STEW

Africa is the homeland of America's soul food cooking and this kind of stew is common to both countries. Twelve ounces of cooked beef cut in 1-inch squares could replace an equal amount of tripe. Then cook the beef and tripe together.

1½ pounds precooked tripe, cut in 1-inch squares
Salt to taste
Water
4 cups fresh collard greens or spinach, washed, stemmed and finely chopped
8 ounces onions
2 medium tomatoes
2 hot green or red chili peppers, stemmed and seeded
½ teaspoon nutmeg (optional)
4 ounces enriched dry cornmeal, prepared according to package directions

Place tripe and salt in a large saucepan. Add enough water to cover. Bring to a boil; reduce heat to medium; cover and cook 45 minutes or until tripe is very tender. Just before meat is ready, heat 1 cup salted water in a medium saucepan. Add collard greens or spinach; cover and cook over medium heat about 5 minutes or until tender. Drain and discard liquid. Add greens to tripe mixture. Chop onions, tomatoes and peppers very fine and combine in a large nonstick skillet. Heat, stirring occasionally, until most of the liquid from the tomatoes is evaporated, and flavors blend. Add to tripe mixture; stir to combine. Add nutmeg, if desired, and stir. Simmer for 1 hour uncovered. Drain and reserve liquid. Divide meat, vegetables and cornmeal into 4 equal portions. Measure liquid and pour ¼ of the liquid over each portion. Makes 4 servings.

COUSCOUS

This thick meaty stew, rich with vegetables, grains and legumes, is served throughout Africa. Wheat is the grain most often mentioned in American cookbooks, but couscous made with corn is traditional in Africa. Our version uses hominy grits, a corn product. Couscous can be made ahead and reheated just before serving. If hominy grains are lumpy, rub them between your fingers until they separate, then steam as directed.

24 ounces cooked dried chick peas	6 ribs celery
12 ounces cooked frankfurters	6 sprigs parsley
3 cups sliced zucchini	⅛ teaspoon turmeric
3 cups sliced Swiss chard or cabbage	⅛ teaspoon red pepper
2 cups carrots, cut in chunks	1 cup beef bouillon
2 cups turnips, cut in chunks	4½ cups cooked enriched hominy grits
6 ounces sliced onion	¼ to ½ teaspoon cinnamon
	¼ teaspoon whole cloves

Place chick peas, franks, zucchini, Swiss chard, carrots, turnips, onion, celery, parsley, turmeric and red pepper in bottom of couscousiere or heavy pot. Add beef bouillon and enough water to barely cover. Combine cooked hominy grits with cinnamon and cloves, and put into the top of the couscousiere or a steamer or colander lined with cheesecloth. Cover pan and steam 30 minutes or until vegetables are tender and grits have absorbed the various flavors. No steam should escape from the pot; to insure this, layers of cheesecloth are sometimes used between the steamer and its cover. Serve the grits on a large platter with a mound of vegetables and the frankfurters. Makes 6 servings.

SKEWERED PORK, FRUIT AND VEGETABLE (Sosaties)

An Arabic-style recipe adapted by the South African Dutch.

1½ pounds pork loin or fillet, cut in 1-inch pieces
1½ medium green peppers, cut in 1-inch pieces
15 cherry tomatoes
¾ medium pineapple, cut in 1-inch pieces
3 ounces onion, chopped fine
½ cup water
¼ cup white vinegar
½ teaspoon salt
½ teaspoon curry powder
¼ teaspoon turmeric
¼ teaspoon paprika
¼ teaspoon pepper
¾ cup tomato puree
Browning sauce (optional)
1½ cups cooked enriched rice
3 large skewers

Place pork, peppers, tomatoes, pineapple and onions in large mixing bowl. Add water, vinegar, salt, curry, turmeric, paprika and pepper. Mix well and marinate for 4 hours. Divide first 4 ingredients into 3 equal portions and thread alternately on skewers. Broil on a rack 4 inches from heat, 12 to 15 minutes, turning frequently until meat is cooked. Pour marinade in a saucepan; add tomato puree and cook until thick; add browning sauce as desired. Place each skewer on ½ cup of rice; divide sauce into 3 equal portions and serve over meat and rice. Makes 3 servings.

RICE SALAD

Serve as a separate course. Cook the rice so grains are separate, not mushy. If necessary, fluff them with a fork or separate by rinsing quickly in colander.

2 cups cold cooked brown rice
1 cup chopped fresh parsley
8 ounces diced scallions
¼ to ½ cup chopped fresh mint
¼ cup vegetable oil
¼ cup lemon juice
Salt, pepper and cumin to taste
4 medium tomatoes, chopped
8 radishes, sliced
1 head romaine lettuce, quartered

In wooden salad bowl combine rice with parsley, scallions, mint, oil, lemon juice, and seasonings. Chill. Just before serving, toss well. Add tomatoes and radishes; serve over romaine lettuce. Makes 4 servings.

MANGO AND PINEAPPLE SALAD

Two sweet peppers can replace the hot red peppers if you prefer a milder salad.

½ fresh medium pineapple, peeled
2 small ripe mangoes, peeled and seeded
1 medium banana, peeled

2 fresh hot red peppers, seeds removed, and finely diced
¼ cup vinegar
⅛ teaspoon salt
Watercress sprigs

Cut pineapple, mangoes and bananas into ¾-inch pieces. In salad bowl combine peppers, vinegar and salt. Add cut fruit, mixing well. Chill for 1 hour. Garnish with crisp watercress sprigs and serve as side dish for roast meat or poultry. Makes 8 servings.

Australia and New Zealand

Australia and New Zealand, its next-door neighbor, were colonized by the English, who also transplanted English customs and eating patterns. Morning and afternoon teatimes, double breakfasts, and after-dinner savories, really meals in themselves, are habitual.

Yet for all its British roots, the food in these countries down under the equator has its own very distinctive quality. New recipes have developed from the tastes of Asian and non-British Europeans, and from the abundance of exotic fruits, vegetables, and Pacific Ocean fish and shellfish. In our sampling, you'll find such authentic specialties as barbecued pork chops with a spiced fruit topping and such typical desserts as Pavlova. There are many other "down under" treats you can feast on at home while you get your weight down.

"CREAM" OF CHICKEN SOUP*

Trace this back to the English, the great settlers in this part of the world.

2 tablespoons imitation (or diet) margarine
2 slices enriched white bread, made into crumbs
4 cups chicken bouillon

¾ cup evaporated skimmed milk
8 ounces cooked or canned chicken, shredded
Salt, pepper and minced chives

Melt margarine in top of double boiler over water. Stir in bread crumbs and bouillon; slowly add evaporated milk; cook over boiling water until smooth and thickened. Add chicken; season to taste with salt and pepper. Serve topped with chives. Makes 4 servings.

CHICKEN CURRY SOUP: Add ½ teaspoon curry powder to melted margarine.

"CREAM" OF LETTUCE SOUP

3 cups water
1 tablespoon dehydrated onion flakes
1 teaspoon dehydrated bell pepper flakes

1 teaspoon chopped fresh parsley
4 packets instant beef broth and seasoning mix
1 quart shredded lettuce
1 cup skim milk

In saucepan, heat water to boiling; stir in onion, green pepper, parsley and beef broth mix. Add lettuce; simmer 15 minutes. Add milk; heat. Makes 4 servings.

PINEAPPLE FRENCH TOAST

Fruit is plentiful in New Zealand as are members with a sweet tooth, so this is a favorite eye-opener.

1 medium egg
¼ teaspoon cinnamon, divided

¼ cup canned crushed pineapple, no sugar added
1 slice raisin bread

In a shallow dish, beat the egg and ⅛ teaspoon cinnamon. Drain juice from pineapple into egg mixture; beat again. Prick both sides of bread with a fork. Soak bread in egg mixture, turning several times until as much egg mixture as possible is absorbed. Carefully transfer to a nonstick baking sheet. Combine drained pineapple and remaining ⅛ teaspoon cinnamon with any leftover egg mixture. Spread on top of bread. Bake at 400°F. for 20 minutes. Makes 1 serving.

BARBECUE WITH CHUCK WAGON SAUCE

Australians like the free and easy camaraderie and informality of this kind of meal. It is easy on the hostess too because most of the work is done the day before.

3 pounds well-trimmed boneless beef roast (use chuck or round or other inexpensive cut), about 2½-inches thick	Chuck Wagon Sauce (recipe follows)

Put roast on a rack in a roasting pan; cover top with foil and bake in slow oven (300°F.) for 2 hours. Remove foil and continue baking until roast is done and brown. Let roast cool, then refrigerate overnight. The next day, combine the ingredients for the sauce and cook 20 to 30 minutes. Meanwhile, shred the beef roast into string-like pieces. Add to the sauce in pan and simmer gently for at least one hour. Watch pan and stir as necessary. For longer periods, set saucepan on asbestos pad over low heat. Can also be simmered in casserole in 300°F. oven or over a charcoal fire, placed to receive only moderate heat from bed of coals. Add more water as necessary to keep sauce from drying out. Makes 6 servings.

Chuck Wagon Sauce

¾ cup tomato puree	¼ cup vinegar
¾ cup water	1 teaspoon paprika
1 tablespoon dehydrated onion flakes	1 garlic clove, minced
	2 teaspoons dry mustard
1 tablespoon Worcestershire	1 teaspoon chili powder

Mix ingredients and simmer slowly together in covered saucepan at stove or at side of the grill about 20 to 30 minutes. Makes 6 servings.

BILLABONG BEEF RING

16 ounces frozen peas
2 envelopes unflavored gelatin
¼ cup cold water
8 slices canned pineapple, cut in
half, with ½ cup juice, no
sugar added

1½ pounds cooked diced beef
12 radishes, cut into "roses"

Cook peas in a minimum amount of salted water; drain; set aside to cool. In saucepan, sprinkle gelatin over water; add pineapple juice and heat over very low flame to dissolve gelatin. Coat a 7-inch ring mold (rinsed in water) with one-third of the gelatin and arrange 8 pineapple halves in mold. Refrigerate until gelatin becomes set. (Keep remaining gelatin in warm place.) Put cooled, drained peas on pineapple layer; spread evenly. Pour in one-third of the warm gelatin. Let set in refrigerator. When this layer is set, combine remaining warm gelatin with meat and spoon evenly into mold. Cover with 6 pineapple halves and let set. When ready, dip mold into hot water, put serving plate on top, reverse quickly. Serve with lettuce border and 2 remaining halves of pineapple. Fill center with radishes. Makes 4 servings.

NEW ZEALAND MUTTON PIE

A fine little dinner dish, prepared this way.

2 medium tomatoes, sliced
12 ounces cooked mutton (or
lamb or beef), sliced thin
6 ounces peeled, cooked potatoes,
sliced thin

Salt and pepper to taste
¾ cup beef bouillon

In pie pan make a layer of sliced tomatoes, add a layer of cold mutton, and a layer of sliced potatoes. Repeat layers. Season each layer with salt and pepper. Pour in beef bouillon. Bake at 350°F. about 30 minutes or until bubbly and hot. Serve immediately. Makes 2 servings.

COLONIAL ROAST BABY LAMB WITH MINT SAUCE

1 boned and trimmed leg of lamb, about 4 pounds net
½ lemon
Salt and pepper to taste
½ cup chicken or beef bouillon
Mint Sauce (recipe follows)
Garnish: Cherry tomatoes and fresh mint sprigs

Rub lamb with lemon and sprinkle with salt and pepper. Place lamb on a rack in roasting pan. Insert meat thermometer in center. Roast in 300° to 325°F. oven following the chart below. Baste occasionally with bouillon. Remove from oven and let roast stand 15 minutes at room temperature to make carving easier. Serve 6-ounce portions, with Mint Sauce accompaniment and garnish. Makes about 8 servings.

	Meat Thermometer	*Minutes per pound*
Rare	140°F.	25 to 30
Medium	160°F.	30 to 35
Well	170° to 180°F.	35 to 40

Mint Sauce

½ cup water
½ cup white vinegar
⅓ cup chopped fresh mint

Place water, vinegar and mint in saucepan; bring slowly to a boil. Remove from heat. Serve with Roast Lamb. Makes 8 servings.

ZESTY CHICKEN-LIVER ROLLUPS

1 pound chicken livers, cut in thirds, rinsed quickly with boiling water and dried
½ cup sliced mushrooms
2 ounces sliced onion
¾ teaspoon salt
Dash pepper
8 lettuce leaves

In nonstick covered pan, cook chicken livers, mushrooms and onion until tender. Uncover and let juices cook down. Turn into chopping bowl and chop fine. Add salt and pepper. Blend well; cool. Divide mixture into 8 lettuce leaves. Fold in sides and roll up leaves as in egg rolls. Serve with flaps underneath. Makes 2 servings.

BARBECUED PORK CHOPS WITH SPICED FRUIT SAUCE

Meats are often cooked with fruit; hundreds of different varieties grow in a climate that includes a tropical north and a temperate south.

2 well-trimmed center-cut pork chops, 10 ounces each
Salt and pepper to taste

1 garlic clove, peeled and cut
Spiced Fruit Sauce (recipe follows)

Trim off fat; lightly season and rub with garlic. Barbecue or broil on a rack, four inches from source of heat for 10 to 15 minutes or until pork is done with no trace of pink showing either in meat or juices when pork is cut; turn chops several times. Serve with sauce. Makes 2 servings.

Spiced Fruit Sauce

½ cup orange juice
¼ cup tomato puree
1 teaspoon white wine vinegar

1 teaspoon dry mustard
Dash cinnamon
Browning sauce (optional)

Combine all ingredients in saucepan. Place over heat and simmer 10 minutes to blend flavors. Divide equally into two portions and serve hot with chops. Makes 2 servings.

SARDINE SALAD WELLINGTON

1 pound 2 ounces peeled potatoes
12 ounces canned drained sardines
2 medium cucumbers, peeled and diced
1 medium sweet green pepper, seeded and chopped
6 ounces onion, chopped
3 tablespoons chopped fresh parsley
Lettuce leaves

¼ cup vegetable oil
¼ cup vinegar
½ teaspoon salt
⅛ teaspoon black pepper
3 medium hard-cooked eggs, chopped
3 medium hard-cooked eggs, halved
Capers, rinsed

Cut potatoes in halves, cover with salted boiling water and cook until potatoes are tender, about 30 minutes. Drain, cool, and cut in ½-inch dice. Lightly mash half of the sardines and combine with potato, cucumber, pepper, onion and parsley. Line a salad bowl with lettuce leaves. Add sardine mixture. Mix oil, vinegar, salt, pepper and chopped hard-cooked eggs. Sprinkle over sardines. Garnish with remaining whole sardines, hard-cooked egg halves and capers. Makes 6 servings.

TOMATO PIE

4 slices enriched white bread, made into soft crumbs
1 tablespoon chopped fresh parsley
1 teaspoon chopped fresh thyme
¼ teaspoon chopped fresh marjoram
4 ounces onion, chopped
Salt and pepper to taste
Juice of 1 lemon
4 ripe medium tomatoes, peeled and cut in thick slices

Mix bread crumbs, chopped herbs, onion, salt, pepper and lemon juice. Put a layer of tomato slices into an ovenproof pie dish; cover with a layer of seasoned bread crumbs, then repeat tomato layer, and finish with bread crumbs. Bake covered in moderate (350°F.) oven for 20 to 25 minutes. Makes 4 servings.

SUNSHINE CARROTS

4 cups carrots, sliced about 1-inch thick
2 small oranges, peeled and diced (reserve juice, about ½ cup)
¼ teaspoon salt
¼ teaspoon ginger
4 teaspoons imitation (or diet) margarine

Cook carrots in boiling salted water until just tender; 15 to 20 minutes. Combine orange juice, salt and ginger in small saucepan. Boil 1 minute. Stir in orange dice. Pour over hot carrots, tossing to coat evenly. Remove from heat. Add 1 teaspoon margarine to each serving. Makes 4 servings.

PINEAPPLE SURPRISE

Orange Sherbet (recipe follows)
1 ripe medium pineapple
2 medium bananas
2 tablespoons brandy or rum extract

Prepare sherbet. Cut the pineapple in half lengthwise. Cut out all the pulp and dice it. Reserve the shell. Peel and slice the bananas. Combine diced pineapple and bananas with rum extract; stuff the shell with the fruit mixture. Serve at the table into fruit cups. Top each serving with a scoop of Orange Sherbet. Makes 8 servings.

ORANGE SHERBET

⅓ cup nonfat dry milk   2 cups orange juice

Combine milk and orange juice in bowl. Mix thoroughly. Pour into ice-cube tray and put in freezer until slightly frozen. Transfer to a bowl and beat rapidly until smooth and creamy. Make 8 scoops. Return to tray and freeze slightly. Defrost slightly to serve. Makes 8 servings.

PAVLOVA*

4 medium eggs, separated
¼ teaspoon cream of tartar
Dash of salt
1 tablespoon plus 2 teaspoons vanilla extract, divided
½ cup evaporated skimmed milk
Artificial sweetener to equal 6 teaspoons sugar

1 teaspoon unflavored gelatin
¼ cup cold water
1 medium papaya, peeled and sliced
1 cup blueberries (optional)

Preheat oven to 200°F. Beat egg whites with cream of tartar and salt until stiff but still shiny. Fold in 1 tablespoon vanilla. Spoon out or pipe onto a nonstick baking sheet which has been sprayed with a release agent and shape into an 8-inch circular mound with an indentation 4 inches wide and 1 inch deep. Bake for 40 to 60 minutes. In top of double boiler combine egg yolks, milk, sweetener and remaining vanilla. Heat over simmering water, beating constantly with a wire whisk until mixture is a light lemony color and slightly thickened. Soften gelatin in cold water. Add to egg yolk mixture; stir to dissolve thoroughly. Whip 2 to 3 minutes. Remove from heat. Chill until mixture thickens to pudding consistency. Pour into indentation in egg white mound, allowing the excess to run over sides, if desired. Surround with papaya slices, reserving 1 slice. Dice the slice and use to garnish pudding. Serve with blueberries if desired. Chill. Makes 4 servings.

RUTABAGA-APPLE PUDDING, TASMANIA STYLE*

Apples and rutabagas are popular crops in Southern Australia, where this pudding recipe originates.

4 slices raisin bread, made into crumbs
4 medium apples (tart), pared, sliced thin
8 ounces cooked rutabaga, mashed
1 teaspoon cinnamon

Dash salt
½ teaspoon apple pie spice
4 medium eggs
1 cup skim milk
1 teaspoon imitation butter flavoring
¼ teaspoon vanilla extract

Combine bread crumbs, apples, rutabaga and salt in a mixing bowl. Add cinnamon and pie spice and mix lightly together. Beat eggs with milk; add butter flavoring and vanilla extract. Fold into the apple mixture. Pour into a 9x9-inch nonstick pan and bake at 350°F. for 1 hour and 15 minutes, or until firm. Remove; cool. Makes 4 servings.

APPLE SUNDOWNER CAKE*

4 cups skim milk
Artificial sweetener to equal 12 teaspoons sugar
4 ounces enriched dry cornmeal
4 medium eggs
1 teaspoon imitation butter flavoring

½ teaspoon cinnamon
½ teaspoon vanilla extract
4 medium apples, pared, thinly sliced
⅔ cup cooked, mashed carrots

In a saucepan combine milk and sweetener and place over low heat. When milk begins to simmer, sprinkle in cornmeal, stirring until mixture thickens. Cook for 1 minute and remove from heat; cool. Beat eggs and stir into mixture. Add butter flavoring, cinnamon and extract. Fold in apples and carrots. Pour into nonstick baking pan and bake in hot (400°F.) oven for 45 minutes. Remove from oven and cool. Remove cake from pan, place on rack and let stand for 4 hours before serving. Divide equally into 4 portions. Makes 4 servings.

Austria and Hungary

For some six hundred years before the First World War, Austria and Hungary were united as part of the Austro-Hungarian Hapsburg Empire, so a commingling of their recipes is in a long-established tradition. Viennese pastry was part of that tradition, too, but for obvious reasons you won't find it here. What you will find is a Tangerine Sponge Cake, a tempting treat, especially if you thought *Gebäck* (baked goods) were behind you (we mean it both ways). Of course, we've included a *paprikash*. Would we dare not to, even in the knowledge that no Hungarian menu ever features more than one course flavored with the native mild sweet paprika, and many Hungarian meals are prepared without it?

Other typical foods of this corner of Europe have been included. Enough, we hope, to give you a taste, however tiny, of the interesting cuisines which developed when Turkish, Slavic, Italian, French, Spanish and German food tastes met over the centuries in these two now-separate countries.

CHERRY SOUP (Cseresznyeleves)

10 large sweet cherries, with pits
Water
½ cup buttermilk

1 slice enriched white bread, toasted and diced

Cover cherries with water and cook until they are soft. Remove pits if desired, and put cherries back into pan. Add buttermilk and simmer but do not boil. Top with diced toast; serve hot. Makes 1 serving.

EMPEROR SOUP (Kaisersuppe)

2 cups shredded cabbage
2 ounces diced leek
1 cup diced carrot
1 cup diced cauliflower
2 ounces onion, diced

5 cups chicken bouillon
2 cups cooked enriched rice
Salt and freshly ground pepper to taste

Combine vegetables in kettle; add bouillon; cover and cook until vegetables are tender, 25 to 30 minutes. Add rice. Simmer 10 minutes more. Season with salt and freshly ground pepper. Serve hot. Makes 4 servings.

TYROLEAN LIVER SOUP (Lebersuppe)

1 pound liver (remove any membranes), sliced
2 cups chicken bouillon or homemade stock (see page ix)
1 cup diced carrots
1 cup diced turnips

1 cup diced celery
2 ounces diced onions
1 bay leaf
Garnish: 1 tablespoon minced parsley, chives or watercress

To wash the liver, put in strainer and pour boiling hot water through it. Drain, dry and transfer to preheated nonstick pan. Brown liver quickly on all sides, 3 to 4 minutes; dice fine. Add bouillon, vegetables and bay leaf; cover pan and cook about 20 minutes or until vegetables are tender. Discard bay leaf. Serve soup and liver in bowls with garnish sprinkled on top. Pass the pepper mill. Makes 2 servings.

FISHERMAN'S SOUP—DANUBE RIVER (Halaszlé)

Danubian carp and whitefish are famous throughout Hungary.

1½ pounds carp (including bones and skin)
2 cups diced celery
1 cup diced carrots
1 cup diced string beans
4 ounces diced onions
4 ounces peas
4 ounces diced parsnips
2 tablespoons lemon juice or mild vinegar

1 tablespoon mild paprika
Bouquet garni (1 small garlic clove, bay leaf, 4 peppercorns, 1 sprig thyme, 2 sprigs dill, 4 sprigs parsley, tied in cheesecloth)
1 pound whitefish and pike fillets, cut in 2-inch pieces

Put carp, celery, carrots, string beans, onions, peas, parsnips, lemon juice, paprika and bouquet garni in saucepan. Cover with water, bring to boil, then simmer 45 minutes. Remove the carp to a strainer. Cut away flesh of carp and transfer 3 ounces to each of 4 soup bowls. With wooden spoon, press back into saucepan all liquid from carp bones in strainer. Add pieces of pike and whitefish to pan and simmer gently for 6 to 7 minutes. Discard bouquet garni. Divide whitefish, pike, vegetables and liquid into the 4 bowls holding the carp. Makes 4 servings.

CHICKEN PAPRIKA

Buttermilk adds the typical tangy piquant flavor.

2 pounds skinned and boned chicken
8 ounces onion, finely diced
1 medium green pepper, diced

2 cups chicken bouillon
1 tablespoon sweet Hungarian paprika
1 cup buttermilk

Layer the chicken in an oven-to-table casserole. Brown onion and pepper in heated nonstick skillet at moderately high heat for about 5 minutes, stirring to prevent scorching. Add chicken bouillon and paprika and bring to boil; pour over chicken in casserole. Cover and bake at 375°F. for 1 hour or until chicken is tender. Ten minutes before serving, add buttermilk to casserole. Mix well and bake 10 minutes more or until buttermilk is heated. Serve the chicken with the sauce well mixed. Makes 4 servings.

HUNGARIAN VEAL GULYAS

Onions, peppers, tomatoes and sweet mild paprika are the basic ingredients of Hungarian gulyas. One cup sliced mushrooms could be browned with the onions to expand the dish.

2 pounds trimmed veal,
   cut in cubes
1 tablespoon mild Hungarian
   paprika
8 ounces chopped onions
2 medium tomatoes, peeled and
   each cut in 8 wedges

1 cup tomato puree
2 medium green peppers,
   cut in squares
1½ teaspoons salt
2 cups hot cooked enriched
   noodles

Dredge veal with paprika and brown on all sides in nonstick skillet. Remove veal; wipe out skillet. Return veal to skillet. Add onions and lightly brown. Add tomatoes, tomato puree, green pepper and salt. Cover pan and simmer gently about 1 hour or until veal is tender. Serve with noodles. Makes 4 servings.

VIENNESE GULYAS

Using mortar and pestle, grind 1 garlic clove, 1 teaspoon caraway seeds and the rind of ½ lemon. Stir into veal about 10 minutes before it is done. Makes 4 servings.

TOKANY MEAT LOAF AND VEGETABLE (Pörkölt)

Pörkölt—from the Hungarian word meaning "broil and stew."

2 pounds ground beef
¼ cup water
1 teaspoon salt
¼ teaspoon rosemary or dill
⅛ teaspoon pepper
1 cup carrots, scrubbed
   and sliced
4 ounces onion, peeled and sliced

4 ounces diced parsnips
¼ cup diced celery
1 large garlic clove, crushed
½ cup water
2 medium tomatoes, diced
1 tablespoon mild paprika
4 ounces fresh or frozen
   young peas

Mix ground beef with water, salt, rosemary and pepper; shape into one long, large patty. Broil on rack about 4 inches from source of heat 15 minutes or until cooked throughout. Turn once during broiling. Meanwhile combine carrots, onions, parsnips, celery and garlic in skillet with cover. Add water, tomatoes and paprika. Cover and simmer 15 minutes or until vegetables are almost tender and sauce cooked down and quite thick. Add meat to skillet. Top with peas. Simmer, covered, for 10 minutes or until beef is piping hot and peas are done. Serve immediately. Makes 4 servings.

HUNGARIAN WEDDING RICE

2¼ pounds chicken livers, cut in halves
Salt and freshly ground pepper to taste
1½ cups sliced mushrooms, sprinkled with lemon juice
3 cups cooked enriched rice

2 cups cooked tiny whole carrots
12 ounces cooked tiny white onions
¼ cup chicken bouillon
3 medium green peppers, roasted, peeled and cut into 12 rings

Wipe chicken livers dry; sprinkle with salt and pepper and brown with mushrooms in a large preheated nonstick skillet. Turn livers often to cook evenly on all sides. Do not overcook; liver should remain juicy. Remove from pan and place in the center of a serving platter. In a large saucepan combine remaining ingredients except green pepper, and heat through, stirring occasionally to prevent sticking. Spoon rice mixture around the chicken livers. Arrange green pepper slices, overlapping at the edges, over rice. Makes 6 servings.

NOODLE-CHEESE-APPLE PUDDING

1 cup cooked enriched noodles
⅔ cup cottage cheese
2 tablespoons vegetable oil
2 medium apples, pared, thinly sliced
¼ teaspoon cinnamon
1½ cups skim milk

Artificial sweetener to equal 8 teaspoons sugar
2 teaspoons lemon juice
⅛ teaspoon almond extract, or to taste
2 medium eggs, well beaten

Combine noodles, cheese and oil in a mixing bowl. Mix well. Lay half the mixture in a 1-quart baking dish; arrange the apples on top. Sprinkle with cinnamon. Cover with remaining noodle mixture. Add milk, sweetener, lemon juice and almond extract to eggs. Pour over noodles and bake at 350°F. for 45 minutes. Remove and let stand for ½ hour before serving (can also be served cold). Makes 2 servings.

SALZBURG NOODLES

Toast ½ teaspoon caraway or poppy seeds in nonstick skillet, stirring constantly. In serving bowl, combine with ½ cup freshly cooked enriched broad noodles and 1 teaspoon margarine. Mix until margarine melts. Makes 1 serving.

PEARL ONIONS IN TOMATO SAUCE

2 cups water
1 teaspoon salt
4 ounces pearl onions

¼ cup tomato puree
1½ teaspoons vinegar

In a medium saucepan, bring water and salt to a boil. Add onions and cook until tender. In another saucepan combine tomato puree and vinegar. Place over low heat until heated through. Drain and rinse onions in a colander; add to tomato mixture and stir to coat. Heat for 2 to 3 minutes. Makes 1 serving.

MUSHROOMS IN CAPER MAYONNAISE, VIENNA STYLE

1 cup mushrooms, cut in half
1 tablespoon lemon juice
½ cup water

⅛ teaspoon salt
Caper Mayonnaise (recipe follows)

Wipe mushrooms and sprinkle with lemon juice. In saucepan (not aluminum) bring water to boil. Add salt and mushrooms; stir. Cover pan and cook quickly for 3 to 4 minutes. Drain mushrooms (save liquid and use in soup). Let mushrooms cool, stir in Caper Mayonnaise. Makes 2 servings.

Caper Mayonnaise

¼ medium dill pickle, diced
3 capers, rinsed and halved
2 tablespoons mayonnaise
1 teaspoon chopped fresh parsley

1 teaspoon chopped fresh or
  frozen chives
2 teaspoons prepared mustard

Combine. Makes 2 servings.

HAM, APPLE AND WILTED LETTUCE SALAD (Häuptelsalat)

2 heads Boston lettuce or romaine
(remove large outer leaves and
use in mixed salad)
2 tart medium apples, peeled,
cored and sliced
1 tablespoon lemon juice

1 cup diced celery
6 ounces cooked ham, sliced
4 teaspoons vegetable oil
1 tablespoon vinegar
1 teaspoon chopped fresh chives
1 teaspoon chopped fresh parsley

Tear washed lettuce into pieces and arrange in 2 salad bowls. Brush apples with lemon juice. Divide evenly over lettuce. Add celery. Stack ham slices and cut into julienne (matchstick) pieces. Divide evenly over apples. Combine remaining ingredients, mix well and serve equally divided over each salad. Let stand about 15 minutes to wilt lettuce. Makes 2 servings.

CUCUMBER PICKLE SLICES

12 medium cucumbers, sliced
12 ounces onions, sliced
¼ cup salt
2 cups celery, cut in matchstick
pieces
1½ cups wine vinegar

Artificial sweetener to equal
8 teaspoons sugar
1 teaspoon celery seeds
1 teaspoon dry mustard
1 teaspoon cinnamon

In medium bowl combine cucumbers and onions. Add salt, toss, and refrigerate overnight. Rinse and drain cucumbers and onions thoroughly. Place in saucepan with remaining ingredients. Cover, simmer 5 minutes, stirring occasionally. Serve chilled. Makes 12 servings.

AUSTRIAN LENTIL (OR SOYBEAN) SALAD (Linsensalat)

8 ounces cooked dried lentils
or soybeans
2 ounces finely chopped scallion
2 teaspoons vegetable oil

2 teaspoons vinegar
¼ teaspoon savory
Salt and pepper to taste

Combine ingredients, mix well. Chill until ready to use. Makes 1 serving.

SPINACH AND MUSHROOM SALAD WITH POPPY SEED DRESSING

1 cup tomato puree
1 teaspoon prepared horseradish
1 teaspoon poppy seeds
1 teaspoon lemon juice

¼ teaspoon salt
1 cup mushrooms, sliced
4 cups spinach leaves, thoroughly washed and dried

In medium bowl combine tomato puree, horseradish, poppy seeds, lemon juice and salt; add mushrooms and marinate 1 hour. Place spinach leaves in large bowl and toss with poppy seed dressing. Makes 4 servings.

TANGERINE SPONGE CAKE*

4 slices enriched white bread, made into crumbs
1⅓ cups nonfat dry milk
Artificial sweetener to equal 8 teaspoons sugar
2 teaspoons baking powder
2 tablespoons imitation (or diet) margarine

4 medium eggs
¼ teaspoon orange extract
2 tablespoons water
½ cup orange juice
1 envelope unflavored gelatin
2 large tangerines, peeled and sectioned

Preheat oven to 425°F. Combine first 4 ingredients in a mixing bowl; blend in the margarine. Place eggs, extract and water in blender container. Process 10 seconds and fold thoroughly into bread crumb mixture. Pour into nonstick round shallow cake tin (8½ x 1½ -inches), and bake 12 to 15 minutes or until golden brown. Cool. Place on wire rack. Pour orange juice in saucepan; add unflavored gelatin. Place over low heat; stir until gelatin dissolves. Chill until gelatin mixture is slightly thickened. Arrange tangerine sections on top of cake; top with gelatin mixture. Chill several hours. Makes 4 servings.

APPLESAUCE PUDDING WITH CHERRY SAUCE

1 recipe Whipped Topping (see page x)
1½ cups applesauce, no sugar added
⅛ teaspoon cinnamon

½ cup pitted, canned sweet cherries, no sugar added
2 tablespoons water
1 teaspoon cornstarch
½ teaspoon lemon juice

Prepare Whipped Topping. Combine applesauce and cinnamon in bowl. Fold in Whipped Topping. Pour mixture into four sherbet dishes. Chill several hours or overnight. Drain liquid from cherries and heat with water, cornstarch and lemon juice in small saucepan, stirring constantly until mixture comes to a boil, thickens and changes from cloudy to clear. Add cherries to thickened juice. Divide evenly and serve sauce with pudding. Makes 4 servings.

APRICOT BAVARIAN*

1 medium egg
1 cup skim milk
Artificial sweetener to equal 8 teaspoons sugar
1 teaspoon freshly grated lemon rind
½ teaspoon sherry extract

¼ teaspoon lemon extract
1 envelope unflavored gelatin
2 medium apricots, peeled, pitted and chopped
¼ cup chilled evaporated skimmed milk

In a mixing bowl combine egg, skim milk, sweetener, lemon rind and extracts. Mix well with beater. Sprinkle gelatin over mixture and let stand to soften. Pour mixture into saucepan. Place over low heat and stir until gelatin dissolves and mixture begins to thicken. *Do not boil.* Remove and cool. Add apricots. Beat evaporated skimmed milk with rotary beater until stiff peaks form. Fold into apricot mixture before it sets. Transfer to a small mold and chill for 2 hours before serving. Makes 1 serving.

CAFE VIENNESE

We've taken the whipped cream out of jause, *the Viennese afternoon coffee hour, and given you a palatable alternative.*

For two large cups:

½ cup evaporated skimmed milk   1 cup freshly percolated hot coffee
½ cup skim milk

Heat the milks in a small saucepan (do not boil). Pour coffee and milk divided equally into coffee cups. Serve hot. Makes 2 servings.

Belgium and The Netherlands

Sooner or later, say the travel advertisements, you'll get hooked on booking a vacation flight to the Netherlands. Whether you land there in the spring, in time for the tulips, or in the summer, when the annual flowers are up, you'll find a country ablaze with color, and friendly, rosy-cheeked people who could have stepped right out of a Frans Hals painting, except for a change to modern dress.

Of course, you'll also want to visit Belgium, the Netherland's neighbor on the North Sea. When you do, be sure to try the Waterzoi, famous meal-in-one-dish, which can be made with fish, as our recipe does it, or with chicken, substituting chicken bouillon for the clam juice. Keeping in mind that a sweet tooth is the most international of all tastes, we end our gastronomic tour of Belgium and the Netherlands with two splendidly rich but "legal" dessert treats.

BELGIAN FISH SOUP (Waterzoi)

2 cups water
6 ounces peeled whole new potatoes
1 cup celery, diced
1 cup sliced carrots
2 ounces onion, diced
2 tablespoons parsley sprigs
5 crushed peppercorns

½ bay leaf
¼ teaspoon thyme
½ cup clam juice
1 pound assorted fillets of carp, eel, perch or pike (at least two kinds), cut into 1½-inch pieces
2 teaspoons white wine extract

In saucepan combine water, potatoes, celery, carrot, onion and bouquet garni. (To make the bouquet put the parsley, peppercorns, bay leaf and thyme in double-layer cheesecloth square and tie with string; or put into tea-infusion strainer.) Cook vigorously about 20 minutes or until potatoes and vegetables are almost soft. Discard bouquet. Add clam juice, fish and wine extract. Cover pan loosely and simmer until fish is done, about 10 minutes. Divide into two soup bowls. Makes 2 servings.

FISH IN ENDIVE BOATS

8 ounces codfish
3 ounces cooked potato
1 cup large Belgian endive leaves, separated
1 tablespoon tomato puree
1 teaspoon margarine, melted

1 teaspoon chopped fresh parsley
¼ teaspoon chopped fresh chives
¼ teaspoon salt
⅛ teaspoon chopped fresh dill
Dash onion powder

Put fish and potatoes through meat grinder. Fill individual endive leaves with fish mixture. Arrange in a shallow flameproof casserole. In a small bowl, combine remaining ingredients. Pour over fish boats. Bake in a moderate oven (350°F.) 15 to 20 minutes or until fish is done. Serve in casserole. Makes 1 serving.

CURRIED SEAFOOD SALAD

Curry and ginger are widely used in Holland . . . seasonings and tastes acquired when the Dutch East Indies were colonized.

1 tablespoon vegetable oil
1 teaspoon lemon juice
¾ teaspoon curry powder
½ teaspoon salt
6 ounces cooked shrimp
½ cup cooked enriched rice

¼ medium green pepper, diced
2 tablespoons chopped fresh parsley
Lettuce leaves
Parsley sprigs for garnish

Combine first 4 ingredients in medium bowl. Mix in remaining ingredients, except lettuce and parsley sprigs. Cover and chill. Serve on lettuce leaves and garnish with parsley sprigs. Makes 1 serving.

KALE AND SAUSAGE (Boerenkool met Worst)

4 cups stemmed and cleaned kale
Salted water

12 ounces roasted pork
6 ounces peeled potato, diced

Cover kale with salted water (about 1 teaspoon salt) and cook until kale is tender. Drain kale (reserve liquid) and chop fine. Put kale back into saucepan with ½ cup liquid. Add roast pork which has been put through meat grinder or food processor and diced potato. Simmer for 30 minutes or until potatoes are tender. Makes 2 servings.

GOLDEN VELVET CARROTS

2 tablespoons imitation (or diet) margarine
3½ cups whole baby carrots, divided
¾ cup orange juice

¼ teaspoon vanilla extract
⅛ teaspoon cinnamon
Chopped fresh parsley to garnish

Melt margarine in top of double boiler over boiling water; pour margarine into blender container. Add ½ cup carrots, all the orange juice, vanilla and cinnamon; process at medium speed until smooth. Return margarine mixture to double boiler; add remaining carrots; heat. Garnish with chopped parsley. Makes 6 servings.

COOKED ESCAROLE

1 large head escarole	1 slice enriched white bread,
2 cups water	made into large crumbs
½ teaspoon salt	Dash grated nutmeg
2 teaspoons margarine	

Cut escarole in small pieces, using entire head except for the root end. Wash thoroughly. Cook rapidly in salted water until tender, 20 to 30 minutes. Drain; add the margarine, sprinkle with crumbs, and season with nutmeg. Makes 2 servings.

"CREAMED" MUSHROOMS

Creamed dishes, which reflect the influence of German cuisine, are much appreciated in the Netherlands.

Herbed White Sauce	1 tablespoon chopped fresh
(recipe follows)	parsley
4 cups raw mushrooms	1 tablespoon chopped chives
1 tablespoon lemon juice	

Prepare Herbed White Sauce and keep hot in double boiler. Trim a thin slice from ends of mushrooms (reserve ends and use in making stock or soup); wipe the mushroom caps with damp towel. Cut in thin slices through cap and stem. Cover with water, add lemon juice and cook until done, about 10 minutes. Drain. Add to sauce and sprinkle with parsley and chives. Serve hot. Makes 4 servings.

Herbed White Sauce

1 tablespoon margarine	Salt and freshly ground white
1 tablespoon flour	pepper to taste
1 cup skim milk	Thyme and marjoram to taste

Melt margarine in top of double boiler over boiling water. Stir flour thoroughly into melted margarine until mixture is smooth. Slowly add milk, stirring with wooden spoon. Add seasonings. Cook until mixture is thick and smooth. Makes 4 servings.

INDIVIDUAL ONION TART (Tarte à l'Oignon)*

Popular in Belgium as in neighboring France.

8 ounces chopped onions
¼ cup bouillon
2 medium eggs
½ cup evaporated skimmed milk
¼ cup water

1 teaspoon salt
¼ teaspoon pepper
1 slice enriched white bread, made into fine bread crumbs

Preheat oven to 350°F. Cook onions in ¼ cup bouillon over low heat until onions are tender, about 15 minutes. Divide onion mixture evenly into two individual casseroles or baking dishes. Beat eggs, evaporated skimmed milk, water, salt and pepper until light. Pour an equal amount into each casserole over onions. Sprinkle with bread crumbs, equally divided. Set casseroles in pan holding 1 inch of hot water. Bake about 25 to 30 minutes, or until set. Serve hot. Makes 2 servings.

PINEAPPLE DESSERT "CREAM"

Trade with their colonies brought pineapple to the Netherlands, along with coconut and curry. We've taken the avoirdupois out of this Dutch dessert treat but left in all the flavor.

1 envelope unflavored gelatin
½ cup water
¾ cup buttermilk
½ cup canned crushed pineapple, no sugar added

½ teaspoon vanilla extract
¼ teaspoon pineapple extract (optional)
3 ice cubes

Sprinkle gelatin over water in small saucepan; heat slowly until gelatin dissolves. Pour dissolved gelatin into blender container; add remaining ingredients except ice cubes; process at medium speed until smooth. Turn blender to high speed; add ice cubes one at a time. Pour pineapple mixture into a medium bowl—a Delft blue one would be nice. Chill until set. Makes 1 serving.

NOTE: Some of the crushed pineapple may be reserved for garnish.

STRAWBERRY CHEESE MOUSSE

1⅓ cups cottage cheese
⅔ cup nonfat dry milk
¾ cup water
2 tablespoons lemon juice
½ teaspoon vanilla extract

½ teaspoon salt
Artificial sweetener to equal 6
   tablespoons sugar
2 envelopes unflavored gelatin
2 cups strawberries, sliced

In blender container, process cheese, milk, ½ cup water, lemon juice, extract, salt and sweetener until smooth. Transfer to bowl. Pour remaining water into small saucepan. Sprinkle gelatin over it to soften. Place over low heat, stirring until dissolved. Pour into cheese mixture and mix well. Fold in strawberries. Pour into bombe mold and chill until set. Makes 2 servings.

The British Isles

Sturdy food—good plain fare—is what you can expect of the typical British meal, with special emphasis on well-roasted and perfectly carved beef. ("Carving," said Mrs. Beeton, famed British household arbiter and cookbook author of the nineteenth century, is "indispensable to the education of every gentleman.")

Travel through England, Scotland, Wales and parts of Ireland will convince you that simple fare has its own appeal. Since British cooks season only sparingly in the kitchen, you'll find a lot of cruets, condiments and bottled sauces at the table. One comment for travelers through Shakespeare country: If your inns include breakfast as part of the lodging, don't pass it up, and don't, if you are a member of Weight Watchers, exceed Food Program limits, which you will be tempted to do.

For stay-at-home enjoyment, there's honest fare in the recipes that follow. Start with a vigorous Cock-A-Leekie and go through the chapter, picking out favorites. There's a trace of thyme in our Welsh Cawl, a lift of lemon on the Brussels sprouts. And for desserts there are Strawberry Fool and Rhubarb Fool to dream about. And finally, you can enjoy "a spot of tea" before we leave the British Isles.

SCOTCH BROTH

6 ounces cooked lamb, cut into small pieces
1½ cups water
1 cup diced celery (including leaves)
½ cup diced carrots
½ cup diced turnip

1 tablespoon dehydrated onion flakes or 1 ounce diced onion
Salt and pepper to taste
½ cup cooked barley
2 tablespoons chopped fresh parsley

Place all ingredients except barley, salt, pepper and parsley in a saucepan. Bring to a boil. Reduce heat, add salt and pepper. Simmer covered until vegetables are tender. Stir in barley; serve generously sprinkled with chopped parsley. Season to taste. Makes 1 serving.

JELLIED BEEF BOUILLON

¾ cup homemade beef stock (see page x), beef bouillon or water with 1 packet instant beef broth and seasoning mix

1½ teaspoons unflavored gelatin
Lemon wedge
Watercress or parsley

Pour stock, bouillon, or water and beef broth mix into small saucepan; sprinkle with gelatin. Heat, stirring, until gelatin dissolves. Pour into small bowl; cover and chill until almost set. Stir just before serving. Serve with lemon wedge and greens. Makes 1 serving.

CELERY "CREAM" WITH BREAD SQUARES

Cauliflower florets may be cooked this same way. In England, sweetener is frequently added to these soups.

3 cups diced celery (including leaves)
2 cups water
2 packets instant chicken broth and seasoning mix or
2 bouillon cubes

Nutmeg (freshly grated if possible) to taste
½ cup evaporated skimmed milk
¼ cup water
1 slice enriched white bread, toasted and cut into 8 pieces

Cover celery with boiling salted water and let stand for 2 minutes. Drain and put into saucepan with 2 cups water. Cook for 20 minutes;

add broth mix or crushed bouillon cubes and nutmeg; cook for 10 minutes longer. Place in blender container. Process at medium speed until smooth. Return to saucepan; stir in milk and water; heat without boiling and spoon evenly into 2 bowls. Float 4 pieces of toast in each bowl. Serve hot. Makes 2 servings.

COCK-A-LEEKIE

This Scottish soup is named for the chicken and leeks which compose it. Be sure the leeks are thoroughly washed. Remove some of green top and roots before weighing.

1 cup chicken bouillon
2 ounces leeks, diced
Bouquet garni (see page 109)
12 ounces cooked chicken, shredded

1 tablespoon chopped fresh parsley
Freshly ground pepper to taste

In small saucepan combine bouillon, leeks and bouquet garni. Bring to a boil; simmer 20 minutes. Remove bouquet. Divide chicken evenly into 2 warm soup bowls. Pour soup over chicken. Garnish with parsley. Season at table with freshly ground pepper. Makes 2 servings.

NOTE: ½ cup cooked enriched rice may be served with each portion of Cock-A-Leekie.

CARROT-CELERY SOUFFLE*

½ cup skim milk
1 slice enriched white bread, made into crumbs
1 medium egg, separated

½ cup cooked mashed carrots
½ cup finely chopped celery
Salt and pepper to taste

Combine milk, bread crumbs and egg yolk in a small saucepan. Place over low heat. Heat, stirring, until thick. Remove from heat and add carrots and celery; season to taste. Beat egg white with rotary beater until stiff peaks form. Fold into mixture. Turn into a soufflé or other ovenproof dish. Bake in 400°F. oven for 30 minutes. Makes 1 serving.

BUCKINGHAM EGGS

2 teaspoons margarine
2 slices enriched white bread, toasted

2 medium eggs
¼ teaspoon Worcestershire
2 1-ounce slices hard cheese

Spread margarine over the toast. Scramble eggs in preheated nonstick skillet (slightly underdone). Sprinkle with Worcestershire. Spread on toast and top with cheese. Bake in hot oven (450°F.) until cheese melts. Makes 2 servings.

COD-TURNIP BAKE, DUBLIN STYLE

1 pound cod fillets
4 ounces onion, chopped
1 teaspoon lemon juice
2 packets instant chicken broth and seasoning mix
4 ounces cooked rutabagas

6 ounces cooked potato
¼ teaspoon salt
2 teaspoons imitation (or diet) margarine
Paprika

In nonstick skillet, cook cod, onion, lemon juice and broth mix, turning occasionally, until fish flakes. Mash the rutabagas and potatoes together; stir in salt. Spread ¼ of the turnip mixture on the bottom of each of 2 individual heatproof casseroles; top each evenly with fish mixture and remaining turnip mixture. Dot each casserole with 1 teaspoon margarine; sprinkle with paprika. Bake in 350°F. oven for 30 minutes. Makes 2 servings.

FINNAN HADDIE STEW

1 pound cooked finnan haddie
3 cups homemade chicken stock (see page ix) or bouillon
1½ cups cooked mushrooms, sliced through cap and stem
1 tablespoon chopped fresh chives

1½ teaspoons lemon juice
1 teaspoon fresh basil
¼ teaspoon onion powder
1 cup evaporated skimmed milk
Salt and pepper to taste
2 teaspoons chopped fresh parsley

Flake fish and place in saucepan. Add stock, mushrooms, chives, lemon juice, basil and onion powder. Simmer over low heat for 5 minutes; add milk. Reheat, but *do not boil*. Season. Sprinkle with parsley and serve. Makes 4 servings.

BAKED SALMON WITH CAPER SAUCE

4 10-ounce salmon steaks (or
bream, cod, flounder, haddock,
mackerel, etc.)
4 medium tomatoes, peeled
and chopped
2 tablespoons chopped fresh
chives ·

Salt and pepper to taste
Dash grated nutmeg
½ cup water
Caper Sauce (recipe follows)
Lemon wedges and dill for garnish

Place steaks in baking dish. Top with tomatoes. Sprinkle with chives, salt, pepper and grated nutmeg. Add water. Bake at 350°F. for 20 to 30 minutes, basting fish several times with liquid. Serve with Caper Sauce. Garnish with lemon wedges and dill. Makes 4 servings.

Caper Sauce

4 teaspoons margarine, melted
1 teaspoon capers, rinsed and
cut in half
¼ teaspoon lemon juice or
mild vinegar

½ teaspoon chopped fresh parsley
Salt and pepper to taste

Combine ingredients for sauce in ovenproof custard cup. Set cup in hot water bath and let stand for 10 minutes while fish bakes. Stir occasionally. Makes 4 servings.

JELLIED WHITEFISH

1¼ pounds dressed whole
whitefish (net weight after head,
tail and fins are removed)
or 1 pound fillets
⅓ cup cider vinegar
3½ cups water
½ teaspoon salt

1 bay leaf
2 teaspoons whole mixed pickling
spice
½ teaspoon dehydrated onion
flakes
¼ lemon, sliced
4 ounces onion, sliced

Cut fish into 1½-inch squares; refrigerate. In a saucepan combine vinegar, water, salt, bay leaf, pickling spice and onion flakes; boil 15 minutes. Add lemon, cook 5 minutes more. Remove lemon. Add fish and simmer 10 minutes. Layer fish and sliced onions in a dish and add the liquid. Cool. Chill at least 1 hour before serving. Makes 2 servings.

PRESSED CHICKEN

2 envelopes unflavored gelatin
1½ cups chicken bouillon
2 tablespoons mayonnaise
12 ounces diced, cooked or
   canned boned chicken (no skin)

8 ounces cooked peas
½ medium dill pickle, chopped
Lettuce

In a saucepan, soften gelatin in ¼ cup bouillon; add remaining bouillon; place over low heat and stir occasionally until gelatin is dissolved, 3 to 4 minutes. Cool slightly. Add mayonnaise; stir to combine. Add chicken, peas and pickle; mix well. Pour into loaf pan or 2-quart mold; chill until firm. Slice into 2 equal portions and serve garnished with lettuce. Makes 2 servings.

BUBBLE AND SQUEAK

When six ounces of beef are left on the marvelous British roast—and British roasts and roasting experts are among the gastronomic marvels of the world—it's time for the dish with this engaging name.

3 ounces peeled potato, diced
2 ounces diced onion
½ cup onion bouillon or water
1 cup cooked broccoli or
   cabbage, chopped

2 teaspoons vinegar (optional)
6 ounces cooked lean roast beef,
   cut in pieces

Use a flame-to-table ramekin or casserole for easy cleanup. Cover the potato and onions with onion bouillon or water and cook until liquid is almost evaporated and potato is tender. Mix in broccoli or cabbage and vinegar (optional); heat thoroughly. Stir in pieces of meat and serve hot. To hold, put ramekin on asbestos pad over low flame. If liquid evaporates, add more onion bouillon as necessary. Serve with dill gherkins. Season to taste at the table, as is the British custom, rather than in the kitchen. Use salt, pepper, Worcestershire, steak sauce, or whatever you prefer. Makes 1 serving.

SHEPHERD'S PIE

4 cups water
12 ounces peeled potato, diced
3 cups diced celery
2 tablespoons dehydrated onion
flakes
Salt and freshly ground pepper
to taste

1½ pounds cooked beef or lamb,
cut into thin, even slices
2 cups fresh sliced mushrooms
½ cup reserved potato liquid
1 packet instant beef broth and
seasoning mix
1 tablespoon Worcestershire

In a large saucepan, combine water, potato, celery and onion flakes. Cook over medium heat until potato is tender, about 15 minutes. Drain and reserve liquid. Place potato-celery mixture in a food processor, food mill or blender container, and process to form a puree. Season with salt and pepper. Line the bottom of a 9x5x3-inch loaf pan with half of the puree. In a large bowl combine beef, mushrooms, ½ cup reserved liquid, broth mix and Worcestershire. Mix well. Transfer to loaf pan. Top with remaining potato-celery mixture. Score top lengthwise and crosswise. Bake at 375°F. for 30 minutes or until heated through and top begins to brown. Makes 4 servings.

SWEETBREAD AND CUCUMBER SALAD

Savory. Summery.

6 ounces cooked calf sweetbread,
sliced thin (see page 125 for
directions for cooking
sweetbreads)
1 cup shredded lettuce
2 ounces cooked peas or diced
artichoke hearts
2 tablespoons imitation
mayonnaise

1 teaspoon lemon juice
1 tablespoon chopped fresh herbs
(chives, tarragon, dill or
parsley)
1 medium cucumber, peeled and
thinly sliced

In a salad bowl, arrange the sweetbread on lettuce. Sprinkle peas or artichoke hearts on top. Combine mayonnaise with lemon juice and herbs. Mix well and pile on to sweetbread. Make a border of cucumber slices. Refrigerate until ready to use. Makes 1 serving.

SPICED GRILLED BEEF

If proper allowance has been made in the daily menu plan, each portion may be served with a 1-ounce enriched white roll.

½ cup cold water
1 small bay leaf, crumbled
¼ teaspoon grated lemon rind
¼ teaspoon allspice
¼ teaspoon ginger

⅛ teaspoon mace
⅛ teaspoon ground cloves
2 pounds beef steak (or good quality chuck, round, rump)

Combine water, bay leaf, lemon rind, allspice, ginger, mace and cloves in saucepan. Bring to boil, then pour over steak. Marinate several hours or up to 2 days. Turn steak several times, if it is not completely immersed in marinade. Drain before use: reserve marinade. Grill steak on a rack 5 minutes on each side, basting with marinade, close to charcoal that has turned ash-gray. Remove steak to carving board and cut thin slices diagonally across the grain. Makes 4 servings.

JELLIED BEEF MOLD

8 ounces boneless lean shin beef (or chuck)
⅓ cup chopped celery
2 ounces onion, diced
½ medium dill pickle, diced
1 teaspoon chopped fresh parsley

6 strips pimento
1 envelope unflavored gelatin
2 tablespoons water
1½ cups beef bouillon
Salt and pepper to taste
Lettuce

Broil beef on rack 4 inches from source of heat. Put through meat grinder (coarse blade) or steel blade of food processor; set aside. Cook celery and onions in water until tender but firm; drain, add to meat with pickle and chopped parsley. Arrange pimento strips on the bottom of a small loaf pan. Spoon in beef mixture. Sprinkle gelatin over water in small saucepan to soften. Add bouillon; place over low heat (2 to 3 minutes). Stir until dissolved. Remove; season if necessary. Pour over beef; chill for 2 to 3 hours. Unmold on lettuce and serve. Makes 1 serving.

SHERRIED KIDNEYS AND MUSHROOMS

8 ounces veal kidney, cut in
½-inch cubes
2 ounces chopped onion
½ cup mushrooms, quartered
¼ medium green pepper, finely
chopped

¼ cup tomato puree
½ teaspoon sherry extract
Browning sauce (optional)
Salt and pepper to taste
1 cup beef bouillon
1 teaspoon chopped fresh parsley

Broil kidney on rack, 4 inches from source of heat, until done, about 5 minutes. Turn once. Combine in skillet with onions, mushrooms, pepper and bouillon. Simmer until pepper is tender. Add tomato puree, extract and browning sauce, if desired. Simmer an additional 10 minutes or until mixture thickens slightly. Season to taste with salt and pepper. Serve garnished with chopped parsley. Makes 1 serving.

WELSH CAWL

8 ounces lean boneless lamb
(shoulder, chop, etc.) or 6
ounces roast lamb
3 ounces peeled potato, diced
1 ounce onion, chopped
1 rib celery, chopped
1 medium carrot or 2 ounces
parsnips, cut in 2 pieces
⅛ teaspoon thyme

⅛ teaspoon rosemary
2 cups water
Salt and pepper to taste
1 ounce cooked peas or diced
artichoke hearts
1 cup cooked asparagus,
cauliflower, green beans, etc.,
cut up
1 teaspoon chopped fresh parsley

If using uncooked lamb, broil on a rack 4 inches from heat, about 5 minutes on each side. Remove; cool and cut into 1-inch pieces. If using roast lamb, cut into 1-inch pieces. In a saucepan, combine lamb with potato, onion, celery, carrot (or parsnips), thyme and rosemary. Pour in water; bring to a boil, season to taste. Simmer, uncovered, 25 minutes or until sauce is thick and lamb tender. Add peas or artichoke hearts, and asparagus, etc. Reheat. Sprinkle with parsley and serve. The meat is served in the middle of the plate, surrounded by the vegetables. The pan liquid can be combined with beef bouillon and used as a separate course or served over the meat and vegetables. Makes 1 serving.

LAMB BROCHETTE WITH RICE

1 pound boned leg of lamb,
  cut in 1-inch pieces
1 medium green pepper, cut in
  1-inch pieces
10 cherry tomatoes
½ medium pineapple, cut in
  1-inch pieces
2 ounces onion, finely chopped
½ cup water
¼ cup white vinegar

1 teaspoon curry powder
½ teaspoon salt
¼ teaspoon turmeric
¼ teaspoon paprika
¼ teaspoon pepper
½ cup tomato sauce, no sugar
  added
Browning sauce (optional)
1 cup cooked enriched rice

Combine lamb, green pepper, tomatoes, pineapple and onions in large mixing bowl. Add water, vinegar, curry powder, salt, turmeric, paprika and pepper. Mix well and marinate for 4 hours. Drain off liquid and reserve. Thread even amounts of lamb, pepper, tomato and pineapple alternately on each of two skewers. Broil on a rack 4 inches from heat, 12 to 15 minutes, turning frequently until meat is cooked. Add marinade liquid to tomato sauce and cook over low heat until thick; then add browning sauce as desired. Place each skewer on ½ cup of rice. Divide sauce evenly and serve. Makes 2 servings.

BOILED BRUSSELS SPROUTS WITH LEMON BALLS

Lemon Balls (recipe follows)
1 pound Brussels sprouts

½ teaspoon salt

Prepare Lemon Balls and refrigerate. Cut a cross at the base of each sprout to speed cooking. Cover sprouts with boiling water and add salt. Bring to boil. Cook until tender, 10 to 14 minutes. Drain and keep hot for a few minutes until ready to serve. Serve with a separate lemon ball for each portion, to be stirred into the vegetable at the table. Makes 4 servings.

Lemon Balls

8 teaspoons imitation (or diet)
  margarine

2 teaspoons grated lemon rind
2 teaspoons chopped fresh parsley

Cream ingredients together. Shape into 4 equal balls and refrigerate until ready to use. Makes 4 servings.

VEGETABLE HOTCH POTCH

3 cups water
3 packets instant beef broth and seasoning mix, or 3 beef bouillon cubes
3 tablespoons dehydrated onion flakes or 3 ounces diced onion
½ cup finely chopped carrot
½ cup diced turnip
1 cup cauliflower florets
1 cup drained canned fresh lima beans or green beans
½ cup celery
1 bouquet garni (see page 109)
½ cup shredded lettuce
1 tablespoon chopped fresh parsley

In saucepan combine water, broth mix, onion flakes, carrot, turnip, cauliflower, lima beans, celery and bouquet garni. Simmer, covered, 20 minutes. Add lettuce and simmer 10 minutes. Remove bouquet and serve hot with parsley garnish. Makes 2 servings.

SPINACH AND EGG SALAD*

1 cup young spinach leaves
1 cut garlic clove
2 ounces diced scallions
2 teaspoons vinegar or lemon juice
1 tablespoon vegetable oil
Salt and pepper
1 medium hard-cooked egg, quartered

Wash the spinach until free from grit, dry thoroughly. Rub salad bowl with cut clove of garlic. Add spinach and scallions. Add vinegar to oil; season with salt and pepper, pour over the spinach, and mix well. Border with sections of egg and serve. Makes 1 serving.

PEACH RICE CUSTARD*

½ cup cooked enriched rice
½ cup canned sliced peaches, no sugar added, drained (reserve juice)
1 medium egg
1 cup skim milk
¼ teaspoon lemon juice
Dash nutmeg

Combine rice and peaches in casserole. In small bowl, beat egg with milk and juices. Stir into rice; sprinkle with nutmeg. Place casserole in pan containing approximately 1 inch of water. Bake at 350°F. for 25 minutes or until set. Serve hot or cold. Makes 1 serving.

STRAWBERRY FOOL

Fool—a term of endearment in Olde England.

4 cups ripe whole strawberries
Artificial sweetener to taste
1 teaspoon lemon juice or sherry
   extract (optional)

1 recipe Whipped Topping
   (see page x)

Slice all but 4 strawberries. If they are sweet and ripe, added sweetener may not be necessary. Otherwise sprinkle it and juice or extract on fruit as desired. Let stand a few minutes while you prepare Whipped Topping. Fold sliced fruit into topping; divide evenly into 4 pretty glass dessert cups. Top each with 1 reserved strawberry. Chill until ready to serve. This can be prepared just before dinner. Makes 4 servings.

RHUBARB FOOL

1 recipe Whipped Topping
   (see page x)
2 cups cooked rhubarb
Artificial sweetener to taste
2 slices dried enriched white bread
   (remove and reserve crusts)

1 teaspoon vanilla extract
Cinnamon and artificial sweetener
   (optional)

Prepare Whipped Topping. Puree the rhubarb in blender or through food processor. Add sweetener. Transfer to bowl. Cut trimmed bread into 16 pieces and mix with rhubarb and vanilla extract. Fold in Whipped Topping and spoon evenly into 4 parfait glasses. Refrigerate. Make crumbs of bread crusts and mix with cinnamon and artificial sweetener, if desired. Sprinkle over parfaits before serving. Makes 4 servings.

A SPOT OF TEA

Tea is a boon. You may have it as often as you like, and in varied ways. Try the many different tea varieties and herb teas which are on the market. Add lemon juice or dehydrated lemon and orange rinds. Pick up the flavor with extracts and seeds like caraway, poppy and

cumin. Try tea with spice powders and curries. Serve it hot or iced,
and in bouillons too. Add artificial sweetener if you wish and, if you
like it white, be sure to use measured amounts of skim milk.

Scald an earthenware pot with hot water, add ½ teaspoon of tea
leaves for each serving, pour on freshly boiled water, and let steep
3 to 4 minutes. Serve immediately.

Herb teas can be made the same way. Use about 1 tablespoon or
more of crushed herb leaves for each serving and let steep 10 to 15
minutes.

Canada

~~~

The Canadian cuisine is hard to classify. Like a stew in which none of the ingredients lose their distinct form, it is a mixture of English, French, Indian and other separate national groups, each living in its own geographical pocket and each, therefore, preserving its own food customs.

But throughout Canada, everybody enjoys the fish which comes from its abundant lakes and streams and the syrup tapped from its towering maples. Canadian fish include bass, pike, salmon, trout and whitefish, much of it frozen and exported to the United States. The maple syrup is exported, too, but it is not on the Food Program, so we've substituted maple extract to give you the flavor without the flab.

PEA SOUP QUEBEC STYLE

Potage St. Germain in France. It is best with fresh peas but frozen may be used. A cup of combined vegetable trimmings (Boston lettuce, celery leaves, parsley, watercress, etc.) may be shredded and cooked with the peas. Curry powder is a popular seasoning for this soup, or use hot pepper sauce or Worcestershire for added zip.

2 cups water (see note)
1 packet golden seasoning and broth mix or chicken broth and seasoning mix
7 ounces fresh or frozen green peas

1 ounce diced onion
Salt and pepper to taste
Green food coloring, if desired
2 sprigs fresh mint

In saucepan, combine water, broth mix, peas and onion. Simmer, covered, for 30 minutes. Put through food mill or strainer, or process in blender until smooth. Add seasoning and coloring, if desired. Serve hot, garnished with mint. Makes 2 servings.

NOTE: Or replace 2 cups water and broth mix with 1½ cups homemade chicken stock (see page ix for recipe) and ½ cup water.

"CREAM" OF PEA SOUP

Heat ¼ cup evaporated skimmed milk in double boiler. Add Pea Soup Quebec and heat thoroughly. Season to taste with nutmeg or hot pepper sauce or Worcestershire. Makes 2 servings.

FRANKFURTERS STUFFED IN MAPLE SQUASH

1 12-ounce acorn squash (yields 8 ounces)
½ teaspoon maple extract

8 ounces cocktail frankfurters
2 teaspoons margarine
Dash cinnamon

Wash and cut acorn squash in half. Remove seeds. Bake squash cut-side down on foil-lined shallow baking pan in 375°F. oven for 40 minutes. Remove from oven. Stir ¼ teaspoon maple extract into each half. Stand 4 ounces of cocktail franks side by side in each squash. Return to baking pan. Reduce oven to 350°F. and bake 30 minutes. Dot each half with one teaspoon margarine and dash of cinnamon and return to oven for a minute. Makes 2 servings.

SCOTIA STEW

Just one of the many ways in which Canadians serve the products of their lakes and rivers. If frozen fillets are used, defrost first. Half a cup of green beans or asparagus could be cooked with the carrots.

¾ cup water
3 ounces peeled potato, diced
⅔ cup diced carrots
1 ounce diced onion or 1 tablespoon dehydrated onion flakes
Salt and pepper to taste

8 ounces fish fillets, cut in chunks
½ cup evaporated skimmed milk
1 tablespoon imitation (or diet) margarine
Freshly ground pepper
Chopped fresh parsley

In medium saucepan heat water to boiling. Add potato, carrots, onion and salt. Cover and simmer until potatoes and carrots are tender; 25 to 30 minutes. Add fish, simmer, covered, 10 additional minutes or until fish flakes when tested with fork. Stir in milk. Heat through; *do not boil.* Remove from heat. Stir in margarine. Sprinkle fresh pepper and parsley on top. Makes 1 serving.

HAM AND MACARONI SALAD

3 ounces boiled ham, cut into ¼-inch strips
⅔ cup cooked enriched elbow macaroni
1 tablespoon mayonnaise
1 tablespoon diced pimento
2 teaspoons white vinegar

1 teaspoon chopped fresh parsley
1 ounce diced onion or ½ teaspoon dehydrated onion flakes
Salt and pepper to taste
Lettuce

Combine all ingredients except lettuce in mixing bowl. Allow to chill at least one hour. Serve on a bed of lettuce. Makes 1 serving.

"CREAMY" CARROT PUDDING

4 medium eggs
1⅓ cups cottage cheese
1 cup finely shredded carrots

½ teaspoon vanilla extract
¼ teaspoon salt

In medium bowl beat eggs. Stir in remaining ingredients. Pour into four 6-ounce custard cups. Bake at 325°F. for about 1 hour. Makes 4 servings.

CAULIFLOWER AND CHEESE PUFFIT

1 cup cauliflower florets
2 ounces cheddar cheese, grated
1 slice enriched white bread
2 teaspoons prepared mustard
2 teaspoons mayonnaise

2 medium eggs
1 cup skim milk
½ teaspoon paprika
Dash salt and pepper

Cook cauliflower florets in boiling water to barely cover; drain, and transfer to 9x5x3-inch nonstick loaf pan. Top with grated cheese. Slice bread horizontally to make two slices. Spread one side of each slice with 1 teaspoon mustard and the other side with 1 teaspoon mayonnaise. Place bread, mustard side up, over cheese. Beat remaining ingredients in small bowl; pour over bread. Bake at 400°F. 35 to 40 minutes. Remove from oven. Increase oven temperature to broil. Place loaf under broiler, 4 inches from source of heat until top is golden brown. Makes 2 servings.

SPINACH-CHEESE RING

1 envelope unflavored gelatin
¼ cup cold water
½ cup boiling water
⅔ cup cottage cheese
2 ounces bleu cheese
1 packet instant beef broth and
seasoning mix

1 tablespoon chopped fresh chives
2 cups chopped spinach
¼ cup finely chopped celery
Shredded lettuce
10 cherry tomatoes
Spinach leaves
Radish roses

In blender container, sprinkle gelatin over cold water to soften. Pour in boiling water. Process at low speed until gelatin is dissolved. Add cottage cheese, bleu cheese, broth mix and chives; blend at medium speed until smooth. Chill until the consistency of unbeaten egg whites. Fold in spinach and celery. Pour into a 3-cup ring mold. Chill until firm. Unmold. Fill center with cherry tomatoes. Garnish with spinach leaves and radish roses. Makes 2 servings.

BLUEBERRY TARTLETS

1 slice raisin bread, cut in quarters
2 teaspoons unflavored gelatin
¼ cup water

½ cup blueberries
¼ teaspoon lemon juice

Roll bread with a rolling pin, until quite thin. Press 2 pieces of bread in each of 2 sections of a muffin pan, keeping the crust around the top edge. Sprinkle with water, if necessary to make it pliable. Bake at 300°F. for 10 minutes or until firm. Remove from pan; set aside and cool. In a saucepan sprinkle gelatin over water and add blueberries and lemon juice. Place over low heat and stir until gelatin dissolves. Remove from heat. Strain, reserving liquid, and cool. Divide berries evenly into each tartlet. Chill liquid until it becomes syrupy. Spoon evenly divided into tartlets and chill. Makes 2 servings.

THREE-LAYER MOLDED APPLE CUSTARD*

1½ cups water, divided
3 envelopes unflavored gelatin, divided
Artificial sweetener to equal 10 teaspoons sugar, divided
1 medium apple, pared, diced and sprinkled with 1 teaspoon lemon juice
3 drops red food coloring
2 medium eggs, slightly beaten
1 cup skim milk
½ cup evaporated skimmed milk
1 teaspoon freshly grated lemon rind
3 drops green food coloring
Mint sprigs for garnish

Pour 1 cup water into saucepan. Sprinkle 1 tablespoon gelatin over water to soften. Add sweetener to equal 6 teaspoons sugar. Place over low heat and stir until gelatin is dissolved. Remove from heat. Add apple and red food coloring. Mix to combine. Pour into a 2-quart mold and chill until firm. Sprinkle 1 tablespoon gelatin over ¼ cup water; set aside. In top of double boiler, combine eggs, skim milk and sweetener to equal 2 teaspoons sugar and heat over boiling water, stirring until mixture is slightly thickened. Add softened gelatin, stirring until dissolved, and pour over apple mixture. Chill until firm. Sprinkle remaining 1 tablespoon gelatin over ¼ cup water in small saucepan to soften. Place over low heat and stir until gelatin dissolves. Remove from heat. In a large mixing bowl combine evaporated skimmed milk, lemon rind, remaining sweetener to equal 2 teaspoons sugar, dissolved gelatin and green food coloring. Beat with rotary beater until peaks form. Spread evenly over egg layer in mold. Chill until set. Unmold; garnish with mint. Makes 2 servings.

ROSY RHUBERRY MOLD WITH LEMON "CREAM" TOPPING

4 cups fresh rhubarb, sliced
2 cups water, divided
Artificial sweetener to equal 12
  teaspoons sugar (or to taste)
2 envelopes unflavored gelatin

½ teaspoon strawberry extract
Red food coloring
2 cups strawberries, sliced
Lemon wedges to garnish
Lemon "Cream" (recipe follows)

Combine rhubarb and 1½ cups water in a saucepan. Add sweetener; simmer over low heat until rhubarb is tender but firm. Sprinkle gelatin over remaining water and let stand to soften. Add to rhubarb, stirring gently until gelatin dissolves. Remove from heat. Add extract and color as desired. Let cool slightly. Fold in strawberries. Pour into 1-quart mold rinsed in cold water, and refrigerate until set. Unmold. Garnish with lemon wedges. Serve with Lemon "Cream." Makes 4 servings.

Lemon "Cream" Topping

1 envelope unflavored gelatin
¼ cup cold water
½ cup boiling water
⅔ cup nonfat dry milk
1 teaspoon freshly grated
  lemon rind

1 teaspoon lemon juice
6 to 8 ice cubes
Lemon slices

In blender container soften gelatin in cold water. Add boiling water; process until smooth. Add remaining ingredients except ice cubes and lemon slices. Process. Add ice cubes one at a time, processing after each addition. Pour into serving dish. Garnish with lemon slices. Serve immediately. Makes 4 servings.

Caribbean and West Indies

Have you lost your heart to one of the enchanting islands of the West Indies? Most of us have. Like all island buffs, you'll go there to sail, swim, shop, sunbathe, gamble or just loaf . . . and, of course, to enjoy the native foods. The foods of the West Indies are exceedingly varied, since the islands are inhabited by many different kinds of people including African, British, Chinese, Dutch, French, Indian, Scandinavian, Spanish and North American groups with culinary traditions and preferences of their own. But overall there is a lively West Indian cuisine which accents native fish and seafood, tropical fruits and vegetables and some typical spices. All are sampled in recipe form in the next pages.

PUMPKIN SOUP (Sopa de Zapallo)

8 ounces cooked pumpkin puree, fresh or canned
2 cups tomato juice
1 cup chicken bouillon
1 medium green pepper, diced
1 tablespoon dehydrated onion flakes
Pinch of cayenne pepper
½ bay leaf
½ cup evaporated skimmed milk
Salt and pepper to taste
1 tablespoon chopped fresh parsley

Combine pumpkin, tomato juice, bouillon, green pepper and onion flakes in a saucepan. Bring to a boil; add cayenne and bay leaf. Simmer until green pepper is tender. Add milk; season to taste. Reheat, but *do not boil*. Sprinkle with parsley. Makes 4 servings.

CALALOO SOUP-STEW

A Caribbean favorite, originally made with crab.

4 cups spinach or turnip greens, coarsely chopped
12 ounces fresh, frozen or canned drained okra
½ cup finely chopped celery
3 cups water
¾ cup tomato puree
¼ teaspoon thyme
½ bay leaf
Salt and pepper to taste
½ small hot red pepper (optional)
1½ pounds fish fillets, cut in 1-inch pieces

In saucepan combine spinach or turnip greens, slices of fresh or frozen okra and celery with water; bring to boil and cook for 6 minutes. Add tomato puree, thyme, bay leaf, salt, pepper and red hot pepper if desired. (If you are using canned okra, add it now.) Place the fish pieces on top; bring to boil and lower heat to simmering temperature. Let simmer until fish flakes, about 10 minutes, basting several times with liquid from pan. Makes 4 servings.

BAKED LEMON-LIME BASS OR TROUT

8 ounces ground trout or bass fillets
Salt and pepper (or hot pepper sauce) to taste
¼ cup chicken bouillon
¼ cup chopped celery
1 tablespoon lime juice
4 to 5 parsley sprigs
1 slice enriched fresh white bread, made into crumbs
1 teaspoon chopped fresh parsley
1 teaspoon imitation (or diet) margarine
1 lemon wedge, peeled and finely chopped

Season fish with salt and pepper. Place in baking dish. Add bouillon, celery, lime juice and parsley sprigs. Bake in hot (400°F.) oven for 20 minutes or until easily flaked with fork, basting frequently. Place fish on a platter. Mix together bread crumbs, parsley, margarine and lemon. Sprinkle on fish. Reheat in oven or under broiler for about one minute, and serve. Makes 1 serving.

SHRIMP HAITI

Haitian dishes have a French or—as this one—a Creole accent.

2 ounces finely chopped onion
½ cup chicken bouillon
¼ cup tomato puree
½ garlic clove, crushed
1 medium tomato, peeled and chopped
¼ medium green pepper, blanched and diced
Salt and pepper to taste
6 ounces cooked shrimp
½ cup cooked enriched white rice
2 teaspoons chopped fresh parsley

Lightly brown onions in nonstick skillet. Add bouillon, puree, garlic, tomato and green pepper. Simmer 5 minutes or until pepper is tender; season to taste. Add shrimp, rice and parsley. Heat and serve. Makes 1 serving.

CHICKEN CURRY TRINIDAD

Curries are popular in Trinidad where so many Indians have settled and where they continue to make their own curry powder, in the old tradition, and as you can do, following our recipe. As a general rule, allow 1 tablespoon curry powder for every 2 pounds of meat and poultry; a lesser amount for fish, shellfish and vegetables—and for people with timid palates. Hot curries are usually served over bland rice.

6 ounces onions, finely chopped
2 cups chicken bouillon, divided
2 garlic cloves, pressed
1 or 2 tablespoons Caribbean Curry Powder (recipe follows)
2¼ pounds diced cooked chicken or turkey
6 ounces peeled and sliced West Indian pumpkin or Hubbard squash
3 cups peeled and diced eggplant
3 cups peeled and sliced christophene (chayote)
1 or more fresh hot chilies, seeded and chopped
1 teaspoon lime juice
Salt to taste

Cook onions in large skillet in small amount of bouillon until golden; add garlic and curry powder and cook, stirring, for 3 to 4 minutes. Add all remaining ingredients except lime juice and salt. Cover and simmer gently until vegetables are cooked. Stir in lime juice and add salt to taste. Makes 6 servings.

Caribbean Curry Powder

2 tablespoons cumin seeds
1 tablespoon coriander seeds
1 tablespoon poppy seeds
1 tablespoon mustard seeds, preferably brown
1 tablespoon whole cloves
1 tablespoon peppercorns
2 tablespoons ground turmeric
1 tablespoon ground ginger, preferably Jamaican

Toast the cumin, coriander, poppy and mustard seeds in a heavy iron skillet until the mustard seeds begin to jump about. Add cloves and pepper; grind in a mortar or in an electric blender; then mix with the turmeric and ginger. Put through a fine sieve and store in a glass jar. Makes about 1 cup.

BAKED HAM WITH PIQUANT ORANGE-FLAVORED SAUCE (Jambon à la Bigarade)

The orange, Haiti's national fruit, inspired this recipe which tastes mighty like France's Jambon à la Bigarade.

3 to 5 pounds smoked ham
Whole cloves
Brown sugar replacement to taste
¾ cup (6-ounce can) frozen
   orange juice concentrate
6 ounces sliced onions or
   2 tablespoons dehydrated onion
   flakes reconstituted in water
2 tablespoons water

2 garlic cloves, minced
2 packets instant beef broth and
   seasoning mix
3 cups water
¼ cup tomato paste
2 teaspoons prepared mustard
1 teaspoon dehydrated orange
   peel

Place ham on a rack in roasting pan. Score it with a knife; stud with cloves; sprinkle with brown sugar replacement. Bake at 325°F. 15 to 18 minutes per pound, or 1½ to 2 hours. Baste with orange juice. In large nonstick skillet heat onions, garlic and broth mix until slightly brown. Add water and tomato paste; cook until sauce is reduced by one-third or to desired consistency. Stir in mustard and orange peel. Serve weighed portions of ham with equal portions of sauce. Makes 12 servings.

PUERTO RICAN MOLDED HAM SALAD (Jamón en Gelatina)

3 ounces cooked ham, finely
   chopped
¼ cup finely diced celery
1 tablespoon chopped pimento
2 teaspoons chopped fresh parsley
½ teaspoon mustard
Dash pepper

2 teaspoons unflavored gelatin
2 tablespoons water
⅓ cup chilled evaporated
   skimmed milk
Lettuce
½ medium tomato, sliced
Parsley sprigs

Combine ham, celery, pimento, parsley and mustard in small mixing bowl. Season with pepper. Sprinkle gelatin over water in small saucepan to soften. Dissolve over low heat. Remove. Add milk and beat with hand whisk until 3 times its volume (soft peaks). Fold into ham mixture; transfer to a pint mold and refrigerate 2 hours or until firm before serving. Unmold on lettuce and garnish with tomato and parsley. Makes 1 serving.

COCONUT RICE AND BEANS OCHOS RIOS

For two dinner portions, decrease cooked dried kidney beans to 8 ounces and add 6 ounces of cooked pork. Makes 2 servings.

4 ounces diced onion
¾ cup chicken bouillon
½ hot red chili pepper
⅛ teaspoon thyme
Salt to taste
1 cup cooked enriched rice

12 ounces cooked dried
   kidney beans
2 tablespoons evaporated
   skimmed milk
½ teaspoon coconut extract

Brown onion over high heat in saucepan, stirring to prevent scorching. Add chicken bouillon, chili pepper, thyme and salt if desired. Bring to boil. Stir in rice and beans; reduce heat and simmer uncovered for 20 minutes or until beans and rice have absorbed flavors and liquid. Stir in evaporated milk and coconut extract; heat gently and serve hot. Makes 2 servings.

CARIBBEAN FRUIT AND CHEESE SALAD RING*

1 small orange, peeled and
   sectioned, or ½ cup canned
   mandarin orange sections, no
   sugar added
1 medium banana, diced
½ cup canned pineapple chunks,
   no sugar added
2 envelopes unflavored gelatin

2 cups water
2 teaspoons orange extract
1 teaspoon coconut extract
2 to 3 drops yellow food coloring
Lettuce
1⅓ cups cottage cheese
Sprigs of mint

Combine orange sections, banana and pineapple and arrange in a ring mold. In a saucepan, sprinkle gelatin over 1 cup of water to soften. Place over low heat and stir until gelatin is dissolved. Remove from heat; stir in remaining water, extracts and color as desired. Pour over fruit in mold and chill. Unmold on bed of lettuce. Fill center of ring with cottage cheese and garnish with sprigs of mint. Makes 4 servings.

BANANAS ANTILLEAN WITH LIME-WHIPPED TOPPING

Lime-Whipped Topping
  (recipe follows)
2 medium bananas
1 cup water
1 cup canned crushed
  pineapple, no sugar added

2 tablespoons lime juice
1 teaspoon grated lime rind
½ teaspoon rum extract
4 teaspoons margarine

Prepare Topping. Peel and cut bananas in half lengthwise. In large skillet heat to boiling, water, pineapple and lime juice; reduce heat and stir in lime rind and rum extract. Add bananas; heat. Remove skillet from heat. Place each banana half on an individual serving dish. Stir margarine into pineapple mixture until margarine melts; divide evenly and pour over bananas. Serve with Topping. Makes 4 servings.

Lime-Whipped Topping

1½ teaspoons unflavored gelatin
¼ cup water
½ cup boiling water
1 teaspoon vanilla extract
⅔ cup nonfat dry milk

Artificial sweetener to equal
  4 teaspoons sugar
1 teaspoon lime rind
8 ice cubes

Pour water in blender container; sprinkle gelatin over water to soften. Add boiling water and process at low speed until gelatin dissolves. Add vanilla, dry milk, sweetener and lime rind. Add ice cubes, one at a time, and process at high speed. Pour topping into a small bowl; chill. Stir topping just before serving and divide equally. Makes 4 servings.

PINEAPPLE RICE PUDDING (Arroz con Leche y Piña)*

1 cup cooked enriched white rice
1 cup evaporated skimmed milk
½ cup water
¼ teaspoon almond extract

½ cup canned crushed pineapple,
  no sugar added
2 medium eggs
¼ teaspoon cinnamon
¼ teaspoon nutmeg

Combine rice, milk and water in top of double boiler. Add extract. Cook 30 minutes over boiling water or until mixture thickens. Drain pineapple and reserve juice. Add pineapple, simmer for 10 minutes.

Remove. Place eggs and reserved pineapple juice in blender container. Process until smooth. Stir into rice; reheat, do not boil. Pour into two dishes. Sprinkle with cinnamon and nutmeg; cool. Chill 2 to 3 hours in refrigerator before serving. Makes 2 servings.

KINGSTON TONIC

From Jamaica, where the British tradition is strong.

½ cup (4 fluid ounces) iced tea
3 to 4 ice cubes
Artificial sweetener to equal
  2 teaspoons sugar

½ cup (4 fluid ounces) dietetic
  tonic water
1 slice lemon

Place tea in a tall glass; add ice cubes, sweetener and tonic water. Stir and serve with lemon. Makes 1 serving.

COCONUT TROPICAL

½ cup (4 fluid ounces) dietetic
  tonic water
½ cup (4 fluid ounces) club soda
1 teaspoon lemon juice
½ teaspoon coconut extract

¼ teaspoon tropical fruit or
  berry extract
Artificial sweetener to equal
  2 teaspoons sugar
½ cup shaved ice

Combine all ingredients in a tall glass and serve over ice. Garnish with a flower blossom. Makes 1 serving.

FAMOUS CARIBBEAN PUNCH

Slake your thirst Caribbean style . . . rum extract replaces the rum poured with a lavish hand in the West Indies.

⅔ cup dietetic ginger ale
⅓ cup lime juice
4 teaspoons rum extract

1 cup crushed ice
Artificial sweetener to taste

Combine in blender container. Process until smooth. Serve in highball glasses. Makes 2 servings.

RUM MILK

¾ cup buttermilk
½ teaspoon coconut extract

½ teaspoon rum extract
3 ice cubes

Place all ingredients in blender container; cover and process at high speed until all traces of ice disappear. Serve in tall glass. Makes 1 serving.

GRAPEFRUIT JUICE MINT COCKTAIL

½ cup grapefruit juice
1 small piece lemon rind

1 sprig of fresh mint

Using well-chilled 4-ounce cocktail glass, pour in juice. Twist lemon rind to release its oils and add to juice. Top with mint sprig. Makes 1 serving.

CAFE PUERTO RICO

1 cup cold strong coffee
2 cups canned crushed pineapple,
no sugar added

1 cup skim milk

Combine all ingredients in food processor (steel blade) or in blender container, in two batches. Process until smooth. Chill. Stir before serving. Makes 4 servings.

China

The wisdom of Confucius has been famous for more than 2,500 years, but did you know that he was also an epicure, as were many Chinese sages? Is it any wonder, then, that the Chinese—with a national proclivity for excellence in food and with thousands of years of practice—have created a cuisine which ranks among the two or three best in the world? It is a perfect cuisine for the weight-conscious.

Chinese table etiquette follows a strict pattern. Although a dozen or more dishes are served at important meals, the diners, who are taught restraint from childhood, help themselves to only small portions from each central dish. Meal customs in general slow down the whole act of eating. Ingredients are cut into small pieces in the kitchen, sizes just large enough to be managed with chopsticks. As you know if you've used them, it's hard to gulp greedy mouthfuls with chopsticks as the sole implements, especially since table manners dictate that the chopsticks be put down at frequent intervals during the meal. So, in effect, the Chinese practice the kind of disciplined eating which we advocate.

An ancient Chinese proverb, this one not attributed to Confucius, says, "Good food brings happiness." We hope our recipes will make you blissfully happy.

CLEAR SOUP

Serve it in your pretty Chinese porcelain soup bowl with its short-handled spoon.

1 cup chicken bouillon
½ slice ginger root, minced
½ teaspoon sherry extract

Soy sauce to taste
Chopped fresh parsley or
    shredded spinach to garnish

In small saucepan, combine bouillon and ginger. Heat to boiling. Stir in sherry extract and serve at once with soy sauce (to be added at the table). Garnish with parsley or spinach. Makes 1 serving.

EGG DROP SOUP*

1 cup chicken bouillon
1 teaspoon cornstarch, dissolved
    in 1 tablespoon cold water
1 medium egg, beaten

1 small slice ginger root, diced
1 ounce scallion, including part
    of green top, finely chopped

Bring chicken bouillon to boil; stir in cornstarch mixture. Remove from heat. With a chopstick in one hand stir the soup. With your other hand, slowly pour the beaten eggs into soup, stirring to create egg shreds. Remove from heat. Put ginger in soup bowl and add soup. Top with scallion. Serve at once. Makes 1 serving.

SIZZLING MUSHROOM SOUP

3 Chinese dried mushrooms
    (½ cup reconstituted)
1 cup beef bouillon
½ cup chopped fresh or
    frozen spinach

1 tablespoon chopped fresh
    parsley or chives
½ teaspoon sherry extract

Clean mushrooms by rinsing in cold water. In saucepan, combine bouillon and dried mushrooms. Let stand 15 minutes or until softened. Lift out mushrooms, cut away stems, and slice mushrooms. Bring bouillon to boil, add mushroom slices. Simmer, covered, for 20 minutes. Stir in spinach and cook 2 minutes more. Stir in parsley and sherry extract. Serve hot. Makes 1 serving.

OYSTER SOUP

A delicacy we first tasted at a Chinese restaurant.

1 cup beef bouillon (or use part mushroom liquid)
½ cup sliced fresh mushrooms or 3 dried reconstituted in hot water and sliced
½ cup diced celery
¼ cup sliced bamboo shoots or carrots
1 small slice ginger root, diced

4 ounces canned drained oysters, sliced or 2 ounces oysters and 2 ounces shredded roast pork
2 ounces pea pods
2 ounces scallions, including green top
1 teaspoon sherry extract (optional)

In saucepan combine bouillon, mushrooms, celery, bamboo shoots and ginger root. Bring to boil; cover and simmer 10 to 15 minutes or until vegetables are tender. Add oysters (or oysters and pork) and pea pods; heat gently 2 to 3 minutes. Turn off heat, add scallions and sherry extract, if desired. Serve at once. Makes 1 serving.

WINTER MELON SOUP

3 cups chicken bouillon
2 cups winter melon, cut into 1-inch cubes, discarding rind and seeds

1 pound cleaned and deveined shrimp, cut into bite-size pieces, or 1 pound raw shredded skinned chicken

Place bouillon, winter melon and shrimp in large saucepan. Bring slowly to a boil. Reduce heat and simmer covered 15 to 20 minutes or until melon is tender. Makes 2 servings.

HOT AND SOUR CHICKEN SOUP WITH BOK CHOY SHREDS

To serve this as a complete luncheon soup, add 4 ounces bean curd cut into slivers and heated along with shredded vegetables.

½ cup Chinese cabbage, Swiss chard or watercress with stems removed
1 cup chicken bouillon

2 ounces cooked chicken, sliced in matchstick strips
1 small piece lemon rind, shredded

To prepare cabbage, cut it in half lengthwise, then slice into thin diagonals. Shred Swiss chard or watercress if used. In small saucepan bring bouillon to boil, add shredded vegetable, and cook until cabbage is wilted, but still crunchy, about 3 minutes Pour over shredded chicken in soup bowl. Garnish with lemon rind. Makes 1 serving.

CHINESE EGGROLL

Wrappers

1 medium egg   Filling (recipes follow)
1 tablespoon water

Combine egg and water in blender container. Process for 10 seconds. Pour mixture into a cup with a spout, such as a liquid measuring cup, and let it stand until bubbles subside, at least 15 minutes. Heat a 7-inch nonstick skillet. Pour half the egg mixture into skillet, tilting skillet until the entire bottom is covered with a thin sheet of egg. Cook until egg is firm enough to turn, but not yet crispy. Turn; cook on second side for 10 to 15 seconds or until just solid. Remove from skillet. Repeat procedure with remaining egg mixture. Prepare one of the fillings. Place half the filling in the center and roll wrapper around filling, first folding in the sides. Place seam-side down on a nonstick baking sheet. Bake at 350°F. for 15 minutes or until wrapper becomes crisp and filling is thoroughly heated. Makes 1 serving of 2 eggrolls.

Shrimp Eggroll Filling

2 ounces cooked shrimp, finely diced
1 ounce finely chopped, cooked snow peas
1½ tablespoons finely chopped, cooked bean sprouts
1½ tablespoons finely chopped cooked mushrooms

1 teaspoon finely chopped celery
⅛ medium green pepper, finely chopped
1 teaspoon soy sauce
½ teaspoon sherry extract
Salt to taste

Combine all ingredients in a small mixing bowl. Filling for 2 eggrolls.

Chicken Eggroll Filling

In this recipe, ¼ cup grated cabbage, crisp-cooked, may be used instead of the spinach-mushroom-bean sprouts mixture.

2 ounces cooked chicken, finely diced
2 tablespoons finely chopped, cooked spinach
1 tablespoon finely chopped, cooked mushrooms
1 tablespoon finely chopped, cooked bean sprouts
1 tablespoon soy sauce
Dash salt (optional)

Combine all ingredients in a small mixing bowl. Filling for 2 eggrolls.

BASS OR PERCH SZECHUAN

1 pound fillets of bass or perch, cut in 1-inch pieces
2 ounces scallions, including green tops, cut in ¼-inch slices
2 garlic cloves, minced
1 cup beef bouillon
2 to 3 tablespoons soy sauce
2 teaspoons minced ginger root
2 teaspoons sherry extract
2 teaspoons cider or rice vinegar
¼ teaspoon crushed red pepper flakes, Szechuan pepper or hot pepper sauce to taste

In preheated nonstick skillet or wok with lid, combine fish, scallions and garlic. Brown fish on both sides over moderate heat. Add bouillon, soy sauce, ginger, sherry extract, vinegar and pepper. Cook covered over low heat 20 minutes or until fish flakes easily, basting it several times. Makes 2 servings.

SLICED FLOUNDER WITH GARLIC, GINGER AND SPINACH

1 pound flounder fillets
Salt and pepper to taste
Boiling water
1 cup fresh spinach, trim off tough stems
1 medium tomato, sliced
2 tablespoons beef bouillon
½ teaspoon finely minced ginger root
1 garlic clove, minced

Slice fish into 2x3-inch pieces. Sprinkle with salt and pepper. Pour boiling water over spinach and let stand, covered, for 3 minutes. Drain well, pressing out moisture. Shred or chop fine. Divide spinach evenly and top each piece of fish with a spoonful. Roll up fish from short end to enclose stuffing and fasten with toothpick. Place fish rolls in a heatproof serving platter or small shallow casserole. Add sliced tomatoes. Combine bouillon, ginger and garlic; spread on fish. Place platter in a Chinese steamer or on a rack in a Dutch oven containing water at least 1 inch below the bottom of the platter. Place wax paper over platter to keep excess moisture out. Cover steamer or Dutch oven loosely enough so steam doesn't build up and heat to steam cook fish for 15 to 20 minutes or until fish flakes with a fork. Replenish hot water in steamer or Dutch oven if necessary. Makes 2 servings.

RED-SIMMERED FISH WITH MIXED VEGETABLES

Red because it's cooked with soy sauce.

1½ cups water
2 tablespoons lemon juice
2 teaspoons soy sauce
1 slice fresh ginger root, minced
1 teaspoon dehydrated onion flakes
Salt and pepper to taste
Dash of cinnamon

2 10-ounce fish steaks
½ cup cauliflower, broken into florets
½ cup asparagus, cut in 1-inch pieces
4 ounces peas
½ cup diced celery
½ cup sliced mushrooms

In wide saucepan, combine water, lemon juice, soy sauce, ginger, onion flakes, salt, pepper and cinnamon. Add fish. Bring to quick boil; surround fish with cauliflower, asparagus, shelled peas, celery and mushrooms. Return to boil. Cover pan and cook gently until fish and vegetables are done, about 20 minutes. Makes 2 servings.

SWEET-SOUR FISH WITH PINEAPPLE

2 pounds fish fillets
2 cups canned pineapple chunks, no sugar added
¾ cup water
¼ cup cider vinegar
1 tablespoon soy sauce
1 garlic clove, pressed
1½ teaspoons salt

1½ cups canned bamboo shoots, rinsed
1 medium green pepper, cut in 1-inch squares
1 medium tomato, cut in thin wedges
2 cups cooked enriched hot, fluffy rice

Cut fish into 1-inch pieces. Drain pineapple chunks; reserve liquid. In saucepan, combine pineapple juice, water, vinegar, soy sauce, garlic and salt; blend well. Bring to boil. Add fish; cook over low-medium heat until fish flakes when tested with fork. Add bamboo shoots, green pepper and tomato and cook 1 minute longer. Serve over rice, divided onto 4 serving plates. Makes 4 servings.

STEAMED EGGS WITH VEGETABLES

You can vary this custard in many ways. Change the vegetables, use beef broth mix, liquid left from cooking vegetables, tomato juice, or water. However, be sure to boil whatever liquid you use, because it forces out the air bubbles and gives the dish its typically creamy texture.

3 packets instant chicken broth and seasoning mix dissolved in 1½ cup hot water
1 cup green beans, spinach or mushrooms, in thin diagonal slices
4 ounces scallions, including green tops, in thin diagonal slices

½ teaspoon sherry extract
½ teaspoon salt
4 medium eggs, lightly beaten
Boiling water
2 teaspoons soy sauce (optional)

You will need a large deep pot or Dutch oven for steaming. Pour broth into a small flameproof dish and bring to boil. Turn off heat. Stir in green beans (spinach or mushrooms), scallions, sherry extract and salt. Gently mix in eggs. Place dish on a rack set in the large pot on the stove or, instead of a rack, use 2 custard cups, side by side, and balance dish on them. Pour boiling water into the pot to reach 1 inch below the level of the rack. Place a piece of wax paper over egg mixture to prevent steam from dripping into eggs and cover the pot, enclosing the entire mixture in this "steamer." Simmer 20 to 30 minutes or until a toothpick inserted in the center of egg mixture comes out clean. Add boiling water to pot as it evaporates. Top each portion with 1 teaspoon soy sauce, if desired. Makes 2 servings.

STEAMED EGGS WITH FISH

Follow preceding recipe but add 12 ounces finely cut raw fish fillets, stirring them into the stock with the vegetables just before adding the eggs. Steam as directed above for 30 to 40 minutes. Makes 4 servings.

CRAB FOO YUNG

Ingredients like bamboo shoots are popular in Chinese dishes because, while lacking in flavor, their texture and ability to absorb and reflect seasonings is essential to the cuisine. If bamboo shoots are not available, chewy vegetables—parboiled cabbage, bean sprouts, broccoli, cucumbers, carrots, green beans or green peppers—may be substituted. For crabmeat, substitute cooked shredded chicken, pork, shrimp or 3 ounces cooked ham.

2 medium eggs
Dash salt and pepper
4 ounces cooked crabmeat, flaked
½ cup celery, finely diced
¼ cup canned bamboo shoots,
 rinsed and finely diced

¼ cup canned mushrooms,
 finely diced
1 teaspoon soy sauce

In bowl beat eggs. Sprinkle with salt and pepper. Add crab, celery, bamboo shoots, mushrooms and soy sauce. Mix well. Divide into two equal portions. Pour one of the portions into a preheated nonstick skillet. Cook at moderately high heat. When bottom is lightly golden, turn with spatula to brown the other side. Remove omelet and keep warm. Repeat for second omelet. Makes 2 servings.

STEAMED FISH WITH GINGER TOPPING

The Chinese don't like the fishy taste in fish, so they shower them in ginger root, scallion, soy sauce and other strong-flavored ingredients. We've done their thing their way—"defishing" makes fish "delish" for people who don't like fish, and of course for those who do.

8 ounces fish fillet (see note)
1 ounce scallion including crisp
 green top, cut in ½-inch pieces
1 tablespoon chicken bouillon
1 tablespoon soy sauce
1 tablespoon chopped fresh
 parsley

2 teaspoons finely minced
 ginger root
1 garlic clove, finely minced
 (optional)
Artificial sweetener to equal
 ½ teaspoon sugar
Salt and pepper, to taste

Rinse fish and wipe dry. Transfer it to a shallow heatproof individual serving plate. Combine remaining ingredients and spread over fish. Put the plate on a steaming rack (or cake rack atop a coffee can).

Set rack in pan holding boiling water. Water should be at least one inch below the level of the fish. Bring water to boil, loosely cover the pot so steam doesn't build up too heavily and steam fish for 15 to 20 minutes or until fish flakes when tested with a fork, and is white and opaque. Add boiling water as necessary to maintain the water level. Serve fish at once in the plate in which it was cooked. Makes 1 serving.

NOTE: Use bass, bluefish, butterfish, carp, mullet, perch, pike, shad and whitefish, etc.

LOBSTER CANTONESE

For an inexpensive substitute, replace the lobster with codfish or hake. A small piece of ginger root may be cooked in the saucepan to release its essence in the chicken bouillon. Add the ginger just before serving if you want only a trace of it in the sauce. Light soy sauce is preferred in Cantonese cooking.

6 ounces lobster, cut into
  bite-size pieces
1 garlic clove, cut in half
¾ cup chicken bouillon
2 teaspoons cornstarch
2 teaspoons soy sauce

2 medium eggs, beaten
2 ounces scallions, minced
⅛ teaspoon salt
Freshly ground pepper
1 cup hot cooked enriched rice

Rub lobster pieces with cut clove of garlic. Put in saucepan with chicken bouillon. Simmer covered for 6 to 10 minutes. Mix cornstarch with soy sauce and add to lobster, stirring constantly until sauce thickens. Stir in beaten eggs and scallions and cook until eggs coagulate; break them into small pieces with stirring spoon. Season with salt and pepper, and serve each portion over ½ cup rice. Makes 2 servings.

WHITE-COOKED CHICKEN

3 quarts water
1 cup chopped chives
3 slices ginger root, grated
8 packets instant chicken broth
  and seasoning mix

1 (3-pound) whole chicken,
  skinned and trussed
Fresh Ginger Sauce (see page 91)

Combine first 4 ingredients in a large pot or Dutch oven. Place over high heat and bring to a boil. Immerse chicken, breast-side down into

[*80*]

boiling mixture. Return to a boil. Remove pot from heat, cover and let cool 5 to 6 hours or to room temperature. Remove chicken from the pot. Discard truss, drain well and chill. Reserve stock. (See note.) Just before serving, chop chicken into bite-sized pieces; this keeps it moist and juices stay in the meat. Weigh portions and serve cold with Fresh Ginger Sauce. Makes 4 servings.

NOTE: Stock may be chilled in refrigerator, then skimmed to remove congealed fat. Measure ¾ cup portions and freeze. Use in recipes calling for bouillon or stock.

WHITE-COOKED CHICKEN WITH MUSHROOMS AND PEAS

¼ cup chicken bouillon
4 cups fresh mushrooms (halved)
2 cups celery, sliced on the
  diagonal
8 ounces peas

1 pound White-Cooked Chicken
  (see recipe above),
  cut in 1-inch squares
1 tablespoon soy sauce

Place bouillon in a medium saucepan and heat. Add mushrooms, celery and peas; cook, stirring, for 4 minutes or until tender but crisp. Drain. Add chicken and soy sauce; heat through. Makes 4 servings.

LEMON PINEAPPLE CHICKEN, PEKING STYLE

A quintessential Chinese dish. The piquancy of lemon, blandness of rice, tart sweetness of pineapple, crunchiness of green pepper, and tender succulence of chicken create a perfect marriage of harmonious colors, textures, aromas and flavors.

2 8-ounce boned, skinless
  chicken breasts
2 tablespoons chicken bouillon
1 tablespoon soy sauce
1 garlic clove, crushed
¾ teaspoon salt
2 teaspoons cornstarch
2 tablespoons lemon juice
½ cup water

¼ cup plus 1 tablespoon cider
  or rice vinegar
1 cup canned pineapple chunks,
  no sugar added
½ cup grated carrot
1 medium green pepper, cut into
  1½-inch squares
1 teaspoon grated lemon rind
1 cup shredded lettuce

Preheat broiler. Wash chicken and wipe dry. Combine next four ingredients in a shallow dish. Place chicken in marinade and spread with fingers. Let stand 15 minutes, turning occasionally so that entire surface of chicken gets coated. Broil on rack 4 inches from heat, turning once, until done on both sides. While chicken is broiling prepare the sauce: Stir cornstarch into lemon juice; combine with water and vinegar in a saucepan. Add pineapple, carrot, green pepper and lemon rind. Bring to a boil. Lower heat and simmer until thickened. When chicken is broiled, place on two individual serving plates. Pour Lemon-Pineapple Sauce over chicken. Serve immediately with a border of shredded lettuce. Makes 2 servings.

NOTE: In a variation of this recipe, ½ cup tomato puree and 3 ounces diced onion or scallions, or 2 tablespoons dehydrated onion flakes, are stirred into the Lemon-Pineapple mixture before it is brought to boil. Pour this Lemon-Pineapple-Tomato Sauce over broiled chicken breasts in a shallow baking pan and bake in 350°F. oven for 15 to 20 minutes.

FIVE-FRAGRANT BEEF

A Shanghai stew. Nice with a bean sprout salad or, if stew will be served hot, with potatoes. Add 12 ounces of peeled new potatoes cut in even dice to the boiling beef stock. Cook until potatoes are tender, about 20 minutes, before warming the beef in the hot liquid.

1½ to 2 pounds well-trimmed beef stew meat (chuck or other inexpensive cut)	1 sprig Chinese parsley (coriander), see note
2 small pieces ginger root, crushed	2 teaspoons five-spice powder
2 small garlic cloves, crushed	2 tablespoons white vinegar
	¾ teaspoon salt or to taste

Cut meat into 1½-inch cubes, cover with boiling water in saucepan and bring to boil. Cook 1 hour or until beef is tender. Drain off liquid, refrigerate it to congeal the fat. Discard the congealed fat. Reheat the beef stock, bring to boil with remaining ingredients, and cook 10 minutes. Pour over the beef. Beef may be served hot, cold or at room temperature. To serve it hot, let the beef simmer (not boil or it will toughen) 10 minutes in the stock. To serve it cold, marinate the beef in the hot stock until cooled, then refrigerate overnight, turning beef several times. Or serve at room temperature. Makes 4 servings: 4 to 6 ounces each.

NOTE: Or omit this and substitute 4 ounces of whole scallions. Flatten scallions with cleaver, tie each one into a bow and serve with stew.

CHICKEN WITH VEGETABLES AND MUSHROOMS (Moo Goo Gai Pan)

1 cup Chinese cabbage,
cut in thin diagonal slices
(or use broccoli florets)
½ cup celery, cut in thin
diagonal slices
½ cup mushrooms, sliced
¼ cup canned, drained bamboo
shoots, cut in thin slices
1 cup chicken bouillon
12 ounces cooked chicken,
cut in thin pieces

8 ounces fresh or frozen Chinese
snow peas
2 teaspoons soy sauce
1 teaspoon sherry extract
(optional)
1 teaspoon finely minced ginger
root
Salt and pepper to taste

In a preheated wok or a nonstick skillet with lid, stir-cook cabbage, celery, mushrooms and bamboo shoots until heated through, but crisp to the bite. Add bouillon and bring to boil. Reduce to simmering and add remaining ingredients. Cover the pan tightly and simmer for 5 minutes. Makes 2 servings.

CHICKEN DYNASTY

1 pound chicken cutlets (boneless,
skinless chicken breasts),
cut in strips
4 ounces onions, chopped
1 cup chicken bouillon
1 cup shredded Chinese cabbage
1 cup diced celery
¾ cup sliced bamboo shoots

½ cup sliced mushrooms
½ cup bean sprouts
¼ cup soy sauce
½ teaspoon garlic powder
½ teaspoon ginger
¼ teaspoon dry mustard
2 ounces pea pods
1 cup cooked enriched white rice

Cook chicken and onions in nonstick skillet or preheated wok until chicken is tender, turning often. Stir in remaining ingredients, except pea pods and rice. Cover and simmer 8 minutes. Add pea pods. Cook 2 minutes more. Evenly divide chicken mixture and serve each portion over ½ cup hot cooked rice. Makes 2 servings.

RED-COOKED CHICKEN

2½ to 3 pound broiler chicken
1 cup soy sauce (dark preferred)
Water to cover
1 tablespoon chives

1 slice fresh ginger root
1 star anise
½ teaspoon sherry extract

Place chicken in a heavy pan with soy sauce and cold water. Bring to boil over medium heat; add remaining ingredients, then simmer, covered, until done (30 to 40 minutes). Turn once or twice for even coloring. Let cool slightly, remove skin, cut into 2-inch sections. Weigh portions before serving. Makes 4 servings.

LO MEIN

1 cup chicken bouillon
½ cup sliced celery
½ cup cooked or canned bean sprouts (see note) or cooked green beans or broccoli
2 ounces diced scallion including green tops, or ¼ cup shredded lettuce
1 teaspoon minced ginger root or dash of ginger

1 teaspoon dehydrated onion flakes
Salt and freshly ground pepper to taste
6 ounces cooked minced chicken, turkey, pork or veal
½ cup cooked enriched noodles
Mustard-Soy Sauce (recipe follows)

In small flameproof porcelain serving casserole, combine chicken bouillon, celery, bean sprouts, or green beans or broccoli, scallion or lettuce, ginger root, onion flakes, salt and pepper; bring to boil. Stir in chicken and noodles. Heat and serve with Mustard-Soy Sauce. Makes 1 serving.

NOTE: To cook fresh sprouts, cover them with boiling water in saucepan; simmer for 3 minutes. Drain. To use canned bean sprouts, rinse first under running water.

Mustard-Soy Sauce

1 tablespoon dry mustard

1½ teaspoons soy sauce

Combine ingredients to make a paste. Use with Lo Mein.

BEEF WITH PEPPERS AND TOMATOES

2 pounds tender boneless steak
(flank, top sirloin or tenderloin)
¼ cup soy sauce
1 tablespoon water
2 garlic cloves, finely chopped
1 teaspoon sherry extract
(optional)
1 teaspoon salt

½ teaspoon pepper
3 medium green peppers, cut into
1½-inch squares
3 medium tomatoes, each cut into
6 wedges
2 cups cooked or canned bean
sprouts
(see note page 84)

Broil meat on preheated rack in broiling pan, 4 inches from heat, until brown on all sides, 10 to 12 minutes; turn steak once. Cut into thin slices and put on platter. Combine soy sauce, water, garlic, sherry extract, salt and pepper. Pour over steak slices. Lightly brown green peppers in nonstick skillet. Tilt platter holding beef and marinade over skillet so marinade liquid flows into it. Bring to boil and let cook 15 minutes. Add tomatoes and cook a minute or two—until tomatoes are soft but not mushy; do not overcook them. Remove pan from heat, add beef slices, and stir them into vegetable mixture. Serve on warmed serving plates, over lightly cooked bean sprouts. Makes 4 servings.

SOY SAUCE ANISE BEEF

2 pounds lean bottom beef round
4 slices ginger root, minced
¼ cup soy sauce
2 tablespoons chopped chives

1 tablespoon sherry extract
1 teaspoon salt
1 cup cold water
1 star anise

Place meat on rack in open shallow roasting pan. Roast in 350°F. oven to desired degree of doneness. Remove and let stand 15 minutes. Cut in one-inch cubes. Heat 2-quart saucepan and add meat and ginger. Cook, stirring constantly, until meat is browned on all sides. Add soy sauce, chives, extract and salt. Mix; add water and bring to a boil. Cover and cook over medium heat 30 minutes, stirring occasionally. Add star anise, cover and cook another 30 minutes. There should only be ½ cup liquid left. If more, uncover and continue cooking to reduce. Makes 4 servings.

CHARCOAL-BROILED STEAK SZECHUAN

2 pounds flank or shoulder steak
Cut garlic clove
3 tablespoons lemon juice
1 tablespoon soy sauce

1½ teaspoons salt
⅛ teaspoon crushed Szechuan
pepper
Hot Pepper Dip (recipe follows)

With tines of fork, pierce steak on both sides and rub with cut clove of garlic. Combine lemon juice, soy sauce, salt and crushed pepper. Pour over steak and let marinate 4 hours, turning several times. Broil in hinged rack over hot coals until done on both sides. Slice on wooden steak board and serve with a bowl of Hot Pepper Dip set in the center of the table. You could also broil this, guests participating, on individual hibachis. Just slice the marinated steak in serving portions, ready for the flame. Makes 4 servings.

Hot Pepper Dip

½ cup soy sauce
1 tablespoon hot pepper sauce
(or to taste)

2 garlic cloves, crushed
Dash powdered mustard

Combine ingredients in serving bowl. Serve immediately. Makes 4 servings.

GINGER BEEF

1 ounce finely chopped onion
1 cup beef bouillon
¼ cup tomato puree
½ teaspoon ginger
¼ teaspoon chili powder
¼ garlic clove, crushed
¼ teaspoon turmeric
1 medium tomato, peeled and
chopped

6 ounces broiled flank steak, cut
diagonally across grain into
thin slices
Salt and pepper to taste
1 teaspoon chopped fresh parsley
½ cup cooked enriched noodles

Lightly brown onions in nonstick skillet. Add bouillon, tomato puree, ginger, chili powder, garlic, turmeric and tomato; simmer 5 minutes. Arrange the beef slices in sauce, reheat; season to taste. Sprinkle with parsley and serve over noodles. Makes 1 serving.

BARBECUED PORK

With the burnished deep-red color that you expect in Chinese roast pork.

2 pounds lean boneless pork
(or pork tenderloin)
½ cup soy sauce
3 tablespoons vinegar or
lemon juice
1 tablespoon Worcestershire
1½ tablespoons brown sugar
replacement

2 tablespoons tomato puree
1 teaspoon sherry extract
1 teaspoon red food coloring
1 teaspoon salt
1 teaspoon minced fresh ginger
root
Dash pepper

Slice pork with the grain into pieces 1½ inches thick, 1½ inches wide and 4 inches long. With a fork, pierce the pieces on all sides. Combine remaining ingredients and pour over the pork. Refrigerate and let stand overnight, turning pork several times. Remove from marinade reserving liquid. In preheated 350°F. oven, roast pork on rack in aluminum foil-lined roasting pan for 40 to 45 minutes. Cut pork against the grain into slices ⅜-inch thick and serve hot or cold. Heat marinade and serve with pork. Makes 4 servings.

GINGER PORK

To avoid peeling garlic, wrap the clove between two folds of wax paper, smack it with the flat part of the cleaver, and drop it from paper into pan.

½ cup chicken bouillon
2 ounces minced scallions
2 tablespoons soy sauce
1 teaspoon sherry extract
1 small garlic clove, crushed
Artificial sweetener to equal 1
teaspoon sugar

½ teaspoon ginger
Dash pepper
8 ounces cooked pork, cut in
1-inch cubes
1 cup hot cooked enriched rice

In saucepan, combine chicken bouillon, scallions, soy sauce, sherry extract, garlic, sweetener, ginger and pepper. Simmer covered for 15 minutes. Turn off heat. Add pork. Stir well. Serve over rice. Makes 2 servings.

STIR-COOKED PORK WITH CHINESE VEGETABLES

1 pound boneless tender pork, trimmed of all visible fat and cut into thin strips
½ cup soy sauce
1 ounce onion, finely chopped
2 garlic cloves, minced
2 teaspoons grated fresh ginger root (or ½ teaspoon ground)

2 cups diagonally sliced celery
1 cup green beans, diagonally cut into 1-inch pieces
¾ cup thinly sliced bamboo shoots
1 cup cooked enriched rice
1 ounce scallions, finely cut

Place pork in bowl with soy sauce, onion, garlic and ginger. Stir to mix well; cover and let marinate 1 hour. Preheat broiler. Remove meat from marinade, reserving liquid. Place pork on rack and broil about 15 minutes, turning meat once, until pork is thoroughly cooked. Place pork and marinade in a wok or 2½-quart saucepan. Add celery, green beans and bamboo shoots. Stir-cook 5 minutes or until vegetables are tender-crisp. Serve each portion over ½ cup rice. Garnish each serving with ½ ounce scallions. Makes 2 servings.

MEAT SHREDS WITH GREEN BEANS

1 pound cooked pork or beef, sliced
4 cups fresh green beans
2 garlic cloves, minced or pressed
1 cup chicken bouillon

1 tablespoon light soy sauce
1 tablespoon cornstarch stirred in 1 tablespoon water
¼ teaspoon sherry extract

Stack slices of pork or beef. Cut through stacks to make fine shreds. Set meat aside or refrigerate until ready to use. Cut off tips of green beans, wash, dry and cut into 2-inch diagonal pieces. Boil water in large saucepan and drop beans into strainer. Immerse strainer in boiling water and cook until beans are tender but still crisp and bright green. Cool in strainer under cold running water (to set bright color). Drain; refrigerate until ready to use. At serving time, preheat wok or skillet. Stir-cook garlic with blanched beans just long enough to spread garlic essence through the vegetable. Add shredded meat and stir together to combine (all of this takes about 3 minutes). Add bouillon, soy sauce, cornstarch and sherry extract. Heat thoroughly. Serve in individual porcelain bowls. Makes 4 servings.

STIR-COOKED CHICKEN LIVERS WITH
BAMBOO SHOOTS AND WATER CHESTNUTS

1 pound chicken livers (partially frozen to make slicing easier)
5 teaspoons water
1 teaspoon sherry extract
¼ cup chicken bouillon
1 tablespoon soy sauce
¾ cup bamboo shoots, sliced thin, then in ½-inch strips
4 ounces canned, drained water chestnuts, sliced
Salt to taste
1 tablespoon chopped fresh chives

Cut chicken livers in ½-inch slices; add water and sherry extract and toss gently. Let stand 5 minutes. Heat bouillon in saucepan or wok. Add livers and stir-cook until they change color. Add soy sauce; stir to blend. Stir in bamboo shoots and water chestnuts, then add salt and chives and mix well. Serve at once. Makes 2 servings.

FIVE-SPICE POWDER

You can buy this sweet and pungent spice mixture by weight, or make your own using a mortar and pestle, blender, or food processor to crush the following ingredients into a powder: 50 peppercorns; 4 star anise; 2 teaspoons fennel seeds; 3 one-inch pieces of stick cinnamon; 10 whole cloves. Wrap the powder tightly in plastic bag and store in screwtop jar. It will stay fresh for several months. Allspice, or a mixture of powdered cinnamon, cloves, ginger and nutmeg, is sometimes substituted for five-spice powder.

SPROUTING BEANS

The idea for sprouting beans originated in China. Sprouts are nutritious and easy and economical to grow, 1 pound of dried beans making 4 or 5 pounds of fresh vegetable. Here are the simple instructions:

Line a colander with two layers of cheesecloth. Soak 4 tablespoons of mung or soy beans in lukewarm water for 1 hour. Arrange beans in colander, one layer deep. Cover top with paper towel. Put colander into basin to catch dripping water. Sprinkle water over the beans each day. In 4 to 5 days you will have fresh sprouts, all ready to use. Rinse the sprouts a few times so that the dark skins come off (they will usually float to the surface), then drain. Don't worry about the skins which remain on the sprout—they can be eaten. Refrigerate unused sprouts for up to one week. For longer storage blanch them as directed below.

BEAN SPROUT SALAD (Dow Ngah)

1 cup fresh bean sprouts
¼ cup grated carrots
1 ounce chopped scallions, including firm green tops

1 tablespoon soy sauce
1½ teaspoons vegetable oil
1½ teaspoons sesame oil

Blanch fresh sprouts by pouring boiling water over them in saucepan, let stand 2 minutes. Then drain, rinse in cold water and drain again. (To freshen canned bean sprouts, drain and rinse in colander under cold running water.) Refrigerate until ready to use. Combine remaining ingredients, pour over beans; mix well and serve. Makes 2 servings.

PLUM SAUCE

To serve over steamed fish, broiled chicken and roast or barbecued meat. For more pizazz, add a few drops garlic juice (made by crushing clove of garlic) or a few drops hot pepper sauce. Other seasoning possibilities include ⅛ teaspoon allspice, ½ teaspoon dry mustard, ¾ teaspoon browning sauce.

1¼ cups chicken bouillon
2 medium plums, peeled, pitted and diced
½ cup cider vinegar
¼ cup brown sugar replacement
1 tablespoon dehydrated onion flakes

1 teaspoon finely minced ginger root
Salt to taste
2 drops red food coloring

Combine all ingredients (except food coloring) in saucepan. Bring to boil, cook over moderate heat, uncovered, until sauce is thick, stirring frequently. Add food coloring, if desired. Makes 2 servings.

FRESH GINGER SAUCE

Make this recipe only if the ginger is very young and tender and free of fibers.

¼ cup vegetable oil
2 tablespoons peeled and finely minced fresh ginger root

1 tablespoon dehydrated onion flakes, reconstituted
1 teaspoon salt

Place all ingredients in a 2-cup container with lid. Shake to combine, and let stand. Pour into 4 individual dip dishes and use with cold chicken. Makes 4 servings.

BOK CHOY WITH MUSHROOMS AND BEAN SPROUTS

Chinese cabbage is milder and less tough than the American species, which can, however, be used in this recipe.

2 cups Chinese cabbage, cut in 1-inch pieces
¼ cup liquid from soaking mushrooms
Salt to taste

2 cups canned, rinsed bean sprouts
1 cup soaked dried black mushrooms, cut in 1-inch pieces (discard tough stems)
1 tablespoon cornstarch

In a wok or nonstick skillet with cover, stir-cook cabbage in mushroom liquid over medium heat, about 2 minutes. Add salt, bean sprouts and mushrooms; mix. Stir cornstarch into 1 tablespoon water and add. Cover, turn heat down to simmer and cook about 5 minutes, to thicken sauce. Cabbage and sprouts should be crisp. Makes 4 servings.

STEAMED CUCUMBERS

2 medium cucumbers
½ teaspoon salt

Lemon Sauce (recipe follows)

Peel, cut in half lengthwise, and seed cucumbers; slice lengthwise into wedges about ⅜-inch wide and cut into pieces 2½-inches long. Place on individual flameproof serving platter, place on a rack in a pot holding boiling water (at least 1 inch below level of serving platter).

Cover platter with wax paper and fit a cover loosely over pot. Steam about 25 minutes or until tender. Serve with lemon sauce. Makes 2 servings.

Lemon Sauce for Cucumber

1 tablespoon prepared mustard
2 teaspoons lemon juice

2 teaspoons soy sauce

Combine. Mix until smooth. Serve with Steamed Cucumbers. Makes 2 servings.

STUFFED CUCUMBERS

Filling (recipe follows)
4 medium cucumbers
¾ cup chicken bouillon

1 teaspoon soy sauce
½ teaspoon sherry extract

Prepare and reserve filling. Peel cucumbers and cut cross-wise into 2-inch thick slices. Scoop out seeds from one side of each section, not clear through, creating a cup shape to hold filling. Stuff the center of each section with filling, packing it in tightly and rounding out the edges. Place cucumbers in skillet; pour next 3 ingredients over and bring to boil. Then cover and simmer 5 minutes or until cucumber is tender. Makes 4 servings.

Filling for Cucumbers*

8 ounces cooked ground pork
or beef, crumbled
2 slices fresh ginger root, minced

1 tablespoon soy sauce
¼ teaspoon sherry extract
Salt to taste

Combine all ingredients in a medium bowl. With a large mixing spoon, spoon mixture into cucumber shells. Makes 4 servings.

CHINESE CUCUMBER SALAD

2 medium cucumbers, peeled
½ teaspoon salt
1 tablespoon soy sauce
1 tablespoon rice vinegar or
wine vinegar

Artificial sweetener to equal 1
tablespoon sugar
2 teaspoons sesame oil

Cut cucumbers in half lengthwise. Scoop out seeds and slice thin. Sprinkle with salt and let stand about 30 minutes in a colander or strainer, allowing liquid to run off. Place in bowl and toss cucumber slices with remaining ingredients. Allow to stand 5 minutes before serving. Makes 2 servings.

STEAMED EGGPLANT

Tearing the cooked eggplant in this recipe gives it a more interesting texture than chopping or mincing. For luncheon, arrange eggplant shreds on a serving dish radiating out like flower petals. Leave space in center and fill this with 4 medium scrambled eggs, cooked and broken into pieces. Makes 2 servings.

1 medium eggplant	½ teaspoon salt
1 tablespoon soy sauce	
1 teaspoon vegetable oil (optional)	

Wash eggplant. Cut skin with a few lengthwise slashes, about ½-inch deep. Place on heatproof dish. Steam until soft (15 to 20 minutes). Let cool slightly, then strip off skin and discard it. Tear eggplant into lengthwise shreds, discarding seeds. Measure 1 cup of eggplant. Place in small bowl. Stir in soy sauce, oil and salt. Serve hot or cold. Makes 2 servings.

VARIATION: Add 1 or 2 slices minced fresh ginger root and ½ crushed garlic clove to soy sauce.

STIR-COOKED VEGETABLES

½ cup water	½ cup diced celery
1 packet instant chicken broth and seasoning mix	4 ounces shelled peas
2 slices fresh ginger root, minced	½ cup Chinese cabbage, stems diced
½ cup cauliflower, broken into small florets	½ cup diced mushrooms
½ cup asparagus, cut in 1-inch pieces	½ cup diced bamboo shoots, rinsed
	1 tablespoon soy sauce

In a preheated wok or large saucepan, heat water and broth mix; add ginger root, cauliflower, asparagus, celery and peas; stir-cook 2 minutes; add cabbage, mushrooms and bamboo shoots, stir; add soy sauce and stir to blend in. Simmer over low heat about 2 minutes. Do not overcook—vegetables should be tender-crisp. Makes 4 servings.

SIMMERED STUFFED GREEN PEPPER

Stuffing (recipes follow)
2 medium green peppers
½ cup chicken bouillon

1 tablespoon soy sauce
Dash pepper

Prepare one of the stuffings. With a sharp knife, cut the tops off peppers then scoop out the seeds. Stuff peppers with one of the mixtures; replace the tops as lids. Stand stuffed peppers upright in a shallow pan; pour in bouillon and soy sauce; sprinkle with pepper. Bring bouillon to boil; lower heat and simmer, covered, 40 minutes. Serve with liquid as a sauce, poured over peppers. Makes 2 servings.

Vegetable Stuffing

1 cup shredded carrots
1 cup cooked bean sprouts
  (if canned, rinse first)
4 ounces onions, diced
½ cup tomato puree

1 teaspoon rice vinegar or pinch
  onion and garlic powder
1 teaspoon salt
⅛ teaspoon pepper

Combine ingredients. Fills 2 medium peppers. Makes 2 servings.

Fish Stuffing

12 ounces cooked haddock or
   halibut, flaked; or cooked
   diced shrimp
1 slice fresh ginger root, minced

1 teaspoon dehydrated onion
  flakes, reconstituted
½ teaspoon salt
Dash pepper

Blend all ingredients. Fills 2 medium peppers. Makes 2 servings.

CHINESE NOODLES

½ cup cooked enriched thin
  noodles

1 teaspoon soy sauce

Combine noodles and soy sauce. Thinly spread on shallow nonstick pan (10x15-inches) and bake at 350°F. until crisp and brown. Remove from oven and break noodles apart if necessary. Makes 1 serving.

SPINACH WITH PEPPERY SAUCE, PEKING STYLE

Two cups Chinese cabbage, cut in 2-inch pieces, could replace the spinach.

Boiling water
2 cups cleaned spinach, stems removed
1 cup shredded carrots
1 tablespoon sesame oil
1 tablespoon lemon juice

1 teaspoon minced fresh ginger root
1 teaspoon prepared mustard or ¼ teaspoon crushed red pepper, or hot pepper sauce
1 teaspoon salt

Place spinach in a colander. Pour boiling water over it to blanch. Drain well. Chop and transfer to serving bowl or dish. Top with carrots. Combine remaining ingredients and pour over vegetables. Makes 1 serving.

"FRIED" RICE*

For variation add 2 ounces cooked chicken, roasted pork or shrimp— diced or cut in julienne strips.

1 medium egg, slightly beaten
2 ounces onion, diced
½ cup diced celery

¼ cup shredded carrots
½ cup cooked enriched cold rice
2 tablespoons soy sauce

In a preheated wok or a hot nonstick skillet, scramble egg; remove from skillet and cut up into tiny pieces. Set aside. Stir-cook onions, celery and carrots in the same skillet until slightly softened. Stir in rice; add soy sauce. Cook at high heat for 3 minutes, stirring constantly. Stir in scrambled egg, remove from heat and serve immediately. Makes 1 serving.

INDIVIDUAL GRAIN RICE

Here is a good way to prepare cooked rice and have it turn out with each grain separate every time. (You can estimate that 1 part raw rice equals about 3 parts cooked.) Extra rice may be frozen and used at another time.

1¾ cups cold water   1 cup uncooked enriched rice

Combine water and rice in 2-quart saucepan with lid. Bring to boil, lower heat and continue cooking on lowest heat 20 minutes. Turn flame off; let rice "relax" for 20 or more minutes before opening lid. Stir to break rice and measure ½ cup portions before serving. Makes about 6 servings.

ALMOND COOKIES*

For anise cookies use anise extract rather than almond extract in the following recipe.

2 medium eggs
⅔ cup nonfat dry milk
1 slice enriched white bread,
   made into crumbs
Artificial sweetener to equal 15
   teaspoons sugar, divided

1 teaspoon imitation butter
   flavoring
Dash salt
1 teaspoon unflavored gelatin
¼ teaspoon almond extract
½ teaspoon water

Preheat oven to 325°F. Combine eggs, milk, bread crumbs and sweetener to equal 14 teaspoons sugar, butter flavoring and salt. Beat with electric mixer until well blended. Sprinkle in gelatin. Mix 1 minute on medium-high speed. Drop by spoonfuls 1½-inches apart on nonstick cookie sheet. Bake for 15 minutes or until a golden ring appears around the edges of each cookie. Remove from sheet with spatula. Combine almond extract with water and remaining sweetener. Spread on cookies with a pastry brush to form a glaze. Makes 2 servings (about 20 cookies).

VARIATION: Add 1 teaspoon fennel seeds with first 6 ingredients. Pulverize seeds with a mortar and pestle or in blender container before mixing. Eliminate glaze.

FRUIT WITH SESAME DRESSING

1 large tangerine or 1 small orange
¼ medium pineapple
2 medium bananas
1 medium cantaloupe
8 large deep lettuce leaves
2 tablespoons lemon juice
4 teaspoons vegetable oil

4 teaspoons sesame oil
1 teaspoon dehydrated onion
  flakes
⅛ teaspoon Worcestershire
Dash each dry mustard, salt,
  paprika and hot pepper sauce

Peel the fruit over a large bowl to catch juices. Discard skins and rinds and reserve liquid. Cut fruit into uniform bite-size pieces. Place in a medium bowl and toss lightly to combine. Place each portion on a lettuce leaf in individual salad bowls. In jar with tight cover, combine remaining ingredients (including juices from fruit) and shake well. Pour over fruit cradled in the lettuce. Makes 8 servings.

BANANA-PINEAPPLE GELATIN

4 cups water
½ cup agar-agar, chopped
  (see note)
Artificial sweetener to equal 10
  teaspoons sugar

1 cup evaporated skimmed milk
1 tablespoon banana extract
1 teaspoon pineapple extract
Few drops yellow food coloring

Bring water to boil in 3-quart saucepan. Add agar-agar and sweetener and cook, stirring, until agar-agar dissolves and mixture begins to thicken. Strain if lumpy. Stir in milk, extracts and food coloring. Pour mixture into 10x15-inch pan (or ice cube trays). Refrigerate until set. Cut in dice and serve in dessert cups. Makes 8 servings.

NOTE: A dried gelatinous seaweed. If not available, use 2½ tablespoons unflavored gelatin, dissolved in ½ cup plus 2 tablespoons water. Add to boiling water in saucepan and continue as above.

STEAMED SPONGE CAKE

6 medium eggs, separated
Artificial sweetener to equal
    ½ cup sugar
2½ tablespoons water
3 slices enriched white bread,
    made into crumbs

½ teaspoon black pepper
½ teaspoon vanilla extract
½ teaspoon almond extract

In a large bowl, beat yolks until light lemony color, about 5 minutes. Add sweetener and water; beat until fluffy. Combine bread crumbs and black pepper and blend into egg yolks, then add extracts and mix well. Beat whites until they form peaks and are stiff, but not dry. Fold into batter. Line an 8x8x3-inch square cake pan with waxed paper. Pour batter into pan. Rap pan sharply on table several times to remove air bubbles. Cover top with wax paper. Steam until done, 20 to 25 minutes. Makes 3 servings.

ALMOND "JELLY"

A few recipes that would be suitable endings to your Chinese meal are included. They are in the Chinese mood, if not in the absolute tradition.

1 envelope unflavored gelatin
2 cups water, divided
⅔ cup nonfat dry milk

Artificial sweetener to equal 8
    teaspoons sugar
1 tablespoon almond extract

Sprinkle gelatin over ½ cup water in small saucepan; heat, stirring, until gelatin dissolves; pour into medium bowl. Add remaining water, dry milk, artificial sweetener and almond extract; mix thoroughly. Pour into four ½-cup molds. Chill. Makes 4 servings.

France

It is said that one-third of the world prefers Italian food, one-third Chinese, and one hundred percent favors *la bonne cuisine* of France. French culinary genius is reflected in an infinite capacity for taking pains, with homemakers often marketing at least once a day to buy ingredients at the peak of quality. And what a wealth of ingredients is available! More than 400 distinct varieties of cheese alone are produced, each region of France having its own specialties made according to centuries-old formulas.

France, like so many sophisticated countries, is very weight-conscious, and this has encouraged her famous chefs to recreate slimmed-down versions of classic dishes, a practice we applaud and have followed for more than a decade. The French recipes in this chapter are adaptations of classic ones, but they give you the delectable flavor while eliminating heavy creams and unnecessary fats.

Since soup is a daily—sometimes twice daily—tradition in France, we begin with a collection that will help you fill empty tureens and tummies in more than a soupçon of different ways. You'll find thick, hearty potages, smooth purees, creamy bisques and sparkling consommés. All of them are as lip-smacking in appeal as the ones *grandmère* used to make, and all are done our stay-skinny way.

QUICK CARROT BISQUE (Purée de Carottes à la Crème)

A rich "cream" soup thickened with pureed vegetables.

1 cup homemade chicken stock (see page ix) or 1 cup water and 1 packet instant chicken broth and seasoning mix or 1 chicken bouillon cube
1½ cups sliced carrots
½ cup sliced celery
1 ounce diced onion or 2 teaspoons dehydrated onion flakes

½ cup evaporated skimmed milk
¼ cup water
1 sprig parsley or thyme (or ⅛ teaspoon dried)
Freshly ground black pepper

In a medium saucepan, heat stock (or water and broth mix, or bouillon cube), carrots, celery and onions to boiling. Reduce heat; cover and simmer until carrots are tender. Place in blender container and process at medium speed until smooth. Return to saucepan; stir in milk and water; heat. Sprinkle top with parsley and freshly ground pepper. Makes 2 servings.

CELERY CONSOMME
(Consommé de Celeri or Consommé au Fumet de Celeri)

4 cups beef bouillon
2 cups sliced celery including tops

Black pepper to taste

In saucepan, combine bouillon and celery; cover and cook for 10 minutes. Remove several slices of celery and reserve for garnish. Continue cooking celery for 35 minutes. Put through food mill or strainer, pressing out as much liquid as possible from the cooked celery. Or process in blender at medium speed until smooth (however, this will not remove the fibers). Serve hot with celery slices garnishing each serving. Pass the pepper mill. Makes 4 servings.

CONSOMME CHIFFONNADE

Blanch ½ cup shredded green lettuce leaves in boiling salted water to cover. Let stand 5 minutes. Drain. Serve in bowl with 1 cup hot chicken bouillon. Season with salt and pepper and perhaps garlic. Makes 1 serving.

POTATO AND RADISH PUREE

3 ounces peeled potato, sliced
1 bunch radishes, trimmed and sliced

1 teaspoon melted margarine
¼ cup skim milk
Salt and pepper to taste

In small saucepan cover potato with boiling salted water and bring to boil. Cover and simmer until potato is tender. Cook radishes in a separate pan, in boiling water until tender. Drain potato and radishes. Add remaining ingredients. Puree, using food mill, blender or food processor. Serve hot. Makes 1 serving.

SPINACH CONSOMME (Consommé d'Epinards)

Cut 1 cup young spinach leaves (washed and well-dried) into very thin strips or shreds. Sprinkle into saucepan holding 4 cups boiling chicken bouillon. Cook 3 to 5 minutes or until spinach is wilted, then serve hot with a thin slice of lemon and grated nutmeg added to each serving. Makes 4 servings.

JELLIED "WINE" CONSOMME

4 cups chicken bouillon
1 medium green pepper, finely chopped
2 tablespoons each chopped fresh parsley and chives
1 tablespoon dehydrated onion flakes
1 tablespoon chopped fresh chervil, if available, or
1 teaspoon dried

1 envelope unflavored gelatin
2 tablespoons cold water or bouillon
1 tablespoon sherry extract
1 teaspoon hot pepper sauce (or to taste)
4 slices lime or lemon, dusted with paprika

Heat bouillon, green pepper, parsley, chives, onion flakes and chervil, if available, to simmering. Soften gelatin in cold water or bouillon, then add to hot bouillon, and stir until gelatin is dissolved. Add sherry extract and hot pepper sauce. Divide the consommé evenly into 4 mugs or bouillon cups and chill. When jelled, beat with fork to make coarse pieces. Top each mug with a thin slice of lime or lemon sprinkled with paprika. Makes 4 servings.

CONSOMME SUZETTE

1½ cups chicken bouillon
½ cup tomato juice
1 cup julienne (thin matchstick strips) of carrots
½ cup julienne of celery
½ cup mushrooms, cut in thin slices

½ teaspoon chopped fresh herbs or ¼ teaspoon dried (parsley, dill, chives and chervil)

In saucepan, bring to boil bouillon, tomato juice, carrots and celery; cook 5 to 8 minutes (vegetables will be almost done but still quite crisp). Add mushrooms; cook another 2 to 3 minutes; serve, sprinkling each portion with chopped herbs. Makes 2 servings.

CONSOMME A L'INDIENNE

To 1 cup hot chicken bouillon, add ¼ teaspoon coconut extract and a dash (or more to taste) curry powder. Pour over ½ cup cooked enriched rice. Makes 1 serving.

CONSOMME PORTUGAISE

Combine ⅔ cup beef bouillon with ⅓ cup tomato juice. Sprinkle with cayenne pepper and salt, and serve chilled in cups. Makes 1 serving.

WATERCRESS SOUP (Potage au Cresson)

Select rich green crisp watercress. Rinse very well under cold running water in colander, dry thoroughly, keep refrigerated until ready to use. Cut away tough ends before use.

2 ounces white part of leeks, scallions, shallots or onions, diced
2 cups zucchini, diced
4 cups chicken bouillon

1 large bunch or 2 small bunches watercress, cleaned (use only leaves)
2 slices bread, cut into 32 small cubes

In saucepan, combine leeks, zucchini and chicken bouillon. Simmer uncovered until zucchini is very soft, 20 to 25 minutes. Add watercress and bring soup to boil. Process in blender container, a small amount at a time (or hot mixture may overflow), until smooth. Serve hot in bowls. Garnish each serving with 8 cubes of bread. Makes 4 servings.

"CREME" CRESSONNIERE

Follow directions above, but after soup is blended, add ¾ cup evaporated skimmed milk and dash of nutmeg. Reheat but do not boil. Stir well and serve at once. Makes 4 servings.

SPRING VEGETABLE SOUP (Consommé Printanier)

Springtime—printemps—is prime time for this soup made from all the earliest vegetables. Be frugal and use the green trimmings from the salad bowl and the tops of leeks and scallions.

4 cups beef bouillon (4 envelopes beef broth and seasoning mix or 4 beef bouillon cubes dissolved in 4 cups water)
1 cup shredded lettuce or watercress
1 cup young sliced green beans (mixed with ends of mushrooms, if available)
½ cup shredded spinach leaves
½ cup sliced asparagus tips and ends, or ends only

3 ounces shelled green peas
½ cup sliced carrots
2 ounces sliced leeks or scallions
1 garlic clove, minced
4 teaspoons imitation (or diet) margarine (optional)
4 sprigs fresh parsley or ½ teaspoon dried parsley, chives or chervil (for garnish)
Salt and pepper to taste

In soup kettle or saucepan, combine bouillon, vegetables and garlic. Bring to boil; cover pan and simmer 35 to 45 minutes. Stir gently, then divide into 4 soup bowls. Stir a teaspoon of margarine into each bowl and float a parsley sprig or few flakes of dried herbs over each serving. Add salt and pepper if necessary. Makes 4 servings.

BREAD SOUP (Panade)*

Bread soup. Reminds us of Rock Soup which it resembles only in that it includes a lot more than the one ingredient named in the title. It's also very filling, and very country French. A pleasant peasant luncheon.

1 cup finely diced celery including leaves
1 cup shredded spinach
1½ cups hot water
2 slices stale enriched white bread, diced

1 cup evaporated skimmed milk
2 medium eggs
½ teaspoon salt
Freshly ground pepper to taste
Nutmeg

Combine celery and spinach in saucepan; add water; bring to boil, cover and cook for 20 minutes. Add bread, bring to boil then simmer for 10 minutes more. Cool slightly and transfer to blender container. Process and return soup to saucepan. In small mixing bowl, beat milk and eggs together with salt and pepper. Stir into the soup, and let it heat but not boil. Serve in mugs with grated nutmeg. Makes 2 servings.

EGGS BASQUE STYLE (Pipérade)*

A super scramble, also pretty good with ¼ cup pimento substituted for the 2 green peppers.

2 medium tomatoes, diced
2 medium green peppers, seeded and diced (remove white pulp)
2 slices enriched white bread made into crumbs in blender container

1 cup skim milk
4 medium eggs, beaten
Salt and pepper to taste

In upper part of covered double boiler placed over direct heat, steam (*sweat* is what the chefs say) tomatoes and green peppers, until peppers are soft, about 10 minutes. Cover crumbs with 3 tablespoons milk. Add to tomato-green pepper mixture with all remaining ingredients. Stir well. Pour hot water into bottom part of double boiler, insert top and cook covered about 20 minutes, until eggs are done to taste, stirring frequently. Serve on warm plates. Makes 4 servings.

POACHED EGGS WITH LETTUCE* (Oeufs à la Maraîchère)

2 cups shredded lettuce, washed
2 medium eggs

Salt and pepper to taste
1 teaspoon minced fresh chives

In steamer or strainer placed over hot water, steam lettuce until wilted (3 to 5 minutes). Line 2 cocottes or custard cups with wilted lettuce. Break an egg over each bed of lettuce, season with salt and pepper, and garnish top with minced chives. Place cocottes in a shallow pan holding hot water and let cook gently on top of the stove 8 to 10 minutes, or until eggs are done to taste. Serve in the cocottes or custard cups. Makes 2 servings.

EGGS FLORENTINE (Oeufs à la Florentine)

1½ cups (10-ounce package)
  frozen chopped spinach, thawed
1 teaspoon salt
⅛ teaspoon pepper

3 medium eggs
3 ounces freshly grated cheese
  (Parmesan or Swiss)

Drain spinach well and squeeze it dry. Season with salt and pepper. Divide equally among 3 individual (10-ounce) pie dishes. Break an egg over each bed of spinach; sprinkle each with an ounce of grated cheese. Bake in moderate oven (350°F.) until egg whites are firm, about 15 minutes. Serve immediately. Makes 3 servings.

Oeufs à l'Arlésienne

Replace spinach with ratatouille (see recipe, page 133), allowing ½ cup for each serving. Follow directions given above. Makes 3 servings.

OMELET WITH BREAD AND CHEESE (Omelette Grand'mère)

1 slice fresh enriched white bread,
  made into crumbs
½ cup warm skim milk
2 medium eggs, lightly beaten

2 ounces grated Swiss cheese
Freshly grated nutmeg
Salt and pepper to taste

Combine all ingredients in a mixing bowl and stir well. Preheat nonstick skillet. Pour in egg mixture, let it set for several seconds, and stir it with fork, lifting the edges and tilting the pan to let the uncooked mixture flow underneath. Cook the omelet until it is set and the underside is browned; loosen it from the pan with a spatula, and invert it onto a heated platter. Makes 2 servings.

MUSHROOM-ASPARAGUS OPEN OMELET*

One- or two-egg omelets should be made in small skillets (5- to 8-inch bottom diameter). Use a nonstick pan or heavy ironware, and preheat it. You can make an open omelet of 8 to 10 eggs in a 10- or 12-inch pan and serve it in wedges for even division.

2 medium eggs
¼ cup cooked, chopped, drained asparagus tips
¼ cup cooked, chopped, drained mushrooms

¼ teaspoon salt
Freshly ground pepper to taste
1 teaspoon water or liquid left from cooking vegetables

Add eggs to a bowl and beat until frothy. Stir in remaining ingredients. Pour into preheated nonstick skillet. Cook over moderate heat. As mixture sets, with fork lift up edges tilting pan so that uncooked portions flow evenly to bottom. When underside is set, turn it with spatula (or flop it from skillet to plate, then slide back on to skillet so that the top of the omelet is now on the bottom). Cook until the bottom is set and golden brown. Divide in half and serve immediately. Makes 2 servings.

LOBSTER OMELET WITH TOMATO SAUCE

For a satisfying and colorful luncheon entrée, serve with 1 cup cooked zucchini strips.

1 medium tomato, sliced
2 tablespoons tomato puree
1 teaspoon chicken broth and seasoning mix
½ teaspoon mixed dried or fresh herbs to taste (chives, parsley, tarragon or basil)

2 ounces cooked lobster or halibut, or a combination, diced fine
1 medium egg, lightly beaten with ½ teaspoon water
Salt and freshly ground pepper to taste

In small saucepan, cook tomato, tomato puree, broth mix and herbs until tomato is soft. Process in blender container and pour back into saucepan. Add fish and keep saucepan over low heat, so contents stay hot without boiling. **Pour egg into small preheated nonstick skillet,** and cook over moderate heat, lifting edges on all sides and tilting pan so that uncooked portions flow evenly to bottom. When omelet is set, place some of the tomato-fish mixture across the center, fold it in half, and slide it onto a warmed serving plate. Top with remaining tomato-fish mixture. Makes 1 serving.

SCRAMBLED EGGS WITH DICED BREAD
(Oeufs Brouillés aux Croûtons)

For le petit dejeuner *(breakfast) serve with* café au lait: *a mixture of half strong coffee and half hot foaming skim milk.*

1 medium egg
Salt and pepper to taste
1 tablespoon water
1 slice enriched white bread,
    toasted (dried in oven or
    toaster), made into croutons

¼ teaspoon minced fresh herbs
    (parsley, chives, rosemary or
    dash of dried herbs to taste)

Break an egg into a bowl; add salt, pepper and water. Beat thoroughly. Pour into small preheated nonstick skillet or heavy iron pan. Cook over moderate heat, stirring gently. When egg is almost done, sprinkle with croutons and herbs. Scramble and serve. Makes 1 serving.

CODFISH WITH HERBS AND TOMATOES
(Cabillaud à la Provençale)

3 cups water
½ cup sliced celery
1 packet instant chicken broth
    and seasoning mix
½ lemon
2 tablespoons dehydrated onion
    flakes
1 teaspoon chopped fresh
    parsley

½ bay leaf
⅛ teaspoon ground cloves
⅛ teaspoon thyme
4 boned and skinned cod steaks,
    8-ounces each
2 medium tomatoes, cut in half
2 medium green peppers, seeded
    and cut in half

In a 12-inch skillet, combine water, celery, broth mix, lemon, onion flakes, parsley, bay leaf, cloves and thyme. Bring to a boil, then reduce heat to a simmer. Add fish and poach 5 to 7 minutes. Add tomato and green pepper halves, and finish cooking until fish flakes easily. Remove fish and vegetables, keep warm. Cook liquid until reduced by half. Remove lemon and bay leaf. Place liquid and half of the cooked tomato and peppers in a blender container. Puree until smooth. Slowly reheat in saucepan. Pour over fish and remaining tomato and peppers. Makes 4 servings.

FISH STEW BRITTANY STYLE (Cotriade)

Freeze any raw fish left from your weighings. When you have collected a variety, make this specialty. Use bass, blackfish, cod, flounder, fluke, haddock, mullet, perch, red snapper, salmon, swordfish, whiting, even a couple of scallops if any are left from your Coquilles St. Jacques (see recipe page 113).

2 pounds assorted fish fillets, frozen
12 ounces peeled potato, diced
2 cups diced turnips
1½ cups diced carrots
2 tablespoons dehydrated onion flakes
1 tablespoon chopped fresh herbs (marjoram, tarragon, savory, chervil and thyme) or 1½ teaspoons dried

1 garlic clove
1½ quarts water
Salt and pepper to taste
4 teaspoons chopped fresh parsley

While the fish is still frozen, cut into small even pieces and set aside. In saucepan, combine potato, turnips, carrots, onion flakes, herbs and garlic. Cover with water. Bring to boil, cover and simmer until vegetables are tender but not mushy. Add the fish to the liquid and simmer until fish is cooked, about 5 to 8 minutes. Do not overcook. Season with salt and pepper. Divide into 4 serving bowls; sprinkle each portion with parsley. Makes 4 servings.

BOUQUET GARNI

4 sprigs parsley or ⅓ tablespoon dried parsley
½ crushed bay leaf
2 sprigs fresh thyme, or tarragon, or marjoram

2 cloves, crushed
2 teaspoons minced celery leaves or chives

Many different herbs can be used in making a bouquet garni. Gather the herbs in 4-inch squares of cheesecloth and tie with white thread, or put them into metal tea-infusion spoons. Add the bouquet garni during the last half hour of cooking, or as the recipe indicates.

ROLLED FILLETS OF FISH WITH CARROTS
(Paupiettes de Poisson aux Carottes)

Use any skinless fillet: flounder, sole, whiting, etc. Cooked pureed sorrel (sour grass) is a favorite vegetable in France, often served with fish.

2 8-ounce fish fillets, fresh or
   frozen
Salt and pepper to taste
2 medium carrots, cooked firm
Paprika
2 slices lemon

1 small orange, unpeeled and
   sliced thin over bowl to save
   juices
Parsley sprigs or watercress
2 ounces cooked peas (optional)

Thaw fish if frozen. Season with salt and pepper. Roll each fillet around a carrot. Trim length of carrot, if necessary. Place in baking pan, seam-side down. Sprinkle with paprika, top with lemon slices, and any juice from orange. Cover with foil and bake at 350°F. for 15 to 20 minutes or until fish flakes easily with a fork. Remove foil and transfer to serving platter. Cut orange slices into half circles and, dividing evenly, arrange half the orange slices around each fillet with cut edge against fish. In between orange slices arrange clumps of bright green parsley or watercress. Sprinkle 1 ounce of peas over each fillet, if desired. Makes 2 servings.

BAKED STUFFED SOLE

½ cup diced celery
3 ounces onion, diced
¼ cup chicken bouillon
1 ounce peas and carrots,
   cooked
1 tablespoon mayonnaise
¼ teaspoon Worcestershire

¼ teaspoon lemon juice
Few drops hot pepper sauce
Salt and pepper to taste
8 ounces fillet of sole
Paprika
Lemon slices (optional)

Cook celery, onion and bouillon in a saucepan until celery is tender. Remove from heat. Drain well; add peas and carrots, mayonnaise, Worcestershire, lemon juice, hot pepper sauce, salt and pepper to taste and 2 ounces of the sole, finely chopped. Mix thoroughly. Lay fish fillet on a flat surface; spread stuffing mixture over sole and roll securely. Place in an individual baking dish. Sprinkle with paprika and garnish with lemon slices. Cover with foil. Bake at 350°F. for about 15 to 20 minutes or until fish flakes easily with a fork. Makes 1 serving.

SOLE ARGENTEUIL

8 ounces fillet of sole
1 cup cooked or canned white asparagus, divided
½ medium tomato, chopped
¼ cup evaporated skimmed milk

1 tablespoon diced pimento
¼ teaspoon dehydrated onion flakes
Salt and pepper to taste

Place fish in a small nonstick baking dish. Bake at 400°F. for 15 to 20 minutes, or until fish flakes easily with a fork. In blender container, add ½ of the asparagus, tomato, milk, pimento, onion flakes, salt and pepper; process until smooth. Pour into a small saucepan, and heat slowly. *Do not boil.* When cooked, remove fish to serving dish; pour heated sauce over and arrange the remaining asparagus on top. Makes 1 serving.

GRILLED FISH STEAKS WITH GRAPEFRUIT
(Poisson aux Pamplemousse)

Four 8-ounce boned fish steaks (cod, halibut, turbot, pollock)
1½ teaspoons salt
¾ teaspoon pepper
Paprika

½ cup grapefruit sections, no sugar added; drain and reserve juice
2 tablespoons chicken bouillon
Chopped fresh parsley

Sprinkle fish with salt, pepper and paprika, and place in broiling pan. Combine grapefruit juice and chicken bouillon. Spoon half of mixture over fish. Broil about 4 inches from source of heat for 5 to 6 minutes. Turn fish; spoon remaining grapefruit juice mixture on each fish steak. Continue broiling until fish flakes easily with fork, 4 to 6 minutes. Serve with pan juices, sprinkle with parsley and top with grapefruit sections. Makes 4 servings.

MACKEREL STEW BRITTANY STYLE (Maquereau à la Bretonne)

½ bay leaf
¼ teaspoon thyme (or 2 sprigs fresh)
1 tablespoon dehydrated onion flakes
1 small garlic clove
Salt and pepper to taste
2 pounds mackerel fillets, cut into large pieces
Four 3-ounce cooked potatoes
1 tablespoon chopped fresh parsley or chives

Cover the bottom of a shallow saucepan with an inch of water. Add bay leaf, thyme, dehydrated onion flakes, garlic, salt and pepper. Simmer gently 3 to 5 minutes. Add mackerel pieces, cover saucepan and let simmer gently for 15 minutes. Add potatoes; cover and cook 10 minutes. Transfer fish and potatoes to serving platter and keep warm. Quickly boil down sauce until reduced by half. Strain sauce over fish. Sprinkle with parsley or chives. Serve hot. Makes 4 servings.

CARP WITH PARSLEY

Follow preceding recipe but substitute carp chunks for mackerel. Omit potatoes. Serve cold with horseradish and an abundance of minced parsley. Makes 4 servings.

CRABMEAT MOUSSE

6 ounces cooked crabmeat
1 tablespoon tomato juice
1 tablespoon mayonnaise
1 tablespoon chopped pimentos
1 teaspoon lemon juice
1 teaspoon chopped fresh chives
1 teaspoon chopped fresh parsley
¼ cup water
1 envelope unflavored gelatin
Salt and pepper to taste
¼ cup chilled evaporated skimmed milk

Flake crabmeat in small bowl; add next 6 ingredients and mix well. Pour water into a small saucepan, sprinkle gelatin on top and heat until gelatin is dissolved. Stir into crab mixture. Season with salt and pepper. Whip milk with beater until peaks form. Fold into crabmeat. Place in small mold. Chill until ready to serve. Unmold. Makes 1 serving.

COLD LOBSTER CARDINALE

6 ounces cooked lobster, diced
¼ cup tomato juice
¼ cup diced celery
1 tablespoon mayonnaise
1 teaspoon lemon juice
1 teaspoon brandy extract
1 teaspoon chopped fresh chives

1 teaspoon chopped fresh
  parsley
1 envelope unflavored gelatin
¼ cup cold water
Salt and pepper to taste
¼ cup chilled evaporated
  skimmed milk

Combine lobster and next 7 ingredients in a mixing bowl. Mix thoroughly. Sprinkle gelatin over cold water in saucepan. Place over low heat and stir until gelatin is dissolved. Add lobster mixture. Season with salt and pepper. Beat milk with rotary beater until peaks form. Fold into lobster mixture. Pour into small mold. Chill until set. Unmold. Makes 1 serving.

SCALLOPS IN SHELL (Coquilles St. Jacques)

Pretty luncheon for two.

1 pound fresh scallops
Boiling water with ¾ teaspoon
  salt
¼ cup scallop liquid
1 cup mushrooms, sliced thin
1 ounce diced onion or
  1 teaspoon dehydrated onion
  flakes
½ cup chicken bouillon

2 slices enriched white bread,
  made into fine crumbs, divided
Salt and pepper to taste
Dash grated lemon rind
½ cup evaporated skimmed milk
¼ teaspoon lemon juice
4 teaspoons margarine
Garnish: 2 lemon wedges and
  sprigs of parsley

Wash and dry scallops. Cut large scallops into 3 or 4 pieces, cover with boiling water, add salt and parboil for 3 minutes. Remove from heat; drain (reserving some liquid), cover and set aside. In nonstick skillet, brown mushrooms and onions; add chicken bouillon, all but ¼ cup of the bread crumbs, salt, pepper and lemon rind. Cover and let simmer over low heat for 5 minutes. Add milk and continue cooking over low heat until sauce is thick. Stir in lemon juice, salt and pepper. Remove from heat; stir in scallops and transfer to 2 large shells or ramekins. Mix margarine with remaining crumbs and sprinkle on top of scallops. Put under broiler just long enough to brown crumbs (less than 1 minute). Serve piping hot. Garnish with lemon wedges and parsley. Makes 2 servings.

SHRIMP SALAD (Salade de Crevettes)

1 pound cleaned, cooked shrimp, diced
1 medium cucumber, peeled, seeded, and diced
½ cup diced celery
1 tablespoon capers
1 tablespoon chopped fresh chives or parsley
¼ cup mayonnaise
½ teaspoon salt
Dash pepper
Cupped lettuce leaves
10 cherry tomatoes, halved

In mixing bowl, combine shrimp, cucumber, celery, capers and parsley. Add mayonnaise, salt and pepper. Toss lightly. Chill. Serve in lettuce cups. Garnish each serving with 5 cherry tomato halves. Makes 4 servings.

LOBSTER DIVAN

2 frozen rock lobster tails (about ½ pound)
1½ cups frozen broccoli spears
1 slice enriched white bread made into crumbs
1 cup evaporated skimmed milk
2 ounces diced cheddar cheese
Salt and pepper
½ teaspoon sherry extract
2 slices lemon

Drop lobster tails into boiling salted water. Bring water to boil again; cook for 5 minutes, drain immediately, cool under cold water, and drain again. Cut away underside membrane and remove meat from shells in one piece. Weigh 4 ounces. Keep warm. Cook broccoli according to package directions. Drain. Line 2 shallow casseroles evenly with broccoli, and place 2 ounces of lobster tail on top. Combine bread, cheese and milk in blender container; process until smooth; place in saucepan, heat to just below boiling; simmer 3 minutes. Season with salt, pepper and sherry extract. Pour over casseroles. Serve at once or brown lightly in broiler before serving. Garnish with lemon slices. Makes 2 servings.

CHICKEN IN VINAIGRETTE (Poulet au Vinaigre)

The vinegar is often boiled for a few minutes with an equal amount of chicken bouillon and other seasonings listed below. We've eliminated this step in our simplified procedure and increased the marinating time.

2 garlic cloves
2½ to 3 pounds chicken, quartered (skin removed)
1½ cups wine vinegar

Dash each of any of the following ground seasonings to taste: cloves, salt, black pepper, poultry seasoning, juniper berries, tarragon, instant chicken broth and seasoning mix

Push garlic through garlic press onto folds of wax paper. Rub paper over chicken. Stack chicken quarters in mixing bowl. Combine vinegar with any desired seasoning, and pour over chicken in bowl. Let marinate, covered, in refrigerator overnight. Drain; reserve marinade. Broil chicken four inches from source of heat (or over hot coals) until done, 15 to 20 minutes on each side, basting several times with reserved marinade. Weigh 4- to 6-ounce portions. Serve hot or cold. Makes 4 servings.

CHICKEN WITH GRAPES (Poulet Véronique)

Véronique, the glorious French way with chicken and fish, has numerous variations including our yummy version.

2½- to 3-pound chicken
Salt, pepper and poultry seasoning to taste
1 cup orange juice
1 packet instant chicken broth and seasoning mix

1 tablespoon chopped fresh parsley
2 tablespoons grated orange rind
20 small seedless grapes

Sprinkle chicken with salt, pepper and poultry seasoning, inside and out. Place chicken on a rack and roast for 50 minutes at 375°F. or until chicken is done. Meanwhile, prepare the sauce. In saucepan, bring orange juice, broth mix and parsley to a boil, lower heat and simmer for 30 minutes, stirring occasionally. Add orange rind and cook 10 minutes longer or until rind is tender. Transfer chicken to serving platter, remove skin; cut into serving pieces and weigh portions (4 to 6 ounces each). Add grapes to sauce; stir well to combine. Pour over chicken. Serve at once. Makes 4 servings.

CHICKEN MARENGO

To us, the real hero at Marengo wasn't the man in the tri-cornered hat, but the one in the toque blanche. *Napoleon's French chef was supposed to have invented this dish, using ingredients available in the war-torn countryside. In the original version, crayfish and eggs were included, but modern-day recipe writers now omit them. So what we are left with is a stylish chicken-tomato-mushroom-onion mixture in the French-Italian family of continental recipes. Cooked enriched rice or noodles are the usual accompaniment.*

2 pounds boned and skinned chicken breasts, cut in 1½-inch pieces
1 crushed garlic clove
2 cups chicken stock (see page ix)
4 medium tomatoes, peeled and chopped
½ cup diced celery
½ bay leaf

1 tablespoon chopped fresh parsley
½ teaspoon mixed herbs (thyme, basil, tarragon) or
½ tablespoon chopped fresh
Salt and pepper to taste
2 teaspoons sherry extract
2 cups mushrooms, sliced
4 ounces cooked or canned drained pearl onions

In a nonstick saucepan, brown chicken and garlic on all sides. Remove chicken. Add stock, tomatoes, celery and bay leaf. Bring to a boil. Simmer 30 minutes. Add parsley, mixed herbs, sherry extract, salt and pepper, and cook for 5 minutes. Put sauce in blender container or food processor and process. If sauce is too thick, add more stock. Stir in mushrooms and onions. Simmer for 10 minutes. Pour over chicken and serve hot. (Or pour sauce into a casserole, top with chicken and add mushrooms and onions. Refrigerate until ready to use, heat 20 to 30 minutes at 350°F.) Makes 4 servings.

VEAL MARENGO

Thyme, a native herb of the Mediterranean, through history has symbolized bravery, and naturally the "little corporal" was enamored of it. It is traditional both in the chicken and veal Marengo. More may be added if to your taste.

AFRICA: Tripe Stew; Rice Salad

AUSTRALIA AND NEW ZEALAND: Pavlova; Roast Baby Lamb

AUSTRIA AND HUNGARY: Cherry Soup (Cseresznyelves); Tyrolean Liver Soup (Lebersuppe); Hungarian Fisherman's Soup (Halászlé)

BELGIUM AND THE NETHERLANDS: Golden Velvet Carrots; Belgian Fish Soup (Waterzoi)

THE BRITISH ISLES: Baked Salmon with Caper Sauce; Strawberry Fool

CANADA: Three-Layer Molded Apple Custard; Rosy Rhuberry Mold with Lemon "Cream" Topping; Spinach-Cheese Ring

CARIBBEAN AND WEST INDIES: Pineapple Rice Pudding (Arroz con Leche y Piña); Pumpkin Soup (Sopa de Zapallo)

CHINA: Chinese Eggroll with Shrimp Filling; Chicken with Vegetables and Mushrooms (Moo Goo Gai Pan); Clear Soup

FRANCE: Rolled Fillets of Fish with Carrots; Watercress
Soup (Potage au Cresson); Poached Whole Pears

GERMANY: Delicatessen; Potato Salad; Sweet and Sour
Cole Slaw

**GREECE AND
THE OTHER
BALKAN STATES:**
Albanian Lamb Stew
with Okra

INDIA: Easy Chicken Curry with Tomatoes (Murghi Kari); Vegetable Chutney; Rice Apple Chutney; Condiments (sliced bananas, diced oranges, sliced scallions, cantaloupe balls)

Replace chicken with 2 pounds thin sliced veal cut from leg (veal scallopini). Pound thin and cut in 2-inch squares. Follow preceding recipe, but wipe out skillet after browning veal and before adding remaining ingredients. Makes 4 servings.

"BRANDIED" CHICKEN (Poulet Alsacien)

Add a green salad to complete this one-dish meal.

4 skinned and boned chicken breasts or cutlets, 6 to 8 ounces each
4 teaspoons flour
Salt and pepper to taste
1½ cups carrots, cut in thick slices
2 ounces shallots or scallions, finely chopped
6 ounces tiny white onions, peeled and blanched
¼ cup chopped fresh parsley
1 teaspoon salt
½ teaspoon pepper
1 garlic clove
1 cup chicken bouillon
2 cups small mushroom caps
1 teaspoon brandy (or sherry) extract

Sprinkle chicken with flour, salt and pepper. Brown in nonstick pan over moderately high heat, turning frequently. Transfer chicken pieces to platter. Lightly brown carrots and shallots or scallions in same pan. Return chicken pieces to pan. Add blanched onions, parsley, salt, pepper and garlic. Pour in chicken bouillon and simmer, covered for 20 minutes. Add mushrooms and brandy extract and continue simmering until chicken is tender and mushrooms are done, about 10 minutes more. Makes 4 servings.

CHICKEN WITH APPLES (Poulet Normand)

In Normandy, small white onions would be the usual accompaniment.

2½- to 3-pound chicken, cut in quarters, skin removed
¾ teaspoon poultry seasoning
1 to 1½ cups chicken bouillon
1 cup sliced celery
1 medium apple, peeled, cored and sliced
2 tablespoons dehydrated onion flakes
1 tablespoon mixed chopped fresh herbs or 1 teaspoon dried (parsley, tarragon, basil and perhaps a little sage)
¾ cup evaporated skimmed milk
½ teaspoon sherry extract
Salt and pepper to taste

Season chicken with poultry seasoning and set aside. In saucepan cook bouillon, celery, apple and onion flakes about 20 minutes over low heat. Add herbs for the last few minutes. Meanwhile, broil chicken on rack 4 inches from source of heat, 12 to 15 minutes or until firm to touch, turning to cook both sides. When celery and apple mixture is soft, process it in blender container, and put back into saucepan. Mixture should now have consistency of a thick sauce. If not, reduce it by quick boiling. Let cool slightly; add milk and sherry extract. Heat gently (mixture must not boil). Turn off heat. Weigh portions (4 to 6 ounces each). Add hot chicken, season with salt and pepper and serve promptly (or cover and keep warm). Makes 4 servings.

TARRAGON ROAST CHICKEN (Poulet Rôti à l'Estragon)

2½- to 3-pound chicken
1 garlic clove, cut in half
Salt and pepper to taste
½ teaspoon tarragon (or 2 large sprigs of fresh tarragon)

½ cup chicken bouillon
Tarragon Sauce (recipe follows)

Rub cut garlic clove on all sides of chicken. Season with salt and pepper, inside and out. Sprinkle cavity with tarragon. Truss chicken with string or skewers. Using brush or fingers, moisten all sides of chicken with bouillon. Place on rack in roasting pan and bake until chicken is done, 50 to 60 minutes, turning every 15 minutes so back, breast and sides are equally browned and all parts of the bird are juicy and succulent. Remove skin and bones. Weigh portions and serve with Tarragon Sauce. Makes 4 servings.

Tarragon Sauce

4 teaspoons margarine
4 teaspoons flour
¾ cup chicken stock or bouillon
¼ cup evaporated skimmed milk

½ teaspoon tarragon (or 2 large sprigs fresh tarragon)
Salt and pepper to taste

Melt margarine in top of double boiler. Stir flour into melted margarine until mixture is smooth. Slowly add stock or bouillon, stirring with a wooden spoon until smooth. Continue to cook until thickened. Add milk and tarragon. Adjust seasonings. Divide evenly and serve over chicken. Makes 4 servings.

CHICKEN WITH EGGPLANT (Coq Basque)

2½- to 3-pound skinned chicken; marinate as in Chicken in Vinaigrette (see page 115) if desired
1 garlic clove
2 cups peeled eggplant, cut into 3-inch lengths
2 cups diced mushrooms
2 medium tomatoes, quartered
2 medium green peppers, cut into squares (remove seeds and white pulp)
8 ounces small onions, parboiled in water to cover for 10 minutes
¾ cup chicken bouillon
1 bay leaf
1 teaspoon mixed dried herbs, including basil and thyme
1 sliced truffle (optional)

Whether or not you marinate the chicken, be sure to rub it with garlic before cooking. Put chicken in a casserole. Combine vegetables and remaining ingredients and spread over chicken. Cover and bake at 375°F. (moderate oven) for 40 to 50 minutes or until chicken is tender. If necessary, to evaporate excess liquid, continue baking without cover. Mix well before serving. Weigh portions. Makes 4 servings.

DEVILED CHICKEN MOUSSE

4 ounces cooked chicken, finely chopped
⅓ cup finely chopped celery
¼ medium green pepper, diced
1 ounce onion, finely chopped
1 tablespoon chopped fresh parsley
1 tablespoon chopped pimento
1 teaspoon mayonnaise
1 teaspoon Worcestershire
½ teaspoon dry English mustard
½ packet instant chicken broth and seasoning mix
¾ cup cold water
2 teaspoons unflavored gelatin
Salt to taste
Lettuce
Watercress

Combine chicken, celery, green pepper, onion, parsley and pimento in a mixing bowl; add mayonnaise, Worcestershire and mustard; mix well. Add broth mix; stir to combine. Pour water into a saucepan. Sprinkle gelatin over it to soften. Place over low heat and stir until gelatin dissolves. Add to chicken mixture and blend thoroughly. Add salt and continue to blend. Turn into a small mold and chill until set; about 3 hours. Unmold and serve on a bed of lettuce and watercress. Makes 1 serving.

MARINATED ROAST VEAL

In spring serve this with cooked fresh asparagus tips, one cup per serving.

4-pound veal roast
3 cups white vinegar
1 teaspoon peppercorns, crushed
2 garlic cloves, crushed
2 sprigs parsley
1 sprig thyme or tarragon
1 teaspoon celery seed

½ bay leaf
Salt and pepper to taste
2 lemons, cut in quarters
Sprigs of watercress or fresh
  sprightly parsley or even
  celery leaves

Cover veal roast in large bowl with a mixture of remaining ingredients (except lemons and watercress). Refrigerate for 24 hours, turning frequently so all sides of meat are immersed. Remove meat to baking pan, reserving marinade. Roast in slow oven—slow roasting is the secret of this recipe—at 325°F. for 2½ hours, basting frequently with reserved marinade until veal is thoroughly cooked. (Internal temperature on a meat thermometer will be 170°F.) Let roast cool for 10 to 15 minutes to gather juices, then slice and serve with garnish: quarters of lemon and sprigs of watercress, or other leaves. Makes 8 servings.

VEAL CHOPS IN FOIL (Côtes de Veau en Papillote)

4 white veal chops, 10-ounces
  each
4 sheets aluminum foil, each
  12x16-inches
2 medium tomatoes, cut in half
8 ounces tiny canned or cooked
  white onions, drained

4 teaspoons chopped mixed fresh
  herbs (parsley, chives, tarragon,
  thyme) or 2 teaspoons dried
Salt and pepper to taste

Brown chops in preheated nonstick skillet over moderate heat, turning once, until done on both sides, about 15 minutes. Put one chop in the center of each sheet of foil. Top each with a tomato half and ¼ of the onions. Sprinkle each with a mixture of herbs, salt and pepper. Wrap, double-folding the edges to make a tightly sealed package. Bake on sheet pan for 20 minutes in 400°F. oven (or longer at lower temperature if dinner must wait). Serve the foil packages, to be opened at the table. Makes 4 servings.

VEAL CHOPS WITH ORANGE (Côtes de Veau à l'Orange)

4 10-ounce rib veal chops
1 garlic clove, cut
Salt and pepper to taste
4 teaspoons margarine
4 teaspoons chopped fresh basil
   (or tarragon) or 2 teaspoons
   dried

2 cups hot cooked enriched rice
4 small oranges, peeled, cut in
   slices (reserve rind for garnish,
   see note)

Buy the whitest chops you can find. Preheat broiler. Wipe chops dry. Rub them on all sides with garlic. Broil 4 inches from source of heat until cooked throughout, turning once. Season with salt and pepper. Meanwhile cream margarine with basil to make a smooth paste. Transfer chops to individual serving plates, each holding ½ cup rice in center, with a border of orange slices. Spread margarine mixture over each chop and serve at once. Makes 4 servings.

NOTE: *For garnish*—Cut matchstick pieces of orange rind. Place in water until soft and pile in center of veal before serving.

VEAL IN ASPIC

A perfect summer lunch dish.

1 envelope unflavored gelatin
¾ cup cold chicken bouillon
2 ounces grated onion
2 tablespoons mayonnaise
2 tablespoons lemon juice
1 teaspoon Worcestershire
½ teaspoon dry mustard

¼ teaspoon salt or to taste
⅛ teaspoon hot pepper sauce
8 ounces roast veal, diced
¾ cup diced celery
2 tablespoons diced pimento
Garnish: lettuce leaves and
   2 pimento strips

Sprinkle gelatin over cold bouillon in small saucepan. Place over low heat; stir constantly until gelatin dissolves, about 3 minutes. Remove from heat. Combine onion, mayonnaise, lemon juice, Worcestershire, dry mustard, salt and hot pepper sauce; mix thoroughly with gelatin mixture. Chill, stirring occasionally until mixture thickens to the consistency of unbeaten egg whites. Combine roast veal, celery and pimento. Stir into thickened gelatin mixture. Transfer to 1-quart mold. Chill until set. Unmold on a bed of chicory leaves or other greens. Crisscross bright red pimento strips across the top before serving. Makes 2 servings.

BEEF WITH PARSLEY (Persillade de Boeuf)

12 ounces cooked beef, thinly
sliced
2 cups beef bouillon
¼ cup chopped fresh parsley
1 tablespoon dehydrated onion
flakes

1 tablespoon lemon juice
Salt and pepper to taste
1 cup cooked enriched rice
(see note)

With sharp knife, cut stacked slices of beef into strips, and set aside. In saucepan, bring bouillon to boil; add beef, parsley and onion flakes. Reduce heat, cover pan and let simmer 15 minutes. Stir in lemon juice and simmer for 10 minutes more. Season with salt and pepper. Put ½ cup rice into each of two serving bowls and top with beef mixture. Makes 2 servings.

NOTE: To reheat or plump up cold rice, place in strainer and pour hot water over it. If rice is lumpy, gently press out lumps between fingers.

BEEF AND CELERY RAGOUT

2 pounds boneless lean beef (cut
from less tender cuts; rump,
round, chuck, etc.)
1 garlic clove, cut
3 cups sliced celery
2 cups beef bouillon
2 cups mushrooms (sliced
through cap and stem)

8 ounces tiny white onions,
peeled
½ cup chopped fresh parsley
3 cloves, slightly crushed
1 teaspoon thyme
1 teaspoon salt
8 peppercorns, slightly crushed

Preheat broiler and rack. Rub beef with cut garlic clove and cut into 1-inch cubes. Transfer to rack in broiling pan. Brown all sides 4 inches from source of heat for 15 to 20 minutes. Transfer meat to Dutch oven or pan with tight cover. Add remaining ingredients. Bring to boil, reduce heat, cover pan and simmer gently for 1 to 1½ hours or until beef is very tender. Serve hot. Makes 4 servings.

MEAT PATTIES (Hamburgers and Vealburgers, Chickenburgers, Lamburgers, Liverburgers)

When French kids want burgers for dinner, it's not necessarily de boeuf *that* maman *will prepare. We've listed some of the other ground meats commonly served. Seasonings and fillers are varied to taste or omitted, since good meat has its own distinctive flavor when cooked simply. We think salt should be added only after cooking because it seems to draw juices from grilled meat . . . and on our Food Program, we leave behind in the pan the fluids and fats rendered in the first broiling of meats. The following recipe for 1 serving is easily multiplied for a family.*

8 ounces raw lean veal, chicken, lamb, liver or beef
1 tablespoon dehydrated onion flakes, reconstituted in
2 tablespoons water or bouillon
½ tablespoon dehydrated celery flakes, reconstituted

½ teaspoon dried herbs to taste: rosemary, thyme, basil, sage or dill (or twice as much chopped fresh)
Salt and pepper to taste

Put meat through fine blade of grinder with onion flakes and celery flakes. Add herbs and mix well with fork. Shape into 1 large or 2 small flat compact patty(ies). Cook as below. Season at table with salt and pepper. Makes 1 serving.

a) Broil on rack, in pan, 4 inches from source of heat, about 5 to 8 minutes on each side or until done to taste.

b) Bake on preheated rack in pan set in moderate oven (375°F.) until well-browned, about 20 minutes.

c) Only for veal, chicken or liver patties: Brown in preheated non-stick skillet until done to taste, turning once.

BEEF IN A POT (Pot-au-feu)

The kind of potluck meal you might find in a typical French country kitchen. Pot-au-feu was so named because it was made in a pot kept simmering at the back of the stove, where thrifty housewives could toss bits of beef, chicken, carcasses and leftover vegetables. But the French, like the rest of us, have an obesity problem, and ad-libbing with ingredients is now a non-non. *Here's our slimdown version of the provincial favorite.*

2 pounds lean stew beef, cut in
  3-inch pieces
2 cups sliced celery and leaves
2 cups shredded cabbage
2 cups diced carrots
1 cup diced turnips
8 ounces well cleaned leeks,
  white part only, sliced

2 garlic cloves
½ bay leaf
1 clove
Salt and pepper to taste
2 cups frozen lima beans

Cover meat with water, bring to boil and cook 1 hour. Remove beef, refrigerate stock, to congeal the fat. Skim to remove fat and bring 3 cups stock to a boil; add the beef with remaining ingredients, except beans and enough water to cover. Cook 30 minutes longer or until vegetables are tender. Add lima beans and cook until beans are done. Serve soup as first course, meat, vegetables and beans as second course. Makes 4 servings.

STEAK WITH PEPPERCORNS (Bifteck au Poivre)

1½ teaspoons peppercorns
2 boneless 8-ounce steaks,
  trimmed of all visible fat

Piquant Sauce, optional
  (recipe follows)
Salt (optional)

With rolling pin, crush peppercorns on a towel until they are flattened (the pepper mill grinds too fine). Using palm of hand or side of cleaver, push pepper as deeply as possible into both sides of steaks. Let stand ½ hour. Preheat broiler pan and rack. Broil steaks on rack at high heat about 3 inches from source of heat for 8 to 16 minutes or until done to taste, turning once. Serve on heated plates with optional Piquant Sauce or a salt shaker for added seasoning. Makes 2 servings.

Piquant Sauce

2 tablespoons margarine
1 teaspoon Worcestershire

2 teaspoons wine vinegar

Make the sauce in two pipkins, custard cups or even the tiny white *pots de creme* tucked away in the china closet. To 1 tablespoon melted margarine (melted over pilot light or in warming well) add

½ teaspoon Worcestershire and 1 teaspoon wine vinegar. Serve in pipkins with steak. Repeat for each serving. Makes 2 servings.

SAUSAGE WITH POTATO SALAD (Saucisson à la Lyonnaise)

1 pound spicy all-beef sausage, knockwurst or frankfurters, pierced with fork
12 ounces cooked and peeled potatoes
¼ cup vegetable oil

2 tablespoons dehydrated onion flakes in ¼ cup vinegar
1 teaspoon Dijon-style mustard
1 cup shredded Boston or romaine lettuce
Chopped fresh parsley

In a kettle, cook sausage in plenty of boiling water to cover. Cut potatoes into a bowl, in ¼-inch slices. While they are still warm, combine oil, vinegar, onion flakes and mustard, and gently toss with potatoes. Drain the sausage and cut into slices ½-inch thick. (Remove skin covering if necessary.) Serve sausage slices, potato salad and shredded lettuce evenly divided on dinner plates. Garnish with parsley and pass Dijon-style mustard. Makes 4 servings.

SWEETBREADS WITH MELTED "BUTTER"

4 ounces cooked tiny peas (optional)
2 tablespoons imitation (or diet) margarine
2 teaspoons chopped fresh parsley

1 teaspoon lemon juice
Salt and pepper to taste
12 ounces cooked trimmed sweetbreads, cut into bite-size pieces (see note)

In each of 2 individual casseroles, place ½ the peas, if desired, and ½ the margarine, parsley, lemon juice, salt and pepper. Divide sweetbreads evenly into casseroles. At the table, gently turn sweetbreads with a fork to absorb all the sauce. Makes 2 servings.

NOTE: *To prepare sweetbreads,* soak them in salted water to cover for 1 hour. Drain. Transfer to a saucepan, cover with cold water and add 1 tablespoon white vinegar. Bring to a boil. Let simmer for 15 minutes. Drain, dip them quickly into cold water and discard tough parts and membrane. Weigh cooked and trimmed sweetbreads for recipe.

HAM WITH GRAPES (Jambon aux Raisins)

May be served with cooked enriched rice and braised celery.

40 small seedless grapes	Dash cinnamon and nutmeg
1 cup boiling water	4 fully baked ham slices,
1 teaspoon unflavored gelatin	4 ounces each
1 teaspoon lemon juice	

Simmer the grapes in water for 20 minutes. Add gelatin, lemon juice and spices. Serve hot on slices of ham (or roasted pork). Makes 4 servings.

ROAST LAMB WITH BEANS (Gigot Rôti aux Haricots)

Lamb is a young animal and its tender meat is ideal for roasting or broiling, but by French standards Americans overcook it. Try it this way, roasted in a hot oven to a medium-rare stage. You'll find it juicy and pink inside rather than the dried, well-done lamb you may be accustomed to.

5 pounds leg of lamb	Lima Beans I or II (recipes
Cut garlic clove	follow)
Salt and pepper to taste	

Season lamb on all sides by rubbing it with a cut garlic clove. Sprinkle with salt and pepper. Insert meat thermometer; avoid bone. Roast on rack for 12 to 15 minutes per pound or until thermometer reaches 140°F. to 150°F. Let lamb stand 15 minutes before carving (so juices gather). Carve and serve weighed portions with lima beans. Makes 6 servings.

LIMA BEANS I

¼ cup sliced mushrooms	½ cup cooked fresh lima beans
1 tablespoon dehydrated onion flakes, reconstituted	Dash marjoram and parsley
1 medium tomato, peeled and diced	Salt and freshly ground pepper to taste

Brown mushrooms and onion flakes in a medium nonstick skillet. Add tomato and heat until most of the liquid has evaporated. Stir in lima beans, marjoram, parsley, salt and pepper. Cook until heated through. Serve with slices of lamb. Makes 1 serving.

LIMA BEANS II

⅔ cup sliced carrots
2 ounces onions, sliced
Water
Dash thyme
Dash ground cloves

Salt and pepper to taste
2 tablespoons evaporated
   skimmed milk
½ cup cooked fresh lima beans
1 teaspoon margarine

In a saucepan, cook carrots and onions in enough water to cover, with thyme, cloves, salt and pepper added. Cook until carrots are tender and water almost evaporated. Stir in milk and lima beans. Reheat at low temperature; do not boil. Remove from heat and add margarine. Serve with sliced lamb. Makes 1 serving.

LAMB STEW (Navarin d'Agneau)

If any single food can be called the national dish of France, it's this savory stew. Prepare as many individual casseroles as there are members of your family for an easy one-course meal. Lamb left from a roast can be substituted for the first ingredient, and the first step omitted.

8-ounce boneless well-trimmed
   lamb steak, or shoulder of lamb
   with gristle and fat removed
1 cup beef bouillon
1 medium tomato, diced
½ cup sliced green beans
3 ounces peeled potato, sliced

½ cup sliced turnips
⅓ cup diced carrots
1 teaspoon dehydrated onion
   flakes
½ garlic clove
Dash each of thyme and parsley
Salt and pepper to taste

Broil lamb steak on a rack 5 minutes on each side. Cut into 1-inch pieces and place in flameproof casserole. Add remaining ingredients. Cover (use aluminum foil if casserole has no cover) and simmer slowly on top of stove for 35 minutes or bake at 350°F. for 50 minutes or until potato is tender. Add hot water or bouillon if stew shows signs of dryness. Makes 1 serving.

LAMB STEAKS WITH ORANGE AND GRAPEFRUIT

Serve this over cooked enriched rice.

2 boneless lean lamb steaks,
   8-ounces each
1 lemon, cut
1 garlic clove, cut
Dash thyme

1 small orange
½ medium grapefruit
Salt and pepper to taste
2 sprigs of mint for garnish

Order steaks about ¾-inch thick. Wipe them with cut lemon and refrigerate until needed. Before using, rub both sides of chops with cut garlic clove and press thyme into them. Peel orange and grapefruit, and cut into sections over a small broiling pan to catch juices. (To do this, just cut down along each section, and lift out the pieces of fruit discarding the membranes which separate the segments.) Place fruit in pan with juice. Put the lamb on another broiling rack and broil 4 inches from source of heat for 10 to 14 minutes, or until lamb is done to your taste, turning the chops once. Broil fruit for last 5 minutes of broiling time. Serve fruit with lamb, and provide salt and pepper mill for added seasoning at the table. Artificial sweetener for the fruit may also be provided at the table, but this is really not needed as broiling the fruit releases its juices and flavor. If fresh mint sprigs are available, use as garnish. Makes 2 servings.

ROAST PORK (Rôti de Porc)

2 pounds boneless roast pork
   (trimmed of fat)
Salt, pepper to taste

1 teaspoon thyme
Fresh sage leaves if available
   or 1 teaspoon powdered sage

Have butcher bone a pork loin or shoulder and tie it well. Season with salt, pepper and crushed thyme. If fresh sage leaves are available insert them in slits cut into the pork, or use powdered sage with the other seasonings. Place pork on rack in roasting pan. Insert meat thermometer so bulb is in thickest part of roast. Bake at 375°F. uncovered for 1¼ hours, allowing 35 minutes per pound or until internal temperature reaches 170°F. to 185°F.

NOTE: For health reasons, pork must be well cooked with no trace of pink showing either in the juices or in the meat—prick the roast with a fork to test. If pink shows, return to oven and continue cooking. Remove pork to serving platter, slice and serve plain or in any of the following styles. Makes 4 servings.

ROAST PORK WITH CHERRIES (Rôti de Porc Montmorency)

Drain and reserve liquid from 2 cups of canned, pitted sweet cherries, no sugar added. Process ½ cup in blender container until smooth. Combine all whole and pureed cherries in small saucepan with cherry liquid. Simmer for 20 to 30 minutes or until cherries are soft. Add salt and pepper to taste. Pour evenly around 6-ounce servings of roasted pork. Garnish each serving with ½ medium pickle, sliced thin. Makes 4 servings.

ROAST PORK WITH SAUERKRAUT (Rôti de Porc avec Choucroute)

2 cups sauerkraut, washed and drained (2 16-ounce cans)	Dash each of ground cloves, nutmeg and ginger
4 tart medium apples, peeled, cored and sliced	¾ cup beef bouillon
1 teaspoon cinnamon	1 teaspoon lemon juice

In baking dish, arrange a layer of half of the sauerkraut and sliced apples. Sprinkle with spices. Repeat layers. Pour in bouillon and lemon juice. Cover and bake at 375°F. in oven for 40 minutes. Serve hot with Dijon-style mustard and Roast Pork (see page 128). Makes 4 servings.

PORK CHOPS WITH BANANAS (Côtelettes de Porc aux Bananes)

For company . . . for that matter, for the family—decorate the chops with paper ruffs, if available.

4 thick well-trimmed pork chops, 10-ounces each	1 tablespoon lemon juice
Salt, pepper and rosemary to taste	Nutmeg
2 medium green peppers	4 teaspoons margarine, melted
4 ripe medium bananas	

Season chops with salt, pepper and rosemary. Broil on preheated rack in pan 4 inches from source of heat until thoroughly cooked, turning once. Test by piercing thickest part of chop with a fork to be certain no trace of pink shows either in the juice or in the meat. While chops broil, cut peppers in half horizontally (through stem). Remove seeds and white pulp from insides. Cover peppers with boiling water in saucepan and cook over medium heat for 5 minutes. Remove from water, plunge quickly into cold water and drain dry. Mash the bananas, sprinkle with lemon juice and nutmeg. Fill pepper cases with bananas and put under broiler with pork chops for last 5 minutes. Remove from heat. Drizzle 1 teaspoon margarine over banana mixture. Serve hot. Makes 4 servings.

CHICKEN LIVERS CHASSEUR (Foies de Volaille Chasseur)

8 ounces chicken livers	Dash garlic powder, rosemary
4 ounces onion, sliced	and thyme
1 medium tomato, diced	Salt and pepper to taste
½ cup sliced mushrooms	½ cup cooked enriched rice
½ cup chicken bouillon	½ teaspoon chopped fresh parsley
½ cup tomato juice	

Cook livers and onions in preheated nonstick skillet turning often with a spatula until lightly browned, about 5 minutes. Add tomato, mushrooms, bouillon, tomato juice and a pinch each of garlic powder, rosemary and thyme. Cook over low heat for 10 minutes or until mixture thickens. Season with salt and pepper. Serve over rice. Sprinkle with parsley. Makes 1 serving.

CHICKEN LIVERS IN ASPIC (Foies de Volaille en Gelée)

1½ envelopes unflavored gelatin	1 pound chicken livers, cut in half
1 cup bouillon	Pinch of allspice and thyme
4 ounces finely minced shallots,	Salt and pepper to taste
onions or scallions	4 slices truffle (optional)

Sprinkle gelatin over 3 tablespoons cold bouillon in saucepan. Add remaining bouillon and heat, stirring to dissolve. Prepare two 2-cup molds. Pour a ¼-inch layer of gelatin into bottom of each mold and chill until set. Add onions to preheated nonstick skillet. Top with livers. Cover skillet and cook over moderately high heat, turning as necessary to prevent scorching (onions should be soft and liver cooked but still juicy inside). Remove from skillet. Sprinkle allspice, thyme, salt and pepper into skillet, mix well and bring to boil. Remove from heat and stir into cooked livers. Add 2 slices of truffle to chilled gelatin in each mold, if desired. Divide liver equally into the molds. Add remaining gelatin mixture. Refrigerate until set. When ready to serve, unmold over lettuce leaves. Makes 2 servings.

CALF'S LIVER WITH APPLES (Foie de Veau aux Pommes)

2 slices calf's liver (8 ounces each)
Salt and pepper to taste
2 medium cooking apples
2 tablespoons chicken bouillon
1 tablespoon lemon juice
½ teaspoon brandy extract
2 lemon slices
1 teaspoon chopped fresh parsley

Trim any filament, membrane and vessels from the liver. Sprinkle with salt and pepper. Peel, core and cut apples into thin slices. Cook covered in small saucepan at very low heat; they should soften but not turn into sauce. Using a small preheated nonstick skillet, brown the liver on both sides, turning once (about 8 minutes in all). Remove it to 2 individual heated platters. Stir bouillon, lemon juice and brandy extract into pan to pick up juices, heat; divide evenly and pour over liver. Surround each slice of liver with ½ of the apple slices. Serve with lemon slice and chopped parsley. Makes 2 servings.

LIVER PATE SALAD (Salade de Foies de Volaille)

2 pounds chicken livers
¼ cup diced celery
4 ounces onion, diced
2 cups mushrooms, sliced
3 cups chicken bouillon
¾ teaspoon nutmeg
2 teaspoons sherry or brandy extract
2 cups firm-cooked green asparagus
2 cups firm-cooked green beans
4 lettuce leaves
Vinaigrette Dressing (recipe follows)

Brown livers quickly in preheated nonstick skillet (about 2 minutes); remove liver and add celery, onion and mushrooms; cook until lightly brown. Add bouillon and simmer until celery is tender. Return liver to pan and simmer for 2 minutes. Cool. Place in blender container a little at a time; add nutmeg and extract and puree for 30 seconds. Chill in 4 individual molds (or coffee cups) for 1 hour or more before serving. Unmold into center of large lettuce leaf on each of 4 chilled individual salad plates. Surround with asparagus and green beans.

Vinaigrette Dressing

¼ cup vegetable oil
¼ teaspoon lemon juice

1 teaspoon Dijon-type mustard
Salt and pepper to taste

Prepare the vinaigrette dressing by combining the oil, lemon juice, mustard, salt and pepper in jar. Shake well. Spoon over the salads (about 2 tablespoons per serving.) Makes 4 servings.

CELERY VICTOR

2 celery hearts
1 cup chicken bouillon
¼ cup vegetable oil
¼ cup white vinegar
¼ teaspoon salt
⅛ teaspoon pepper

Shredded lettuce
4 capers
1 medium tomato, cut in 4 wedges
Chopped fresh parsley or
    celery leaves

You can sometimes find hearts of celery in the market or use the tender inside ribs only. Split celery hearts lengthwise and put in saucepan with chicken bouillon. Bring to boil and simmer 15 to 20 minutes, or until tender-crisp. Drain and cool. Mix oil, white vinegar, salt and pepper. Add cooled celery hearts. Marinate in refrigerator at least 2 hours. Drain and reserve dressing. On each of 4 salad plates, arrange celery rib on a bed of shredded lettuce. Lay a caper over celery heart. Garnish with tomato wedge and sprinkle with chopped parsley or celery leaves. Serve with evenly divided reserved dressing. Makes 4 servings.

ALSATIAN SAUERKRAUT (Choucroute Alsacienne)

Fully cooked frankfurters or ham (4 ounces for each dinner serving) may be reheated by placing them on top of sauerkraut for last half hour.

1 cup sauerkraut
1 cup water
1 garlic clove

1 tablespoon white wine vinegar
6 juniper berries, cracked
6 peppercorns, cracked

Wash sauerkraut, drain it, pressing out excess liquid. Put it in a heavy saucepan with water and seasonings. Cover and cook slowly for 1½ hours. Serves 4.

RATATOUILLE

There are a number of variations on the theme of ratatouille, or ratatouia—as it is occasionally spelled. In some regions cooked dried white beans are added. In Provence, there's almost as much garlic as eggplant, or so it seems. Herbs vary too. But no matter how you spell it, or modify it, it's still a pretty wonderful dish. Serve it as an appetizer; with melted cheese for luncheon; as a base for scrambled or poached eggs; or as a dinner vegetable. When cold it may be mixed with a little wine vinegar and served as a relish or salad.

2 cups sliced eggplant	2 tablespoons dehydrated onion
2 cups sliced zucchini	flakes
2 medium green peppers	1 teaspoon marjoram or oregano
2 medium tomatoes	2 garlic cloves lightly crushed
2 cups tomato juice	1 teaspoon salt
¼ cup chopped fresh parsley	Pepper to taste

Cut the washed but unpeeled eggplant, well-scrubbed zucchini, green peppers and tomatoes into pieces of about the same size, roughly 1-inch squares. Combine in saucepan with remaining ingredients, heat to boiling point, then lower heat, cover and cook until vegetables are tender, stirring gently to prevent scorching, about 30 minutes (more for a very soft vegetable mixture). If there is too much liquid, uncover and continue cooking until the sauce thickens. Serve hot or cold. Makes 4 servings.

ZUCCHINI QUICHE (Quiche aux Courgettes)

2 slices enriched white bread,	½ cup evaporated skimmed milk
made into crumbs	½ cup skim milk
3 tablespoons water	2 ounces freshly grated Gruyère
2 cups sliced peeled zucchini	(or Parmesan) cheese
1 teaspoon salt	Salt and pepper to taste
2 medium eggs	

Combine crumbs and water, mix to a paste and press into bottom of a 9-inch pie pan or quiche dish. Bake at 400°F. for 10 minutes. Set crust aside to cool. This can be done ahead of time. Wash zucchini, grate it against the coarse blade of grater and place in strainer over bowl. Toss with salt. Let stand 20 to 30 minutes. Drain, pressing out as much liquid as possible. If zucchini is too salty for your taste, wash it. Dry very well. Beat eggs; add to zucchini with skim and evaporated skimmed milk, cheese, salt and pepper. Mix well. Pour into prepared pie shell and bake at 400°F. (fairly hot oven) for 35 to 40 minutes. Makes 2 servings.

ZUCCHINI AND TOMATO QUICHE

Scald 2 medium tomatoes in boiling water for a few minutes; pull off skin and discard; cut open and remove seeds. Cut pulp into pieces and let drain in strainer. Reduce zucchini to 1½ cups. Add drained tomato pulp to eggs (and add to zucchini) in preceding recipe. Fill pie shell and bake as above. Makes 2 servings.

MACEDOINE OF VEGETABLES

3 ounces potato, diced	¾ cup water
2 ounces frozen peas	1 packet instant beef broth and
1 ounce sliced onion	seasoning mix
¼ cup sliced carrots	½ teaspoon dill weed
½ cup sliced celery	1 garlic clove, minced
½ cup frozen cut green beans	

Place vegetables in a 1-quart casserole. Heat water, broth mix, dill and garlic in small saucepan; pour over vegetables. Cover casserole and bake at 350°F. for 45 minutes. Makes 1 serving.

VEGETABLES A LA GRECQUE

Another classic way with vegetables, but we change procedure, adding oil to individual servings for easy tracking. The long way round is often your shortcut to goal.

Court Bouillon (recipe follows)	3 tablespoons vegetable oil
3 cups whole small mushrooms or young green beans (ends trimmed), or celeriac	

Prepare Court Bouillon and add vegetables, bring to boil again, then reduce heat and simmer until vegetables are done but crisp. (They continue to cook in their own steam.) Lift vegetables from liquid with slotted spoon and arrange in serving dish. Using high heat, boil the Court Bouillon down until it has reduced about half. Stir in oil. Pour over vegetables and refrigerate until well chilled. Serve cold as an hors d'oeuvre. Makes 6 servings.

Court Bouillon

3 cups water	3 sprigs parsley
1 lemon, sliced	½ bay leaf
½ cup diced celery, and leaves	1 garlic clove, crushed
1 tablespoon dehydrated onion flakes	½ teaspoon salt
6 peppercorns, crushed	⅛ teaspoon thyme (or 1 sprig fresh)
2 cloves	

In saucepan, bring all ingredients to boil; let simmer 5 minutes. Strain before adding vegetables. Makes 3 cups.

CHATEAU POTATOES

18 ounces cooked potatoes, peeled	½ teaspoon imitation butter flavoring
1 cup chicken bouillon	Salt to taste

Place potatoes in small ovenproof dish; add bouillon, imitation butter flavoring and sprinkle with salt. Bake in 400°F. oven, basting occasionally with bouillon until brown on top. Makes 6 servings.

PEAS WITH LETTUCE (Petits Pois à la Française)

A classic method.

1 cup shredded lettuce (Boston, romaine or iceberg)—do not dry after washing	Dash of salt and pepper
	¼ teaspoon thyme and savory
4 ounces tiny shelled peas, fresh or frozen	3 tablespoons water, or chicken bouillon
1 tablespoon dehydrated onion flakes	1 teaspoon vegetable oil
	½ teaspoon chopped fresh parsley

In small heavy saucepan, with tight-fitting cover, make a layer of lettuce, add peas and another layer of lettuce. Sprinkle with onion flakes, salt, pepper, thyme and savory. Add water or bouillon. Cover pan and cook over moderate heat until peas are tender, 10 to 15 minutes (less if you are using frozen peas which are already blanched by the packers). Remove peas from heat while they are still a fresh green color and slightly underdone. Bring them to the table where they will continue to steam in their own juices. Just before serving, stir in oil and parsley. Makes 1 serving.

NOTE: It is usual in France to sweeten this dish. If you wish, sprinkle the peas with artificial sweetener to equal ½ teaspoon sugar.

TOMATO MOUSSE

1 envelope unflavored gelatin
¼ cup cold water
½ cup evaporated skimmed milk
4 medium tomatoes, peeled, seeded and chopped

1 cup tomato puree
2 teaspoons lemon juice
Salt and cayenne pepper to taste
Bed of lettuce (optional)

Sprinkle gelatin over water in blender container to soften. Scald evaporated skimmed milk in a small saucepan. Pour into blender container. Process. Cook tomato in puree until soft. Season with lemon juice, salt and cayenne pepper. Let cool. Add to blender container and process. Divide into 4 individual molds and chill for 2 hours or until set. Unmold and serve on a bed of lettuce leaves, if desired. For creamier mousse, whip again immediately before serving and pour into individual dishes. Makes 4 servings.

RICE AND RADISH SALAD VINAIGRETTE

Vinaigrette Sauce (recipe follows)
1 cup sliced radishes
1 cup cooked green beans, sliced

1 cup cooked enriched rice
Lettuce leaves

Prepare Vinaigrette Sauce; pour over radishes and beans; toss. Refrigerate 2 hours. Remove vegetables from sauce and arrange on lettuce leaves in two chilled salad bowls; mix remaining sauce with rice; arrange on vegetables and serve. Sprinkle with parsley. Makes 2 servings.

Vinaigrette Sauce

4 teaspoons vegetable oil
2 teaspoons wine vinegar
Dash dry mustard

Salt and pepper to taste
1 teaspoon chopped fresh parsley

Combine ingredients. Makes 2 servings.

RAW MUSHROOM SALAD

Serve as a separate course after the entrée.

2 cups (scant ½ pound) sliced raw mushrooms
2 tablespoons vegetable oil
2 tablespoons lemon juice or wine vinegar

¼ teaspoon dry mustard
1 small head Boston, romaine or Bibb lettuce, washed and torn

Wipe the mushrooms, cut off the tips and slice vertically (through cap and stem) into pieces about ⅛-inch thick. Combine oil, lemon juice and mustard and pour over mushrooms. Let marinate for 30 minutes. Serve over salad greens. Makes 2 servings.

JAPANESE-STYLE SALAD (Salade Japonaise)

1 cup shredded lettuce
¼ medium pineapple
2 teaspoons lemon juice
1 small orange, peeled and sectioned

2 medium tomatoes, sliced
¼ cup plain yogurt

Make a bed of greens on each of two chilled salad plates. Cut pineapple quarter away from skin, remove core and slice fruit into small triangular segments. Sprinkle with lemon juice. Arrange half of the pineapple, orange sections, and the tomato slices in a circle on the lettuce with one-half of the yogurt in the middle. Repeat. Makes 2 servings.

ROQUEFORT CHEESE DRESSING*

For a mixed green salad rub your wooden bowl with garlic. Add crisp dry greens—one kind or a mixture (escarole, Boston, romaine and endive). Toss with watercress or parsley. Serve with this dressing.

¾ cup buttermilk or plain yogurt
2 ounces shredded Roquefort cheese

1 tablespoon lemon juice
¼ garlic clove, pressed
⅛ teaspoon salt

Combine ingredients, mix well and serve over greens. Makes 2 servings.

LEMON FRENCH DRESSING (Sauce Piquante)

A lively French dressing to have in your repertoire for the days when you've consumed your allotment of fat. Use it on freshly cooked greens (asparagus, broccoli, string beans, etc.) and serve the vegetables and dressing at room temperature, not chilled. It will do nicely for salads too.

1 tablespoon cold water	1 teaspoon grated lemon rind
1 teaspoon unflavored gelatin	1 garlic clove
¼ cup boiling water or bouillon	½ teaspoon salt
½ cup fresh lemon juice	¼ teaspoon dry mustard
¼ teaspoon Worcestershire	Dash ground pepper

In container or jar with lid sprinkle gelatin over cold water; then pour on boiling water or bouillon. Screw cover on jar and shake to dissolve gelatin. Open jar and add remaining ingredients; cover and shake well. Serve at room temperature. If made ahead and refrigerated, this will jell. Put the jar into a saucepan holding hot water until dressing is liquefied. Makes 4 servings.

A BOUQUET OF FRUITS AND VEGETABLES

Raw vegetables make marvelous desserts when served with fruit, one flavor enhancing the other. We like to cut the fruits and vegetables into approximately the same sizes. Pick up one of each and eat with your fingers—no added dressing needed. Serve apple with celery curls. Melon wedges with raw cauliflower florets. Halved broccoli florets or Brussels sprouts with cherries or grapes. Tomato slices or small cherry tomatoes with orange segments. Pineapple chunks with fennel slices. Tender peas in pod (to be shelled at the table) with berries. Rolled-up leaves of lettuce or Chinese cabbage with strawberries. Banana slices served in the peel with sea kale. Make your dessert bouquets as pretty and colorful as a flower arrangement . . . a treat for eye and palate.

PEACH MELBA

4 medium peaches, blanched and
peeled
1 teaspoon vanilla extract
1 cup raspberries, or ¾ teaspoon
raspberry extract

Artificial sweetener to equal
2 tablespoons sugar
Whipped Topping (see page x)

Cut peaches in half and remove pits. Place on individual dessert dishes. Sprinkle vanilla over peaches to coat. In a small bowl, mash berries with sweetener. Divide evenly and spoon over peach halves (or mix raspberry extract with sweetener and sprinkle over peach halves). Refrigerate while preparing Whipped Topping. Spoon topping over peaches. Serve immediately or chill 1 hour. Makes 4 servings.

NOTE: To blanch, immerse peaches in boiling water for a minute or two, cool slightly; peel while still warm.

PEACH PIE

Pie Crust

½ cup skim milk
1 teaspoon peach, raspberry or
other fruit extract
1 teaspoon vanilla extract

Artificial sweetener to equal
½ cup sugar
8 slices enriched white bread,
toasted and made into crumbs

In mixing bowl combine skim milk, extracts and sweetener. Add bread crumbs and stir with fork until crumbs are evenly moistened. Press into bottom and sides of a 9-inch pie plate. Bake at 400°F. (hot oven) 10 to 12 minutes. Cool.

Pie Filling

8 medium peaches, peeled and
sliced
1 cup water
Artificial sweetener to equal
½ cup sugar

¼ cup cold water
1½ envelopes unflavored gelatin
Whipped Topping (see page x)

Place peaches in saucepan with water and sweetener. Bring to a boil; reduce heat, simmer 5 minutes. Place water in a small bowl. Sprinkle gelatin over water to soften. Stir into peach mixture; stir until gelatin dissolves. Refrigerate until syrupy. Pour mixture into crumb shell; refrigerate until set. Serve with Whipped Topping. Divide evenly. Makes 8 servings.

POACHED WHOLE PEARS

Perfect summertime dessert. Use ripe pears.

4 ripe small pears	1 small piece cinnamon stick
1 cup citrus-flavored dietetic soda	Artificial sweetener to equal
1 piece lemon rind	6 teaspoons sugar, or to taste

Remove skin from top half of pears. In saucepan, combine fruit with remaining ingredients except sweetener and simmer until soft. Remove fruit to platter. Quickly cook liquid until reduced by half; stir in sweetener and pour sauce over fruit. Serve hot or chilled. Makes 4 servings.

"BRANDIED" PEACHES

Poach peaches as above. Add 1 tablespoon brandy extract to liquid, mix and pour over fruit. Makes 4 servings.

CHERRIES JUBILEE

This is an adaptation of a favorite dessert in haute cuisine. *Don't try to flame the brandy extract. It's not basic to the recipe and the results are unreliable.*

½ recipe Whipped Topping (see page x)	2 cups canned, pitted sweet cherries, no sugar added
Cherry juice plus water to equal ¾ cup liquid	1 teaspoon brandy extract
	½ teaspoon cherry extract

Just before dinner prepare the Whipped Topping and spoon it into 4 dessert dishes. Freeze. Bring the liquid to a boil in a saucepan, add cherries and cook briefly until cherries are just tender, turning them in the liquid so they cook evenly and quickly. This will take just a few minutes, don't overcook. Cool. Stir in extracts. Remove dessert dishes from freezer. Spoon on the fruit sauce and serve immediately. Makes 4 servings.

CHEESE FRUIT BOMBE*

⅔ cup cottage cheese
1 cup strawberries, sliced
⅓ cup skim milk
1 teaspoon strawberry extract
1 medium apple, cored and diced

¼ cup water
2 envelopes unflavored gelatin
⅓ cup evaporated skimmed milk
1 teaspoon grated lemon rind

Place cottage cheese, ½ cup strawberries, skim milk and extract in blender container. Process until smooth. Pour into bowl; add apple and remaining strawberries; mix well. Set aside. Pour water into a small saucepan; sprinkle gelatin over it to soften. Place over low heat and stir until gelatin is dissolved; cool. Combine evaporated skimmed milk and lemon rind; beat with rotary beater until peaks form. Pour gelatin slowly into milk and continue beating; fold into fruit mixture. Pour into medium-size mold and chill 1 hour. Unmold. Makes 2 servings.

STRAWBERRY OMELET (Omelette aux Fraises)*

½ cup strawberries
½ teaspoon vanilla extract

2 medium eggs
Pinch of salt

Hull the strawberries and cut them in half into small bowl. Sprinkle them with half of the vanilla. Beat the eggs until blended; add salt and remaining vanilla. Pour into preheated 6-inch nonstick skillet. As mixture sets, lift up the edges so uncooked portions flow to the bottom edges. When eggs are set, place berries on one half of the omelet and with a spatula fold the other half over fruit. Roll out of pan onto a warmed plate. Divide evenly and serve immediately. Makes 2 servings.

GRAPE OMELET (Omelette aux Raisins)

Follow the preceding recipe, but substitute 20 small grapes for the strawberries, and rum extract for the vanilla. Makes 2 servings.

HOT FRUIT SOUFFLE*

2 medium apples, or peaches, or 2 small pears, peeled and cored or pitted

2 tablespoons water
2 medium eggs, separated
Dash lemon juice

In small saucepan, combine fruit with water; cover and cook until fruit is very soft. Put fruit and liquid in blender container and process; transfer to small bowl. Beat yolks lightly and add to fruit in bowl with lemon juice. Beat whites until stiff and fold them into the first mixture. Transfer to 2 individual soufflé dishes and bake at 350°F. until tops are brown, about 20 minutes. Serve at once. Makes 2 servings.

HOT FRUIT COMPOTE (Compote Composée)

2 cups boiling water
4 medium apricots, halved and pitted
4 medium plums, halved and pitted
2 medium peaches, halved and pitted

40 small seedless grapes
1 2-inch piece of vanilla bean or 2 teaspoons vanilla extract
1 slice lemon
Artificial sweetener to equal ½ cup sugar

In large saucepan pour boiling water over apricots, plums and peaches. Simmer for 12 minutes or until fruit is almost tender. Add grapes and vanilla bean (or extract) and lemon slice. Cook a minute or two longer. Stir in sweetener. Serve hot or chilled. Makes 8 servings.

PLUM MOUSSE

1½ teaspoons unflavored gelatin
½ cup water
2 medium plums, peeled and pitted
⅓ cup nonfat dry milk

⅛ teaspoon vanilla extract
Artificial sweetener to equal 2 teaspoons sugar
2 to 3 ice cubes

Sprinkle gelatin over water in small saucepan. Heat, stirring, until gelatin dissolves. Pour into blender container. Add plums, milk, extract and sweetener; cover and process at low speed until smooth. Add ice cubes, one at a time, processing at high speed until all traces of ice disappear. Pour into dessert dish; chill 5 minutes, or until set. Makes 1 serving.

MACEDOINE OF FRUIT

1 small orange, peeled and sectioned, or ½ ripe medium cantaloupe (remove rind)

2 ripe medium apricots or 4 canned apricot halves (no sugar added) and 2 tablespoons juice

1 ripe medium peach or ½ cup canned peach slices, no sugar added

20 small seedless grapes

Artificial sweetener to taste

1 tablespoon lemon juice (optional)

1 tablespoon brandy or rum extract

Cut the fruits into even pieces. Sprinkle lightly with artificial sweetener. Add lemon juice if mixture seems dry, and stir in brandy or rum extract. Makes 4 servings.

Germany

~~~~~~~~~~

As you can see if you peruse the pages which follow, German fare isn't all sauerbraten and sausage, popular as they are. You can enjoy *Pfannkuchen* (pancakes) for breakfast, *Frischkäse* (cottage cheese, even better with a sprinkling of caraway seed and minced chives) at *Mittags,* and *Kalbsbraten* or *Kalbsleber* (roast veal or calf's liver) and other meats and fish for dinner. And as Germans are as fond of sweets as the rest of us, we have included a few hearty dessert specialties, too.

If you are searching for some foolproof German recipes done the new way but with old-fashioned charm, recipes in the spirit of German *Gemütlichkeit* or conviviality, here they are. *Gesegnete Mahlzeit!*

LENTIL SOUP*

The amount of dried uncooked lentils needed to make 16 ounces cooked varies depending on age and method by which the legume is processed. Weigh the lentils after they are cooked, and use only the amount required in the recipe. The surplus can be frozen and used in combination with other cooked dried beans.

2½ cups water
½ cup freshly chopped celery
2 ounces freshly chopped onion
1 packet instant beef broth and seasoning mix

1 garlic clove, minced
½ bay leaf
¼ teaspoon thyme (or 1 sprig fresh)
16 ounces cooked dried lentils

In a large saucepan, bring water to a boil. Add remaining ingredients except lentils; simmer until vegetables are tender. Add lentils; cook 20 minutes longer. Serve hot. (For a smoother soup, process in a blender.) If soup is too thick, add hot water and reheat; stir to prevent burning. Makes 4 servings.

FARMHOUSE OMELET

2 ounces onion, finely chopped
3 ounces cooked potato, diced
2 medium eggs, beaten

1 teaspoon freshly cut chives
1 tablespoon water
Salt and pepper to taste

Lightly brown onions in nonstick omelet pan. Add potato and heat for one minute. Combine eggs, chives, water, salt and pepper, and add to omelet pan. As mixture sets at edges, with spatula draw edges toward center so that uncooked portions flow to bottom of pan. Tilt pan. Using a spatula, carefully roll or fold omelet in half and transfer to serving dish. Makes 1 serving.

COUNTRY LUNCH

⅔ cup cottage cheese
1 teaspoon caraway seed
1 tablespoon minced fresh chives
3 ounces cooked potato, sliced

Few small red radishes
5 cherry tomatoes
Salt and pepper to taste
¾ cup chilled buttermilk

Sprinkle cottage cheese with caraway and chives, and put in center of chilled plate. Surround with mounds of potato slices, radishes and cherry tomatoes. Salt and pepper to taste. At table, pour some of your buttermilk on top of the salad, and drink the rest of it. Makes 1 serving.

MARJORAM VEAL CHOPS

8 5-ounce veal chops or 4
   10-ounce
2 cups mushrooms
½ cup evaporated skimmed milk
½ cup chicken bouillon

1 teaspoon marjoram
½ teaspoon paprika
1½ teaspoons salt
1 teaspoon sherry extract
   (optional)

Pound veal chops until thin. Brown on both sides over moderate heat in nonstick skillet. Remove chops and wipe out skillet. Brown mushrooms in same skillet and stir in evaporated skimmed milk, bouillon, marjoram, paprika, salt and sherry extract. Do not boil. Transfer to baking pan or shallow serving casserole and bake in moderate oven (350°F.) until chops are tender. Makes 4 servings.

SAUERBRATEN

Sour roast, traditionally served with braised red cabbage, and often with prepared horseradish.

3 pounds well-trimmed beef
   (bottom round or other tender
   roast)
1 cup beef bouillon
½ cup wine vinegar
1 teaspoon salt

¼ teaspoon pepper
5 cloves, crushed
2 bay leaves, crumbled
1 tablespoon burgundy or
   sherry extract

Place meat in shallow heatproof casserole. Combine remaining ingredients and pour over meat. Refrigerate 2 to 3 days, turning frequently. When ready to cook, drain meat (reserve marinade). Bake on rack in roasting pan in 325°F. oven for 2 hours or until meat is very tender, basting frequently with part of the reserved marinade. (Serve with "gravy" of remaining beef marinade.) Slice meat diagonally across the grain and serve hot. Makes 6 servings.

DELICATESSEN

1 pound cold, cooked pork
1 tablespoon chopped fresh
parsley
1 small garlic clove (optional)
½ teaspoon grated lemon rind
¼ teaspoon sage or marjoram

¼ teaspoon grated nutmeg
Sprinkle of black pepper
2 tablespoons unflavored gelatin
1 cup beef bouillon
3 pimento strips
½ medium dill pickle, cut in
3 strips

Put pork, parsley, garlic, lemon rind, sage, nutmeg and pepper through meat grinder with medium blade or chop in food processor. In small saucepan, sprinkle gelatin over ¼ cup cold beef bouillon to soften. Stir in remaining bouillon and heat over low flame until gelatin is dissolved. Stir into pork mixture; mix well. Press ⅓ mixture tightly into a small loaf pan or mold. Arrange 2 pimento strips and 1 pickle strip on top. Press ½ of remaining pork mixture over strips. Arrange remaining strips over mixture. Top with remaining pork mixture, pressed down. Bake 1 hour in 325°F. oven. Refrigerate. Slice evenly and serve cold. Makes 4 servings.

KNOCKWURST SAUCE FOR COOKED KALE

Serve over cooked kale or shredded cabbage.

8 ounces knockwurst
2 ounces diced onion
1 cup sliced celery
1 teaspoon chopped fresh
parsley

¾ cup tomato puree
1 bay leaf
⅛ teaspoon crushed red pepper

Pierce knockwurst with fork and put in saucepan with water to cover. Bring to boil and cook until heated. Pour off water and dry knockwurst by shaking pan over moderate heat. Remove from pan; slice. Return to pan; add onion and celery and brown on all sides, turning as necessary. Add remaining ingredients, cover pan and cook until sauce is thick, about 1 hour. (If necessary, keep warm on an asbestos pad.) Makes 2 servings.

HAM WITH GREEN BEANS

1½ pounds ham
Water
4 cups fresh green string beans

18 ounces potatoes, peeled and quartered
Salt and pepper to taste

Cover the ham with water and simmer slowly for three hours. Add water from time to time during cooking, so ham is covered at all times. After 3 hours, drain the ham and add 1 quart water. Break the beans into small pieces and add to the ham. Continue cooking about 25 minutes. Add potatoes to beans and ham, and cook until potatoes are tender. A few minutes before serving, stir in salt and pepper. Serve hot, with vinegar, mustard and horseradish on the table. Makes 6 servings.

LIVER DUMPLINGS WITH TOMATO SAUCE

8 ounces beef liver, coarsely ground
1 slice enriched white bread, made into crumbs
1 tablespoon skim milk
1 teaspoon chopped fresh parsley

1 teaspoon dehydrated onion flakes
Salt and pepper to taste
2 cups water
1 packet instant beef broth and seasoning mix
Tomato Sauce (recipe follows)

Combine ground liver, bread crumbs, milk, parsley, onion flakes, salt and pepper in medium bowl; form into small balls. In medium saucepan, heat water to boiling; add broth mix. Drop dumplings into boiling beef bouillon; cook until each dumpling rises to the surface; remove dumplings, serve with Tomato Sauce. Makes 1 serving.

NOTE: Sauce may be eliminated if desired and liver may be served in bouillon.

Tomato Sauce

1 cup tomato juice, or ½ cup tomato puree
1 packet instant beef broth and seasoning mix

⅛ medium green pepper, chopped
½ teaspoon hot pepper sauce

Combine all ingredients in small saucepan; cook until pepper is tender and mixture thickens to sauce consistency. Makes 1 serving.

"CREAMED" LIVER RHINE VALLEY

1 pound calf or steer liver
1 cup buttermilk
4 or 5 capers, rinsed and chopped
1 teaspoon grated lemon rind
Salt and pepper to taste
1 cup cooked enriched noodles

Wipe liver clean and brown quickly on both sides in preheated non-stick skillet. Do not overcook (it should remain juicy). Slice. Combine with remaining ingredients, except noodles. Cover and heat without boiling. Serve with hot noodles. Makes 2 servings.

GERMAN POTATO SALAD (Kartoffelsalat)

1 pound 2 ounces cooked potatoes, peeled and sliced thin
Salt and pepper to taste
1 teaspoon chopped fresh parsley
½ teaspoon chopped fresh chives
¼ cup strong chicken bouillon (dissolve ½ envelope instant chicken broth and seasoning mix in ¼ cup boiling water)
2 tablespoons vegetable oil
1 tablespoon wine vinegar
3 medium cucumbers, sliced
6 ounces sliced cooked beets

Layer potato slices in a salad bowl. Season each layer with salt, pepper, parsley and chives. Combine bouillon, oil and vinegar and pour over salad. Mix lightly; serve warm, accompany with slices of cucumber and beets. Makes 6 servings. For carrying to a picnic pack cucumbers and beets separately.

SWEET AND SOUR COLE SLAW

⅓ cup vinegar
¼ cup vegetable oil
1 tablespoon brown sugar replacement
1 teaspoon dehydrated onion flakes
1 teaspoon celery salt
½ teaspoon dry mustard
½ teaspoon salt
¼ teaspoon pepper
2 tablespoons chopped pimentos
4 cups shredded cabbage

Combine all ingredients except pimento and cabbage in a large mixing bowl. Add pimento and cabbage; toss. Cover and chill. Makes 6 servings.

POTATOES WITH CHEESE (Kartoffeln mit Käse)

1 medium egg
½ cup skim milk
3 ounces cooked potato, diced
1 ounce diced American cheese

1 cup diced cooked cauliflower
Salt and pepper to taste
Prepared mustard

For each serving use a good-sized individual casserole. Beat the egg; stir in the milk, potato, cheese and cauliflower. Season with salt and pepper. Bake at 350°F. for 20 minutes or so. Serve hot with prepared mustard. Makes 1 serving.

MIXED VEGETABLES HOTPOT (Allerlei)

1 cup string beans
1 cup shredded cabbage or
  cauliflower florets
1 cup mushrooms sliced
½ cup carrots
4 ounces onion
2 medium tomatoes, sliced
½ to ¾ cup water or chicken
  bouillon

1 garlic clove
¼ cup evaporated skimmed milk
2 teaspoons margarine
1 tablespoon chopped fresh
  parsley
Salt if desired

Cut string beans, cabbage or cauliflower, mushrooms, carrots, onion and tomatoes into approximately even dice; add water and garlic; cover pot and cook until vegetables are tender. Carefully remove vegetables with slotted spoon so they do not mash. Remove and discard garlic clove; boil down liquid in pan, reduce heat, and stir in evaporated milk. Heat but do not boil. Remove from heat. Stir margarine into sauce and pour over vegetables. Sprinkle with parsley. Makes 2 servings.

PEARS AND BEANS (Birnen und Bohnen)

4 small pears, peeled and cored,
  cut in quarters
¾ cup boiling water
1 small piece lemon rind

4 cups frozen cut green or wax
  beans (about 3 packages)
2 teaspoons lemon juice
Pepper to taste

In saucepan, cover pears with boiling water; add lemon rind and cook for 15 minutes. Add beans, and continue cooking for 20 minutes, or until most of liquid has evaporated. If necessary remove cover for the last few minutes and cook rapidly to reduce liquid. Stir in lemon juice and pepper. Serve hot as meat side dish. Makes 4 servings.

GERMAN APPLE PANCAKE (Pfannkuchen)*

1 medium egg
2 tablespoons skim milk
Artificial sweetener to equal
   3 teaspoons sugar

¼ teaspoon cinnamon
1 slice enriched white bread,
   made into crumbs
1 medium apple, pared and grated

Combine egg, milk, sweetener and cinnamon in mixing bowl. Add bread crumbs and beat with whisk or fork 1 minute. Pour into heated nonstick omelet pan. Arrange apple on top. Bake in hot oven (400°F.) for 3 to 4 minutes until set. Remove; fold in half and serve. Makes 1 serving.

APPLE BUTTER

4 medium apples, cored, pared,
   cut in eighths
½ cup water
Artificial sweetener to equal
   ¼ cup sugar

½ teaspoon cinnamon
⅛ teaspoon each, cloves and
   allspice

Place apples and water in medium saucepan; cover; cook slowly, until apples are soft but not mushy. Pour mixture into blender container; add remaining ingredients; process at medium speed just until apples are pureed. Pour into medium bowl; chill. Makes 8 servings.

GERMAN APPLE CUSTARD*

4 medium eggs, slightly beaten
½ cup evaporated skimmed milk
4 teaspoons margarine, melted,
   or vegetable oil
Artificial sweetener to equal
   2 tablespoons sugar or to taste

1 teaspoon grated lemon rind
1 teaspoon almond extract
4 medium apples, peeled, cored
   and sliced

In bowl, combine eggs, milk, melted margarine or oil, sweetener, lemon rind and almond extract. Mix well together. Arrange sliced apples in a 1½-quart casserole. Pour egg mixture over apples. Place casserole in a pan containing one inch of water. Bake in moderate oven (350°F.) 35 to 45 minutes or until eggs are set. Makes 4 servings.

Greece and the Other Balkan States

Travelers love Greece and its fabled islands. All the ancient Hellenic legends come alive for you as you cruise to Crete or Skiathos, romp on the sun-dappled beaches, and swim in the sparkling blue Aegean water. But the next best thing to being there is to cook the sleek, chic Greek way.

Although ethnic hostilities have ravaged the Balkans for many centuries, in the pages of our cookbook Albania, Bulgaria, Romania, Yugoslavia and Greece live a peaceful coexistence. You'll enjoy our sampling of dishes from the countries that share the mountains with Greece.

BULGARIAN VEGETABLE SOUP

1½ cups water
¼ cup carrots, diced
1 ounce parsnips, sliced
½ cup cauliflower florets
½ cup asparagus pieces

½ teaspoon chopped fresh dill
1 packet instant chicken broth
and seasoning mix
Salt and pepper to taste

Combine water, carrots, parsnips, cauliflower florets, asparagus and dill in saucepan. Cook until vegetables are tender. Stir in chicken broth mix and seasonings to taste. Makes 1 serving.

EGG AND LEMON SOUP (Avgolemono)*

Lemon juice flavors almost every course in Greek menus, beginning with a favorite soup, Avgolemono.

4 cups chicken bouillon
4 medium eggs, well beaten
2 cups cooked enriched rice
Juice of 1 lemon

3 tablespoons chopped fresh dill
or parsley
Salt and white pepper to taste

Bring bouillon to a boil. Remove from heat. Slowly (*sica, sica*—as the Greeks say) pour about 1 cup of hot soup into eggs, beating constantly. Pour egg mixture back into remaining hot soup, continuing to beat. Heat but do not boil. Stir in rice and lemon juice, add dill or parsley, and season with salt and pepper to taste. Makes 4 servings.

ROMANIAN FISH SOUP

4 cups water
5 packets instant chicken broth
and seasoning mix
2 pounds bass or carp fillets,
cut into 4 equal pieces
1 small head Boston lettuce,
cut into pieces

4 ounces scallions, cut into
1-inch pieces
1 bay leaf
4 peppercorns
Salt to taste

Pour water into a large saucepan. Bring to a boil; add broth mix. Lower heat; simmer for 2 to 3 minutes or until mix is totally dissolved. Add fish, lettuce, scallions and seasonings; return to boil; lower heat and simmer, covered, 10 minutes. Remove bay leaf. Divide mixture evenly into 4 soup bowls. Makes 4 servings.

LENTIL SOUP (Faki)

This lentil soup, sharpened with vinegar, can be made ahead of time and refrigerated for several days as it improves with age. It also freezes well.

1 quart beef bouillon
1 pound 2 ounces cooked dried lentils
Salt and pepper to taste
6 tablespoons tomato puree
3 ounces onion, finely chopped

¼ cup finely chopped carrot
½ rib celery, finely chopped
½ garlic clove, minced or put through garlic press
1 tablespoon vinegar or lemon juice

Combine bouillon, lentils, salt and pepper in a large saucepan. Bring to a boil. Add remaining ingredients, except vinegar. Return mixture to a boil; reduce heat and simmer for at least 30 minutes, or until vegetables are tender. Divide evenly into 3 soup bowls. Stir 1 teaspoon vinegar or lemon juice into each bowl of soup as it is served. Makes 3 servings.

ROMANIAN CHEESE BALLS

⅔ cup dry cottage cheese
2 medium eggs, beaten
¼ teaspoon salt

Pinch of pepper
6 ounces cooked mashed potatoes
3 cups chicken bouillon

Mash cottage cheese through sieve. Add eggs and seasonings; add potatoes and mix well. Drop by spoonfuls into simmering bouillon. Let simmer gently 8 to 10 minutes. Divide evenly into 2 servings.

SPINACH CHEESE PIE (Spanakopita)

1 teaspoon dehydrated onion flakes
1½ teaspoons water
2 medium eggs
⅔ cup cottage cheese

1 cup cooked, drained, chopped spinach
¼ cup snipped parsley leaves
1 teaspoon salt
½ teaspoon dill weed

Soak onion flakes in water. Beat eggs in medium bowl. Beat in cottage cheese, spinach, parsley, salt, dill and soaked onions. Pour into 2 shallow nonstick casseroles. Place casseroles in a larger baking pan. Pour boiling water into baking pan until it reaches halfway up sides of casseroles. Bake in 350°F. oven for 30 minutes. Makes 2 servings.

CLAM PILAF

4 ounces onion, finely chopped
¼ cup chicken bouillon
12 ounces canned, drained, tiny whole baby clams, or steamed shucked cherrystone clams, cut in half

2 medium canned tomatoes, chopped
¾ teaspoon oregano
Salt and pepper to taste
1 cup cooked enriched rice

In a medium saucepan, cook onion in bouillon until tender. Add remaining ingredients, except rice, and simmer, covered, until hot. Divide into two plates, each holding ½ cup rice. Makes 2 servings.

STUFFED MUSSELS

6 ounces raw mussels (20 mussels in the shell)
2 ounces grated American cheese
1 slice enriched white bread, made into crumbs
¼ cup chopped fresh parsley

2 teaspoons chopped fresh basil or 1 teaspoon dried
1 teaspoon oregano
1 garlic clove, pressed
1 tablespoon water

Using a sharp knife, open mussel shells, running the knife horizontally, to separate shells. Remove mussels and discard half the shell; reserve the other half of each shell. Weigh 6 ounces of the raw mussels and divide equally into the half-shells. Place on a nonstick baking sheet, and set aside. In a small mixing bowl, combine cheese, bread, parsley, basil, oregano and garlic. Sprinkle water over mixture and stir to moisten. Divide mixture evenly into the same number of portions as there are mussel shells. Spoon each portion over mussels and mound slightly. Bake at 500°F. for 5 minutes or until mussels are cooked and cheese is melted. Divide shells evenly. Serve hot. Makes 2 servings.

SCALLOPS WITH RICE

8 ounces onion, finely chopped
¼ cup bouillon
2 pounds scallops, washed

Salt to taste
2 cups cooked enriched rice
Chopped parsley (optional)

In a 3-quart saucepan, cook onions in bouillon until tender. Add scallops; bring mixture to a boil (liquid will accumulate as mixture cooks). Lower heat and simmer for 10 minutes. Divide evenly into 4 portions and serve each portion in an individual bowl over ½ cup rice. Garnish with chopped parsley if desired. Makes 4 servings.

SHRIMP SCORPIO

¼ cup chicken bouillon
4 ounces finely chopped onion
¼ cup finely chopped fresh parsley
1 tablespoon finely chopped fresh dill
1 garlic clove, pressed
⅛ teaspoon dry mustard

4 medium tomatoes, blanched, peeled and chopped
½ cup tomato puree
⅛ teaspoon thyme
12 ounces peeled and deveined raw shrimp
4 ounces feta cheese, crumbled

Heat bouillon in a saucepan; add onion. Cook, stirring, until onion starts to brown. Add parsley, dill and garlic. Stir in the mustard. Do not add salt at any time. Add tomatoes, tomato puree and thyme and simmer thirty minutes. Rinse cleaned shrimp, drain and add to the sauce, cook covered, 3 to 5 minutes. Pour the mixture into a 1½-quart casserole and sprinkle evenly with cheese. Bake 10 to 15 minutes, or until the cheese is melted. Serve immediately. Makes 4 servings.

VARIATION: Grated mozzarella cheese may be substituted for the feta cheese. If so, season the tomato sauce with salt to taste before adding the shrimp.

YUGOSLAV BEEF ROLLS (Čevapčići)

As served in Yugoslavia restaurants, this is accompanied by a spicy cole slaw.

8 ounces chopped beef
½ teaspoon Worcestershire

Salt, pepper and garlic powder to taste

Preheat broiler. Season beef with Worcestershire, salt, pepper and garlic powder. Form into 2-inch long sausage-shapes; place on a rack 4 inches away from source of heat. Broil until well-browned, turning once. Makes 1 serving.

BAKED LAMB CHOPS

4 (8-ounce) broiled loin lamb chops
Salt and pepper to taste
1 cup tomato puree

1 tablespoon Worcestershire
½ teaspoon oregano
¼ teaspoon garlic salt

Sprinkle salt and pepper on both sides of lamb chops and place in a shallow casserole. In a small bowl, combine remaining ingredients, and pour over meat. Cover and bake in moderate oven (350°F.) for 1 hour. Makes 4 servings.

ALBANIAN LAMB STEW WITH OKRA

12 ounces fresh or frozen okra
2 medium green peppers, diced
1 cup celery, diced
4 ounces onions, diced
4 garlic cloves, pressed
Salt and pepper to taste

½ cup water
1 pound roasted lamb, cut into bite-sized pieces
¼ teaspoon thyme
Paprika
Strips of lemon rind for garnish

Cook okra in a skillet, until liquid evaporates, stirring occasionally, for about 5 minutes. Add green peppers, celery, onions, garlic, salt and pepper and cook for 10 minutes longer, stirring to keep vegetables from sticking to the bottom of the pan. Add water, lamb and thyme, and let simmer, covered, on low heat for 20 to 25 minutes or until heated through and vegetables are tender. Sprinkle with paprika and garnish with lemon rind. Makes 4 servings.

BALKAN ONE-POT LIVER AND VEGETABLE DINNER

¼ cup beef bouillon
1 medium green pepper, thinly sliced
2 ounces onion, chopped
1 small piece cinnamon stick (about 1 inch)
2 tablespoons tomato puree

8 ounces steer or calf liver, cut into 1-inch squares
½ cup mushrooms, sliced
½ cup cooked enriched rice
Salt and pepper to taste
1 teaspoon chopped fresh parsley

In skillet, heat bouillon. Add green pepper, onions and cinnamon stick. Cook until vegetables are tender. Stir in tomato puree, mix well, and add liver and mushrooms. Continue to cook, stirring constantly, until liver is done to taste. Remove cinnamon stick. Stir in rice, season with salt and pepper, and heat through. Sprinkle with parsley to garnish. Makes 1 serving.

MIXED VEGETABLE SALAD

Tavernas in Greece serve the famous salads made of heaps of fresh raw vegetables and large bowls of assorted greens dressed with oil and lemon juice—sprinkled over at the table.

Coarse salt to taste
1 garlic clove, peeled and split
4 cups salad greens (escarole, romaine, chicory or other greens) torn into bite-size pieces
8 radishes, cut into "roses"
4 ounces red onion, cut into rings
1 medium green pepper, cored, seeded and cut into thin rings or strips

10 cherry tomatoes, halved
Freshly ground pepper to taste
2 tablespoons lemon juice or vinegar
¼ cup vegetable oil

Pour a little coarse salt into a salad bowl; rub the salt with the garlic clove around the surface of the bowl. Add the salad greens and raw vegetables. Sprinkle with pepper and lemon juice or vinegar and toss lightly. Add oil and toss again. Serve immediately. Makes 4 servings.

EGGPLANT SALAD (Melitzanes Salata)

1 medium eggplant
4 ounces onion, grated
2 medium tomatoes, peeled, chopped
1 garlic clove, minced
2 tablespoons chopped fresh parsley

2 tablespoons vegetable oil
2 tablespoons red wine vinegar
½ teaspoon marjoram
½ teaspoon salt
Pepper to taste
Lettuce leaves
Chopped fresh parsley for garnish

Bake whole eggplant in shallow pan in moderate oven (350°F.) for 1 hour. Dip in cold water; peel off skin. Dice eggplant; measure 2 cups; put in large bowl. Add onion, tomato, garlic, parsley, vegetable oil, vinegar, marjoram, salt and pepper. Mix well. Serve on lettuce; sprinkle with parsley. Serve at luncheon or dinner. Makes 4 servings.

CUCUMBERS GREEK STYLE

1 cup buttermilk
2 medium cucumbers, peeled,
  seeded and diced
2 medium tomatoes, sliced into
  wedges
4 teaspoons vegetable oil
2 teaspoons lemon juice

1 garlic clove, finely minced
1 teaspoon oregano
½ teaspoon mint leaves
Salt and freshly ground black
  pepper to taste
Chilled celery strips

Pour buttermilk into a mixing bowl; add remaining ingredients except celery strips. Let stand 1 hour in refrigerator until ready to serve. Mix well before serving. Serve with chilled celery strips as an appetizer. Makes 4 servings.

ARTICHOKE HEARTS

1 pound frozen artichoke hearts,
  thawed
½ cup water
1 tablespoon lemon juice

½ teaspoon salt
1 teaspoon chopped fresh dill
4 teaspoons vegetable oil

Combine artichokes, water, lemon juice and salt in medium saucepan. Cover; bring to a full boil over high heat, separating artichokes with fork. Reduce heat; simmer covered 5 to 8 minutes until tender. Drain and sprinkle with chopped dill. Mix to combine. Divide evenly onto 4 dishes. Add 1 teaspoon oil to each serving and mix well. Makes 4 servings. Serve with luncheon or dinner.

STUFFED GRAPE LEAVES (Dolmadakia)

4 ounces onions, finely chopped
¼ cup finely chopped celery
1 cup beef bouillon
8 ounces cooked ground beef
8 ounces cooked ground lamb
2 cups cooked enriched rice
¼ cup finely chopped fresh
  parsley

1 tablespoon finely chopped fresh
  mint or 1 teaspoon dried mint
Salt and freshly ground pepper
  to taste
1 cup grape leaves
¼ cup wine vinegar
2 tablespoons lemon juice

Cook onions and celery in ¼ cup bouillon until tender. Place meat in a bowl and add the onions and celery. Add rice, parsley, mint, salt and pepper. Blend well. Gently turn the grape leaves into a colander and rinse them under cold running water, separating the leaves. Dry gently and place one at a time on a flat surface, shiny side down. Place an even amount of filling in the center of each leaf and roll each tightly from the stem end toward the point of the leaf. Arrange the leaves in layers in a heavy saucepan. Add the remaining bouillon, vinegar and lemon juice and cover with a heavy plate to prevent the leaves from opening. Cook tightly covered, over low heat ½ hour. Makes 4 servings.

ROMANIAN RICE PUDDING WITH APPLES

4 medium apples
Water
1 teaspoon lemon juice
2 tablespoons margarine, softened

2 cups cooked enriched rice
  (see note)
Cinnamon

Core, peel and slice apples (see note below for using the peels). Place in medium saucepan with water to cover and lemon juice. Simmer until apple slices are soft but still hold a shape. Remove from heat. Drain and discard liquid. Stir in margarine. Let stand while preparing rice. In a pretty nonstick oven-to-table 1-quart serving dish, place ⅓ rice, ½ apple mixture and sprinkle with cinnamon. Layer another ⅓ rice, remaining apple mixture, sprinkling of cinnamon and top with remaining rice. Bake in moderate oven (350°F.) until edges turn brown, 35 to 45 minutes. Makes 4 servings.

NOTE: Boil the peel in water to cover for 30 minutes. Drain, press out juice. Use this liquid plus additional water as necessary to cook the rice, following package directions.

MOCHA FRAPPE

1 cup strong black coffee
⅔ cup nonfat dry milk
Artificial sweetener to equal
  4 teaspoons sugar

2 to 3 ice cubes

Pour coffee, milk and sweetener into blender container; cover and process at low speed to combine. Add ice cubes; cover and process at high speed until all traces of ice disappear. Pour into two glasses. Makes 2 servings.

India

India is spice merchant to the world, so naturally its foods are pungent with appetizing seasonings of all kinds. If you are a curry buff, this may be your favorite section, but would it surprise you to know that in its own country there is no one spice called curry? Curry powder is a blend of many different condiments. One old recipe calls for 8 ounces turmeric, 6 ounces coriander, 3 ounces each of cardamom, cumin and fenugreek, 1 ounce each of cloves and peppercorns and ¼ ounce cayenne pepper, all reduced to a powder. However, we assume you'll buy the curry blend in your supermarket or specialty store. Since the potency of the curry powder is variable, add it to taste. Start with the minimum suggested amount and then increase as desired.

Curries are not inevitable at an Indian meal, but spicy foods are popular, as is natural in a tropical country, and drinks are an important part of the menu. We don't mean alcoholic beverages—in fact, few Indians drink spirits with their meals. We do mean refreshing cool drinks such as freshly squeezed limes or lemons with ice water, or iced tea . . . Darjeeling and Assam are two very fine teas grown in India. Add a colorful pinch of saffron, a few crushed cardamom seeds or a sprig of mint to tea and you'll give it an authentic Indian touch.

Our chapter concludes with authentic buttermilk and yogurt drinks to help quench the fire which a hot curry might have sparked in your throat.

MULLIGATAWNY

¼ cup diced celery
½ medium green pepper, minced
½ teaspoon dehydrated onion flakes
1 cup chicken or onion bouillon, divided

½ to 1 teaspoon curry powder (or to taste)
1 medium tomato, cut in eighths
⅛ teaspoon ground cardamom

In saucepan cook celery, pepper and onion in ¼ cup chicken or onion bouillon over low heat until tender, about 5 minutes. Stir in curry. Add tomatoes, cardamom and remaining bouillon. Cook 15 minutes. Serve hot. Makes 1 serving.

CHICKEN SOUP WITH LEMON AND MINT

8 ounces cooked chicken, cut into ⅛-inch strips
2 cups onion bouillon
1 cup cooked enriched rice

1 tablespoon fresh lemon juice
Salt and pepper to taste
2 tablespoons chopped fresh mint

Combine all ingredients, except mint, in medium saucepan. Simmer long enough to heat chicken. Place 1 tablespoon mint in each of 2 bowls. Ladle soup over mint and serve at once. Makes 2 servings.

SPLIT PEA SOUP (Dal)*

This can be cooked down to become a stew.

12 ounces cooked drained dried yellow split peas (reserve liquid), see note
4 cups liquid (water plus reserved liquid)
1 cup diced celery
1 tablespoon curry powder

1 tablespoon dehydrated onion flakes
1 teaspoon salt or to taste
2 hot green chili peppers, finely chopped
1 bay leaf
Garnish: chopped fresh parsley

Combine all ingredients in saucepan (except garnish) and bring to a boil. Reduce heat and simmer 45 minutes. Puree in blender container and serve in bowls with garnish. Makes 4 servings.

Cooking Note: Cover 1 pound washed uncooked dried split peas with water; bring to boil, cover pan and simmer gently until peas are tender but still firm. Drain peas (reserve liquid), weigh peas. Freeze serving portions in liquid to cover. Label net weight.

CURRY OF EGGS*

You can omit the eggs and use the curry sauce over cooked vegetables such as cauliflower or broccoli, cooked dried beans; or over cooked chicken, fish, meat or shellfish. Curries are usually served over cooked rice, but you may substitute cooked bean sprouts. Try stirring saffron powder into bean sprouts to heighten the illusion.

8 ounces sliced onions
2 small garlic cloves, minced
4 medium tomatoes, chopped
2 green medium apples, sliced
1 cup chopped celery
1 tablespoon curry powder, or to taste
1 teaspoon fresh ginger root, diced

2 cups chicken bouillon
1½ teaspoons salt
1 teaspoon coconut extract
¼ teaspoon pepper
8 hard-cooked medium eggs, cut in half
4 cups cooked enriched rice

Brown onions and garlic in nonstick skillet. Add tomatoes, apples, celery, curry powder and ginger. Simmer for 5 minutes. Stir in remaining ingredients except eggs and rice. Place eggs and rice in casserole and pour mixture over. Serve very hot. Provide seasoning at table . . . salt, pepper and more curry powder. Makes 8 servings.

CHICKEN TANDOORI

Tandoor is an Indian clay oven, but the term now applies to the spiced chicken dish which was originally made in it.

2½ to 3 pounds skinned chicken
2 garlic cloves mashed or pressed
1 teaspoon allspice
½ teaspoon grated fresh ginger root or ¼ teaspoon ground

¼ teaspoon crushed red pepper
Lemon juice to moisten
1 cup buttermilk

Pierce chicken with fork. Make a paste of seasonings and lemon juice and rub into chicken. Bake chicken on rack in moderate (350°F.) oven for 45 minutes, or until done to taste (or barbecue over hot coals turning frequently). Weigh portions. Serve with ¼ cup buttermilk poured over each portion. Makes 4 servings.

EASY CHICKEN CURRY WITH TOMATOES (Murghi Kari)

1 pound onions, diced
1 cup chicken bouillon
2 tablespoons curry powder
   (more or less to taste)
1 cup tomato puree

Salt to taste
2 pounds boned and skinned
   chicken breasts, diced
¾ cup hot water
2 cups cooked enriched rice

Place onions, bouillon and curry powder in a casserole or large skillet with lid and cook, covered, over low heat for 10 to 15 minutes. Add tomato puree and salt. Stir to combine. Place chicken in sauce; stir sauce over chicken; cook, covered, over medium heat, turning occasionally until chicken is done, about 15 minutes. Add water; stir to combine; replace cover and cook over low heat for 5 minutes. Serve with rice. Makes 4 servings.

VEAL LOAF MADHYA

For a fiery loaf, you can add lots more ginger, paprika and cayenne.

1 pound ground veal
2 tablespoons tomato puree
1½ teaspoons prepared mustard
½ teaspoon paprika
¼ teaspoon grated fresh ginger
   root or dash ground ginger

¼ teaspoon cayenne pepper or
   crushed red pepper
⅛ teaspoon ground cardamom

Combine ingredients. Shape into loaf and place on a nonstick baking sheet. Bake at 350°F. for 35 minutes or until cooked throughout. Makes 2 servings.

CHOPPED MEAT WITH PEAS (Keema Matar)

1½ pounds ground lamb or beef
½ cup beef bouillon
2 tablespoons curry powder
1 teaspoon garlic powder
1 cinnamon stick
1 teaspoon minced fresh ginger
   root or ½ teaspoon ground
   ginger

1 teaspoon salt
12 ounces frozen green peas,
   thawed

Broil, or bake meat at 350°F. on rack in oven. Remove and break into small pieces. Place in a large nonstick skillet. Add next 6 ingredients; cook, stirring constantly, to keep meat crumbly not caked, about 5 minutes or until flavors blend and mixture is hot. Stir in peas, remove cinnamon stick; serve hot. Makes 3 servings.

COOKED CUCUMBER WITH BUTTERMILK

2 medium cucumbers, peeled
½ cup buttermilk
1 tablespoon chopped fresh coriander or parsley
½ teaspoon minced fresh ginger root (or dash ground ginger)
Salt and pepper to taste
Cayenne pepper to taste

Cut the cucumbers in half and remove the seeds if they are large. Slice. Cover with boiling water and simmer until they are tender. Drain. Add remaining ingredients and heat but do not boil. Makes 2 servings.

RAYTA SALAD

In recipe above, add 1 medium diced tomato, 1 seeded diced green chili pepper, and slivers of lemon rind to the cooked cucumbers. Serve on shredded lettuce with lemon or lime wedge. Makes 2 servings.

SPICED OYSTER PLANT SALAD

2 cups oyster plant
2 cups water
1½ teaspoons vinegar
¼ teaspoon each sage and dried mint
¼ cup vegetable oil
2 teaspoons chopped fresh parsley
1½ teaspoons lemon juice
½ teaspoon chili pepper
¼ teaspoon thyme

Cut cleaned oyster plant into long thin strips. In saucepan combine oyster plant, water and vinegar. Let stand 10 minutes. Add sage and mint, and cook until oyster plant is tender; drain well. (If using canned oyster plant, continue from here.) Combine in jar with tight-fitting lid oil, parsley, lemon juice, chili pepper, and thyme. Shake well and pour over oyster plant. Makes 4 servings.

APPLE CHUTNEY

1 medium green pepper
1 tart medium apple
1½ tablespoons lemon juice

¾ teaspoon paprika
¼ teaspoon cayenne pepper
¼ teaspoon salt

Peel and seed pepper; peel and core apple; grate both very fine, mashing or chopping thoroughly (or process in blender container or in food processor until finely chopped). Add lemon juice, paprika, cayenne pepper and salt. Makes 4 servings.

VEGETABLE CHUTNEY

1 medium cucumber
1 teaspoon salt
1 medium green pepper, seeded
2 tablespoons chopped celery

2 tablespoons lemon juice
1 teaspoon paprika
½ small garlic clove, minced
¼ teaspoon pepper

Peel cucumber; cut in quarters and remove seeds, then slice. Sprinkle with salt. Let stand 1 hour; drain and rinse. Blanch green pepper in boiling water. Combine all ingredients; chop fine until mixture is well-blended (or combine all ingredients in blender container, until mixture is finely chopped). Makes 4 servings.

LENTIL AND TOMATO STEW*

4 ounces sliced onion
1 garlic clove, crushed
1 pound cooked dried lentils
2 medium tomatoes, peeled and chopped

¾ teaspoon crushed mustard seed
½ teaspoon salt
¼ teaspoon dried crushed red chili pepper

Cook onions and garlic in nonstick skillet, stirring often until soft. Add remaining ingredients and simmer 10 to 15 minutes. Makes 4 servings.

CURRIED POTATOES WITH STRING BEANS

9 ounces peeled potatoes, sliced
3 cups frozen young string beans,
  thawed
¼ cup chicken bouillon
1 teaspoon curry powder
1 teaspoon salt
Juice of small lemon

In a saucepan, cook potatoes until barely tender; drain off most of moisture. Add string beans, chicken bouillon, curry powder and salt, and cook until string beans are done. Stir in lemon juice and serve. Makes 3 servings.

SPICY BANANA SAUCE

As accompaniment for a poached fish or roast or broiled chicken, lamb or beef.

2 medium bananas, firm but ripe
1 cup buttermilk
1 teaspoon ground cumin
½ teaspoon dry mustard
¼ teaspoon salt

Mash bananas with fork. With egg beater, gradually beat in buttermilk and seasonings. Beat steadily for several minutes until thick. Makes 4 servings.

MINTY APRICOT WHIP

In the mood of India dessert-making.

6 very ripe medium apricots,
  pitted
⅔ cup evaporated skimmed milk
Artificial sweetener to equal
  6 teaspoons sugar
¼ teaspoon lemon extract
1 tablespoon unflavored gelatin
¼ cup water
Mint leaves

Place half the fruit in blender container. Add milk, sweetener and extract. Sprinkle gelatin over water in small saucepan and let stand to soften. Place over low heat; stir until gelatin is dissolved. Add to apricot mixture. Process until smooth. Remove container. Chill for a few minutes in refrigerator. Process further until mixture becomes thick. Dice remainder of fruit and fold into "creme." Divide equally into three sherbet glasses. Chill at least 30 minutes before serving. Garnish with fresh mint leaves. Makes 2 servings.

ORANGE SHAKE (Lassi)

½ cup crushed ice
½ cup orange juice

½ cup plain yogurt

Put crushed ice in blender container and add remaining ingredients. Process and serve at once. Makes 2 servings.

BORANI

This refreshing Kashmir drink is a summertime favorite.

1 cup buttermilk
2 cups crushed ice
Lemon rind, 1 strip
1 tablespoon each chopped fresh mint or basil or ¼ teaspoon dried

Dash chili powder
Salt and freshly ground black pepper to taste
Garnish: Mint or basil leaves

In blender container, combine buttermilk and ice. Add lemon rind, chopped mint or basil, chili powder, salt and pepper. Process at high speed. Serve in sherbet glasses with garnish of mint or basil leaves. Makes 4 servings.

Israel

Like the Jews themselves, the recipes in this section have wandered from one country to another for hundreds and even for thousands of years. This medley of food ideas picked up in scattered countries would be a gastronomical hodgepodge except for the blending and unification which took place as the dishes were modified in obedience to *Kashruth*. Under this ancient rabbinic law, orthodox Jews were required to use only sanctioned foods certified as ritually clean. Shellfish and pork were prohibited. Milk products could not be served with meats. So, adapted to fit these requirements, the old recipes, whatever their origins, acquired a common character and became Jewish. Our recipes from the reestablished Jewish homeland are very old, very new (potato *latkes* without guilt) and very delicious. Naturally, we begin with the famous soup. . . .

CHICKEN NOODLE SOUP

1 cup chicken bouillon
¼ cup diced celery leaves
¼ cup shredded watercress
   or parsley

½ cup cooked enriched noodles

Bring chicken bouillon, celery leaves and watercress or parsley to boil in small saucepan. Strain and serve hot over noodles in small bowl. Makes 1 serving.

CHICKEN NOODLE SOUP WITH REAL CHICKEN

1 skinned broiling or roasting
   chicken, 2½ to 3 pounds
4 cups water
2 ribs celery and leaves, diced
2 teaspoons dehydrated onion
   flakes

2 teaspoons salt
3 peppercorns
2 cups cooked enriched noodles
3 tablespoons chopped fresh
   parsley

Cut chicken into 8 pieces and broil on all sides, turning as necessary. Allow about 20 minutes. Transfer browned chicken to soup kettle, cover with water, and add celery leaves, onion flakes, salt and peppercorns. Cook 1½ hours. Serve soup hot in soup bowls each containing ½ cup noodles. Garnish with parsley. Chicken should be weighed and served (6-ounce servings when cooked and boned) either in the bowls (for chicken in the pot) or as a separate course. Makes 4 servings.

GEFILTE FISH WITH HORSERADISH

1 pound whitefish fillets, cut in
   small pieces
1 pound pike fillets, cut in small
   pieces
1 celery rib, sliced
2 tablespoons dehydrated onion
   flakes
1 teaspoon garlic powder

Salt and pepper to taste
2 tablespoons unflavored gelatin
1 cup cold water
4 lettuce leaves
½ cup drained, cooked, sliced
   carrots
Prepared horseradish

Place fish and celery in food processor and process until finely ground or put through a meat grinder 3 times. Add onion flakes, garlic powder, salt and pepper; mix well. Sprinkle gelatin over mixture. Add cold water, about ¼ cup at a time, mixing constantly, until absorbed. Divide evenly into 4 oval loaves. Bake at 350°F. in 15½ x 10½ x 1-inch baking pan for about 25 minutes or until cooked through; serve on lettuce leaf. Garnish with carrot slices. Serve with horseradish. Makes 4 servings.

POTATO PANCAKE PUFFS (Latkes)*

For applesauce to go with potato pancakes: In saucepan bring to boil 1 diced peeled medium apple in 3 tablespoons water and ½ teaspoon lemon juice. Add a dash of cinnamon and artificial sweetener to equal 1 tablespoon sugar. Cook 2 to 3 minutes. Makes 1 serving.

3 ounces freshly cooked potato, drained and mashed	Dash of pepper
1 medium egg	½ slice enriched white bread, made into fine crumbs
1 ounce grated onion	½ teaspoon baking powder (double acting)
¼ teaspoon minced fresh parsley	
½ teaspoon salt	

In bowl combine potato, egg, onion, parsley, salt, pepper, bread crumbs and baking powder. Mix well. Drop by spoonfuls onto preheated nonstick skillet or griddle and brown until golden on both sides. Makes eight pancakes. Makes 1 serving.

SPINACH PANCAKES*

In recipe above, substitute ½ cup well-drained chopped cooked spinach for the potato, add a dash of nutmeg, and brown as above. Makes 1 serving.

CHILLED FISH AND VEGETABLES (Yakne)

8 ounces onion, sliced thin	¾ teaspoon salt
6 sprigs fresh parsley, cut coarsely	Freshly ground pepper to taste
4 celery ribs with leaves, diced	2 tablespoons water
4 medium tomatoes, peeled, cut in pieces	1½ pounds fish fillets, fresh (or frozen and partly thawed), sliced

Brown onion slices in preheated nonstick skillet. Add parsley, celery and tomatoes; sprinkle with salt, pepper and stir in the water. Cover and simmer over low flame for 20 to 30 minutes until vegetables are tender. Place fish slices on top and cover. Simmer until much of the liquid is reduced and the fish flakes with a fork, about 15 minutes. Refrigerate. Yakne tastes best cold, but can also be served hot. Makes 4 servings.

CHOLENT

1 pound boneless beef chuck shoulder steak	½ bay leaf
4 ounces onion, sliced	Dash paprika
1 cup beef bouillon	Salt and pepper to taste
½ garlic clove	1 cup cooked fresh lima beans
2 cups tomato juice	1 teaspoon chopped fresh parsley

Broil steak 3 inches from source of heat 5 minutes on each side or until brown. Remove and cool. Cut into large pieces. Brown onions in nonstick skillet. Add bouillon and garlic; bring to a boil. Pour into saucepan. Add steak, tomato juice, bay leaf and páprika. Salt and pepper to taste. Simmer 1½ hours or until meat is tender and sauce thickens. Add lima beans; reheat. Remove bay leaf. Divide into 2 equal portions. Sprinkle with parsley. Makes 2 servings.

BEETS PIQUANTE

3 tablespoons lemon juice or vinegar	½ teaspoon salt
1 tablespoon dehydrated onion flakes	⅛ teaspoon whole cloves
	1 small piece grated orange rind
1 tablespoon frozen orange juice concentrate	8 ounces cooked drained beets, diced or sliced

In saucepan heat lemon juice, onion flakes, orange juice and other seasonings. Add beets, stir gently and serve hot or cold. Makes 2 servings.

RED SEA CABBAGE AND APPLE SLAW

½ teaspoon salt	2 tablespoons vegetable oil
5 cups (about 1 pound) shredded red cabbage	Dash pepper
1½ cups boiling water	2 medium apples, peeled and diced
2 teaspoons lemon juice	2 ounces onion, finely diced

Sprinkle salt over shredded cabbage; add boiling water. Let stand 10 minutes; drain. Combine lemon juice, oil and pepper. Add to cabbage along with the diced apple and onion. Mix well. Chill at least 30 minutes before serving. Makes 4 servings.

SQUASH TSIMISS

8 ounces cooked acorn squash
½ cup canned pineapple chunks, no sugar added, drained, reserve juice
2 teaspoons cinnamon

1 teaspoon nutmeg
¼ teaspoon ginger
1 medium apple, cored, pared, diced
1 tablespoon margarine

Combine squash, pineapple juice, cinnamon, nutmeg and ginger in medium bowl. Layer half squash mixture in an 8-inch baking dish. Arrange apple and pineapple over squash layer; top with remaining squash. Dot with margarine. Cover. Bake at 325°F. for 30 minutes. Makes 2 servings.

CHICK PEA CROQUETTES (Falafel)

12 ounces dried, cooked, canned chick peas
½ teaspoon salt
¼ teaspoon each basil, marjoram and thyme

¼ teaspoon hot pepper sauce
1 garlic clove, minced
1 slice enriched white bread, toasted and made into crumbs

Put chick peas through food grinder. In medium bowl, combine chick peas, salt, herbs, hot pepper sauce, garlic and toasted crumbs. Form into balls one inch in diameter. Place on nonstick shallow pan. Bake 20 minutes at 350°F. Makes 2 servings.

PINEAPPLE CHARLOTTE

1 cup canned crushed pineapple, no sugar added, drained, reserve liquid
1 envelope unflavored gelatin

1½ teaspoons lemon juice
Whipped Topping (recipe page x)

Place pineapple juice in small saucepan. Sprinkle gelatin over liquid and place over low heat, stirring with a wooden spoon until gelatin is dissolved. Add pineapple and lemon juice. Stir. Chill until mixture begins to thicken. Fold in Whipped Topping. Transfer to 1-quart mold and chill until set, about 1½ hours, or overnight. Makes 2 servings.

ISRAEL: Gefilte Fish with Horseradish; Fluffy Lemon Pie

ITALY:
Luncheon Antipasto
or Cold Salad Antipasto;
Herb Fingers; Garlic Bread;
Garlic Dressing;
Red Vinegar Dressing;
Mayonnaise

JAPAN: Chicken Liver Teriyaki; Pickled Shrimp; Chinese
Mustard; Clear Soup

LATIN AMERICA: Chili Con Carne; Mexican Carrot Cake;
Spiced Grapes

MIDDLE EAST: "Creamed" Eggplant; Loola Kabob on a Bed of Rice

POLAND AND RUSSIA: Hearty Ukrainian Borscht

PORTUGAL: Sponge Cake Roll and Strawberry Filling; Whipped Topping; Portuguese Baked Chicken

SCANDINAVIA: Swedish Meat Patties (Beef à la Lindstrom) with Yogurt; Danish Cucumber Salad; Cardamon Cookies

THE SOUTH PACIFIC:
Skewered Bananas
with Dipping Sauce;
Philippine Chicken
and Veal Stew
(Adobo)

SPAIN:
Paella;
"Sangria"

SWITZERLAND: Stuffed Tomatoes; Dill Boiled Potatoes

THE UNITED STATES: New England Boiled Dinner; Black
Bottom Cheesecake

FLUFFY LEMON PIE*

3 medium eggs, separated
Artificial sweetener to equal
  14 teaspoons sugar, divided

2 tablespoons cold water
Juice and grated rind of 1 lemon
Few grains salt

Beat egg yolks thoroughly with artificial sweetener to equal 8 teaspoons sugar. Stir in water and lemon. Cook in double boiler until thick. Remove from heat. Add salt and remaining sweetener to equal 6 teaspoons sugar to egg whites and beat until stiff. Fold into hot egg yolk mixture. Fill 8-inch nonstick pie plate. Bake in moderate oven (350°F.) until top is lightly brown. Makes 3 servings.

STRAWBERRY "JELLY"

2 teaspoons unflavored gelatin
¾ cup water
1 cup strawberries, crushed

½ teaspoon vanilla extract
Artificial sweetener to equal
  4 teaspoons sugar

Sprinkle gelatin over water in small saucepan. Heat, stirring, until gelatin dissolves. Add remaining ingredients. Pour into small dish. Chill. Makes 4 servings.

Italy

La cucina Italiana! Magnifica! It offers something for everyone. Earthy, gutsy Sicilian specialties redolent with garlic, heroic soups that are meals in themselves; subtle Northern Italian dishes that appeal to refined palates. In fact, recipes from Italy have such incredibly distinct characteristics that we might more accurately refer not to one Italian cuisine but to the more than two dozen regional cuisines of Italy.

The roots of these regional specialties can be found in the history, geography and agriculture of the country. In Sicily, the Arab conquest is apparent in the use of spices and such savory vegetable stews as Caponata. Artichokes, eggplant and broad green beans are grown and favored in the south; potatoes and polenta in the north. In the Italian Alps, the cuisine shows Germanic influence from its Tyrol neighbors.

Pasta, however, is more or less common throughout Italy, although its shape varies from one place to another. In modern Italy, particularly in cities around Milan and Rome where Weight Watchers classes exist, restaurateurs often give you a choice of delectably cooked vegetables—*contorni*—rather than pasta or soup. We've done as well for you. Try fingers of zucchini splashed with garlic; the parade of pickled artichoke hearts; the crisp bright green flowers of broccoli; crunchy whole green beans *al dente;* mustard-spiced spinach and mushroom salads; and our other wonderfully Italian foods.

COLD ANTIPASTO (As Appetizer)

In Italy, antipasto (literally, before the pasta) is generally served only at elaborate meals. But as it is a popular first course on Italian-American restaurant menus, we've indicated a few methods of serving it to fit the Food Program. Antipasto is as variable as the seasons and regions in which it is eaten. It can include many different foods, or two or three, or even just one. Whatever you choose, serve each food so it is separated from the others on the antipasto plate, arranging forms, colors and sizes with an eye to contrast and eye appeal.

1. *Vegetables and garnishes.* Select in reasonable amounts. Raw (only if garden fresh), blanched or cooked *al dente* broccoli or cauliflower florets, whole green beans, zucchini spears. Raw carrot curls, cucumbers scored with a fork and cut in slices; radishes; tomato wedges or cherry tomatoes; sliced green pepper; fennel. Roasted pimentos or peppers, sliced or shredded. Whole button mushrooms; crisp greens, endive, sprigs of parsley and watercress, all washed, and thoroughly dried.

2. *Limited vegetables.* Select up to 4-ounce servings—raw red onion rings or scallions; whole cooked chilled artichokes, beets, Brussels sprouts, leeks; parsnips; peas.

3. *Fruits.* Select 1 of the following, if desired. Serve whole, halved, or quartered, as appropriate. 2 medium apricots. 1 cup cantaloupe balls. 10 large cherries; 2 small fresh figs. 1 small fresh pear with lemon juice. 2 medium fresh plums.

4. *Salad dressing.* Select 1 per serving (recipes on page 186).

ANTIPASTO (As Luncheon Main Dish)

Select vegetables, limited vegetables, or greens, and a dressing, from the preceding recipe. Add the following:

(Choose 2 per luncheon serving)

1 hard-cooked medium egg, halved, quartered or sliced

1 ounce hard cheese, mozzarella, Swiss, Roquefort, Romano (Pecorino) or fresh Parmesan. (Parmesan is often sliced and eaten as a delicious table cheese in Italy)

⅓ cup skim milk ricotta cheese, in a ball

2 ounces drained tuna fish, in one piece

2 ounces slivered roast beef, evenly diced cooked veal or chicken

1½ ounces ham, rolled around a gherkin

½ recipe Lentil Salad (see page 26)

Bread, Beans or Pasta (Choose 1 per serving, if desired)

½ cup cooked fresh lima beans, chilled

⅔ cup cooked enriched macaroni, chilled

1 recipe Garlic Bread, Herb Fingers or Salty Sticks (see page 218)

3 ounces boiled new potato, whole, halved, sliced; or dice and combine with dice of 2 fresh medium plums or 1 small fresh pear sprinkled with lemon juice to preserve color

DRESSINGS FOR ANTIPASTO OR SALADS

Garlic Dressing: Combine 1 tablespoon vegetable oil, 1 tablespoon vinegar or lemon juice, ½ garlic clove, crushed, salt, freshly ground black pepper and a pinch each of oregano and basil. Makes 1 serving.

Lemony Vinaigrette Dressing: Combine 2 tablespoons white vinegar, 1 tablespoon lemon juice, ½ small garlic clove put through press, ½ teaspoon Worcestershire and Dijon mustard in mixing bowl; mix all ingredients well with fork or wire whisk; add ¼ cup vegetable oil, a spoonful at a time, stirring constantly. Add 2 teaspoons chopped parsley, 1 teaspoon chives, ⅛ teaspoon salt and freshly ground pepper. Makes 4 servings.

Red Vinegar Dressing (No oil): Combine 2 tablespoons red wine vinegar, 2 tablespoons tomato puree, 1 envelope golden seasoning mix,

½ teaspoon Worcestershire, and a dash each of cinnamon and dry mustard. Makes 1 serving.

Mayonnaise: Combine 1 tablespoon imitation mayonnaise with minced washed capers, parsley, dry mustard and chives. Thin with lemon juice or thicken with measured amount of tomato paste or minced vegetables such as cucumber, green pepper, spinach, etc. Good over fish. Makes 1 serving.

FISH SOUP (Brodetto)

Brodetto is Italy's answer to France's bouillabaisse. Or, maybe France copied from Italy when Catherine de Medici married Henry II, and brought, with her dowry, to France, a staff of fine Italian cooks and their fine Italian recipes. On the other hand, "necessity" is mother's invention, and any time fishermen's wives—whatever their port—are given a mess of plentiful fish, you can be certain the fish will end up as a soup or a stew.

In Italy, the local fish used for brodetto might include (but not all at the same time): anguilla (*eel*); cefalo *and* triglie (*types of mullet*); carpa; luccio (*pike*); cernia (*bass*); sgombro (*mackerel*); *and* vongole (*small clams*). *However, there are almost as many recipes for brodetto as there are fishermen's wives, but saffron and tomatoes seem to be the two necessities.*

2½ pounds (if with bones and skin) assorted fish cut in slices or 2 pounds skinned and boned fillets including shellfish, if desired
4 ounces onion, sliced
⅔ cup sliced carrot
1 garlic clove
4 medium tomatoes or 1 cup tomato puree
1 cup diced celery
1 tablespoon chopped fresh parsley
2 cups water
2 cups clam juice
1 teaspoon wine extract
½ teaspoon salt
½ teaspoon saffron
½ bay leaf
¼ teaspoon pepper
¼ teaspoon fennel seeds (optional)

Fish with bones should be cut into slices; fillets into 2-inch pieces; refrigerate until ready to use. In preheated nonstick saucepan brown onions, carrots and garlic for 5 minutes, turning so they do not scorch. Press garlic clove with fork to extract juices, then discard it. Add tomatoes, celery, parsley and remaining ingredients except fish and bring to boil. Cook for 20 minutes. Reduce heat to simmering temperature; add the fish; cover pan and cook 15 to 20 minutes longer. Serve the soup and fish separately—but at the same meal. Makes 4 servings.

CHICKEN SOUP (Zuppa di Pollo)

A hearty meal-in-one-bowl.

2 pounds skinned and boned chicken, in pieces
2 cups cleaned asparagus pieces
1 rib celery, diced
2 teaspoons minced fresh parsley
1 teaspoon dehydrated onion flakes

½ garlic clove
3 peppercorns, crushed
6 cups water
2 cups cooked enriched rice

Brown chicken under broiler, turning as necessary (15 to 20 minutes). Transfer to soup kettle. Add asparagus, celery, parsley, onion flakes, garlic, peppercorns and water. Bring to boil, cover kettle and cook for 1 hour. Remove chicken. Continue simmering soup. Cut chicken into dice and divide pieces evenly into each of 4 large soup bowls. Put ½ cup rice in each bowl. Pour soup into bowls. Makes 4 servings.

"CREAM" OF CAULIFLOWER SOUP (Crema di Cavolfiori)

2 cups water
2 packets instant chicken broth and seasoning mix
1 cup chopped celery
1 tablespoon dehydrated onion flakes

½ teaspoon salt and dash of white pepper
3 cups cooked chopped cauliflower
1½ cups evaporated skimmed milk
Garnish: minced watercress or dash of paprika

In saucepan, heat water to boiling; add broth mix, celery, onion flakes, salt and pepper; cover and cook until celery is tender. Pour celery mixture into a blender container; process at medium speed until smooth. Gradually add cauliflower processing after each addition until smooth. Pour into saucepan; stir in milk; heat. Garnish. Makes 6 servings.

ESCAROLE AND CHICKEN SOUP (Zuppa di Pollo con Escarole)

You can save the white inside leaves for a salad.

1 bunch escarole, well washed
2 cups chicken bouillon
¼ teaspoon minced fresh
   ginger root
¼ teaspoon sauterne or
   sherry extract
Salt and pepper to taste

Shred leaves. Transfer to saucepan containing boiling chicken bouillon and ginger. Cover and simmer 30 minutes. Season with sherry extract. salt and pepper. Serve hot. Makes 2 servings.

LENTIL SOUP (Zuppa di Lenticchie)

6 ounces cooked dried lentils
1 medium tomato, peeled and
   chopped
1 cup chicken bouillon
1 teaspoon dehydrated onion
   flakes
1 garlic clove
Salt and pepper to taste
2 teaspoons minced fresh herbs:
   (½ teaspoon each of basil,
   parsley, chives, and mint,
   or to taste)

Combine cooked lentils, tomato, chicken bouillon, onion flakes, garlic, salt and pepper in saucepan. Bring to boil, stir well. Cover pan and simmer 15 minutes. Stir in herbs and serve hot. Makes 1 serving.

PASTA AND POTATO SOUP (Zuppa di Pasta e Patate)

3 ounces potato, peeled and diced
1 medium tomato, diced
1½ cups chicken bouillon
1 tablespoon chopped chives
   (or 1 teaspoon dehydrated
   onion flakes)
2 teaspoons minced fresh basil or
   ¼ teaspoon dried
Salt and pepper to taste
⅔ cup hot cooked enriched
   elbow macaroni

In small saucepan, combine potato, tomato, chicken bouillon, chives and basil. Bring to boil; reduce to simmer, cover pan and cook 30 to 40 minutes, stirring several times. Season with salt and pepper and serve, divided into two bowls, each holding ⅓ cup elbow macaroni. Makes 2 servings.

EGG AND CHEESE BROTH (Stracciatelle)

Add a dash of cinnamon, as the Romans frequently do.

1 cup beef bouillon
1 medium egg
1 ounce Parmesan cheese, freshly grated
Salt and freshly ground black pepper to taste

1 teaspoon finely chopped fresh parsley and marjoram
Twist of lemon rind or grated lemon rind

In medium saucepan, bring bouillon to a boil. In a small mixing bowl, beat egg with cheese. Pour into bouillon, stirring vigorously with fork or wooden spoon until egg is set. Bring to boiling point; serve hot with salt and pepper to taste. Garnish top with parsley, marjoram and lemon rind. Makes 1 serving.

EGG, CHEESE AND SPINACH SOUP (Stracciatelle con Spinaci)

Follow preceding recipe, but add 1 cup cooked well-drained, frozen chopped spinach to the bouillon before bringing it to boil. Continue as above. Makes 1 serving.

MINESTRONE ALLA GENOVESE

2 quarts beef bouillon
4 ounces minced leeks or onions
⅔ cup diced carrots
½ cup diced celery
¼ cup minced fresh parsley
1 teaspoon minced fresh basil
¾ cup tomato puree
1 small garlic clove, minced
2 cups shredded cabbage

1 cup sliced zucchini or yellow squash
1 cup shredded spinach
1 cup sliced green beans, or peeled diced eggplant
2 cups cooked fresh lima beans
Salt and pepper to taste
Minced basil (or parsley) to garnish

In saucepan, combine beef bouillon with leeks, carrots, celery, parsley and basil, and bring to boil. Add tomato puree and garlic; simmer for half an hour. Stir in cabbage, zucchini, shredded spinach and green beans (or eggplant). Cook for 30 minutes. Add lima beans and salt and pepper to taste. Serve piping hot in deep bowls, sprinkled with more minced fresh basil (or parsley). Makes 4 servings.

SOUP WITH BREAD AND CHEESE, ROMAN STYLE*
(Zuppa con Crostini alla Romana)

1 sliced enriched white bread,
    toasted
1 ounce grated Parmesan cheese
1 teaspoon dehydrated onion
    flakes, reconstituted

⅛ teaspoon garlic powder
1 cup hot bouillon

Place toast in an individual 1½-cup earthenware casserole. Combine cheese, onion flakes and garlic. Sprinkle over toast; brown top lightly in toaster-oven or under broiler. Pour in bouillon and serve hot (or keep hot in oven until ready to serve). Makes 1 serving.

VERMICELLI AND ZUCCHINI SOUP
(Zuppa di Vermicelli e Zucchini)

4 ounces onion, diced
2 medium tomatoes, peeled, diced
4 cups beef bouillon
2 cups diced zucchini
1½ tablespoons chopped fresh
    basil or ¾ teaspoon dried

2⅔ cups cooked enriched
    vermicelli (thin spaghetti) cut
    into 1-inch lengths

In saucepan, simmer onion and tomatoes for 5 minutes. Pour in bouillon and bring to boil. Add zucchini and basil. Cook 30 minutes, or until zucchini is very soft. Divide evenly into 4 soup bowls, each containing ⅔ cup cooked enriched vermicelli. Pass salt and pepper mill at the table. Makes 4 servings.

BROCCOLI OMELET (Frittata di Broccoli)

¼ cup water
1 packet instant chicken broth
    and seasoning mix
½ teaspoon salt
⅛ teaspoon thyme

2 ounces onion, chopped
1 garlic clove, minced
1 medium tomato, chopped
1 cup cooked chopped broccoli
4 medium eggs

In large nonstick skillet, heat water, broth mix, salt and thyme to boiling. Add onion and garlic; cook until onion is tender. Add tomato; cook only until tomato is soft. Remove from heat; stir in broccoli. Beat eggs in medium bowl. Add broccoli mixture. Return skillet to heat; pour in broccoli-egg mixture. Cook until lightly brown on the bottom. Immediately place skillet under broiler (cover handle with foil); cook only until eggs are set. Makes 2 servings.

EGGS FLORENTINE (Uova alla Fiorentina)

2 cups frozen chopped spinach
4 ounces grated mozzarella cheese (reserve 2 tablespoons)
½ cup evaporated skimmed milk
2 slices enriched white bread, made into crumbs
¾ teaspoon salt
¼ teaspoon basil (or 1 teaspoon chopped fresh)
¼ teaspoon nutmeg
¼ teaspoon pepper
4 medium eggs

Cook spinach according to package directions. Drain. Dry out by cooking in saucepan over moderate heat. Add cheese (all but 2 table-spoons), milk, bread crumbs (reserve 2 tablespoons), salt, basil, nutmeg and pepper. Heat, mixing thoroughly. Divide mixture evenly into 4 ramekins or shallow individual oven-to-table baking dishes. Poach 4 eggs in boiling salted water until just set. Remove from water to spinach mixture in ramekins. Combine 2 tablespoons reserved cheese and 2 tablespoons reserved crumbs. Sprinkle ½ tablespoon over each egg. Bake at 375°F. until top is browned and mixture is piping hot. Makes 4 servings.

TUNA-SPINACH OMELET (Frittata con Tonno e Spinaci)

An excellent lunch for two.

2 medium eggs
2 tablespoons skim milk
1 tablespoon mayonnaise
1 tablespoon lime juice
1 teaspoon dill
1 teaspoon dehydrated onion flakes
¼ teaspoon salt
Dash hot pepper sauce
1 cup cooked, drained chopped spinach
4 ounces canned, drained tuna, flaked
2 slices enriched white bread, cut in ½-inch cubes

In medium bowl, beat together the eggs, milk, mayonnaise, lime juice, dill, onion flakes, salt and hot pepper sauce. Combine with spinach and tuna; fold in bread cubes. Pour mixture into an 8-inch nonstick pan. Bake at 375°F. for 10 to 12 minutes, or until mixture is set on the bottom. Transfer pan to broiler; broil about 4 inches from heat source for about 1 minute until lightly golden on top. Makes 2 servings.

CHEESE OMELET (Frittata al Formaggio)

4 medium eggs, separated
4 ounces grated Swiss or
mozzarella cheese

¼ cup evaporated skimmed
milk
½ teaspoon salt

Beat egg whites until stiff. Combine egg yolks, cheese, milk and salt. Fold into the beaten whites. Pour mixture into 9- or 10-inch preheated nonstick skillet and cook over low heat lifting edges of egg as they set, so uncooked part flows to bottom. Turn to brown second side. Serve in wedges. Makes 4 servings.

BAKED VEGETABLE PUDDING (with Eggs and Cheese) (Sformato di Legumi)

Sformato is served usually as a side dish or meat accompaniment. However, we present it as a luncheon main dish. For an optional sauce, heat ¾ cup tomato puree.

2 cups skim milk
2 slices enriched white bread,
made into crumbs
2 cups cooked cauliflower
2 cups cooked green beans
1 tablespoon dehydrated onion
flakes

2 sprigs tarragon or parsley,
minced
4 medium eggs
4 ounces grated Parmesan cheese
Salt and freshly ground pepper
to taste

Heat milk in saucepan until bubbles form around the side but do not let it boil. Add crumbs. Simmer 5 minutes. Remove from heat. Stir in cauliflower, green beans, onion flakes and tarragon. Transfer to blender container and process until smooth (in two batches, so hot mixture does not overflow). Pour into large mixing bowl. Stir in eggs, cheese, salt and pepper. Transfer to 8- or 9-inch square baking pan; cover with foil and bake at 350°F. for 30 minutes. Makes 4 servings.

SFORMATO DI SPINACI

Cook 2 cups frozen chopped spinach according to package directions. Drain well, and add to milk and crumbs in saucepan omitting cauliflower and green beans. Season with grated nutmeg and grated lemon rind. Process in blender container following directions and other ingredients listed above. Makes 4 servings.

[*193*]

SFORMATO

As you can see from the two preceding recipes, these puddings are very versatile, for they can be made with any mixture of leftover vegetables.

To make a lighter, airier company pudding—really a cross between a pudding and a soufflé—beat yolks and whites separately. Stir the lightly beaten yolks with the cheese, salt and pepper. Add green food coloring if desired; fold in egg whites. Transfer to a pudding mold (with cover) and set in a pot. Pour water into the pot so it comes halfway to the top of the mold (at least 1 inch of water). Steam pudding in 375°F. oven with cover on for 1 to 1¼ hours or until a straw inserted in center comes out clean. Turn out on platter and garnish with roasted canned pimento (rinsed, drained and cut into a heart or other shape). Makes 4 servings.

LIGURIAN FISH STEW (Ciuppin)

Like cioppino, its San Francisco cousin, ciuppin, *the Italian fish stew, can be made of one kind of fish or of many. If just one variety is used, it might be crab on Fisherman's Wharf and* vongole (*the tiny-neck clam*) *along the Adriatic. But just as often, you're likely to find in your* ciuppin *an interesting assortment of sea life. If you freeze pieces of fish left from your "weighings," you can put them together this way.*

¾ cup tomato puree
⅔ cup diced carrots
½ cup diced celery
1 garlic clove, minced fine
¼ teaspoon rosemary
¼ teaspoon chives
1 tablespoon chopped fresh parsley
1 packet instant beef broth and seasoning mix
1 pound skinned, boned fish, cut into bite-size pieces
2 teaspoons sherry or sauterne extract or lemon juice

Combine puree, carrots, celery, garlic, rosemary, chives, parsley and beef broth mix in saucepan. Bring to boil; cover and let simmer 20 minutes. Add the fish, cover pan, reduce heat and simmer 20 minutes longer or until fish flakes. Stir in wine extract or lemon juice and serve hot. Makes 2 servings.

QUICK-BAKED FISH WITH OREGANO SAUCE

If frozen fish fillets are usually too fishy for your taste, pour boiling water over them and drain well before proceeding.

9 ounces frozen fish fillets, thawed
Salt and pepper to taste
1½ cups frozen broccoli or spinach, defrosted
1 tablespoon margarine, melted
Paprika
Oregano Sauce (recipe follows)

Season fillets with salt and pepper. Make a bed of the vegetables in bottom of baking dish. Top with margarine and fish. Sprinkle top with paprika. Bake until fish is done. Serve with Oregano Sauce. Makes 3 servings.

Oregano Sauce

1½ cups scalded skim milk
1½ slices enriched white bread, made into crumbs
3 ounces grated Parmesan cheese
½ teaspoon oregano
¼ teaspoon pepper
1 packet golden broth and seasoning mix

Combine all ingredients in saucepan; simmer 5 minutes stirring constantly. Serve hot with fish. Makes 3 servings.

SALMON AND GREEN BEAN STEW

Bravo! With a tossed salad for luncheon.

1½ cups water
1 cup French style green beans, fresh or frozen
½ cup diced celery and leaves
3 ounces diced potatoes
4 ounces canned, drained pink salmon
¼ cup evaporated skimmed milk
1 teaspoon dehydrated onion flakes
1 teaspoon chopped fresh parsley
Dash rosemary

In saucepan, combine water, green beans, celery and potatoes. Simmer until potatoes and green beans are tender. Stir in remaining ingredients and heat, but do not boil. Serve piping hot. Makes 1 serving.

STUFFED SOLE FLORENTINE (Sogliola alla Fiorentina)

½ cup evaporated skimmed milk
½ cup cooked cauliflower
½ teaspoon lemon juice
½ teaspoon dehydrated onion flakes
½ teaspoon salt
2 cups coarsely chopped fresh spinach leaves, divided

½ cup fresh parsley leaves
½ cup canned chopped mushrooms
2 8-ounce sole (or flounder) fillets

In blender container process milk, cauliflower, lemon juice, onion flakes and salt at medium speed until smooth. Gradually add 1 cup spinach and the parsley; process at high speed after each addition, until smooth. Combine remaining spinach and mushrooms with 2 tablespoons spinach sauce from blender; spoon evenly along center of each fillet. Fold ends of each fillet over filling; secure with toothpicks. Sprinkle with additional salt and lemon juice. Place fillets, seam-side down, in shallow casserole. Evenly divide remaining sauce over fillets. Bake in 350°F. oven for 40 minutes. Makes 2 servings.

TUNA AND SPINACH LOAF
(Polpettone di Tonno e Spinaci)

8 ounces canned, drained tuna, flaked
2 cups cooked frozen chopped spinach, press out liquid through strainer until well drained
4 ounces chopped onion
½ cup chopped celery

1 tablespoon chopped capers
2 slices fresh enriched white bread, made into crumbs
4 medium eggs (2 uncooked, 2 hard-cooked, for garnish)
1 tablespoon lemon juice
1 teaspoon Worcestershire
4 slices of lemon, for garnish

Stock

2 tablespoons dehydrated onion flakes
¼ cup coarsely diced celery and leaves

4 sprigs parsley

In mixing bowl, combine tuna, chopped spinach, onion, celery, capers, crumbs, 2 uncooked eggs, lemon juice and Worcestershire. Mix until thoroughly blended. Turn mixture onto a board holding 4 thicknesses of cheesecloth about 14x15 inches. Knead the tuna mixture until it forms a tight roll, about 2 inches in diameter. Wrap in cheesecloth and tie at both ends. Put the roll into an oval pan. Add ingredients for stock and cover with water. Bring to boil, then reduce heat and simmer gently for 40 minutes. Remove roll from stock by lifting ends of cloth; let cool 10 minutes at room temperature, then remove the cheesecloth. Refrigerate the roll and serve cold. Garnish each serving with 2 quarters of hard-cooked egg and slice of lemon. Makes 4 servings.

SPAGHETTI TWISTS WITH TUNA

Mama mia—it's hailing tuna sauce over pasta twists!

8 ounces canned, drained tuna fish, flaked	1 teaspoon salt
1 medium green pepper, chopped	½ teaspoon oregano
2 ounces chopped onion	¼ teaspoon chopped basil
1 garlic clove, diced	¼ teaspoon pepper
¾ cup tomato puree	1⅓ cups cooked enriched spaghetti
½ cup water	twists (cooked al dente)

Heat tuna, green pepper, onion and garlic in nonstick pan, turning to prevent scorching. Stir in tomato puree, water, salt, oregano, basil and pepper. Cook until thoroughly heated, about 5 to 10 minutes. Pour sauce over spaghetti. Makes 2 servings.

EGGPLANT STUFFED WITH TUNA*

2 small eggplant	⅛ teaspoon dry mustard
8 ounces canned, drained tuna fish, flaked	½ garlic clove, finely minced
2 slices enriched white bread, soaked in water and squeezed dry	1½ cups tomato puree
	Dash of hot pepper sauce or cayenne pepper
1 tablespoon minced fresh parsley	½ cup water

Wash eggplant, cut into halves and scoop out, leaving 4 thick shells. Take thin slice from bottoms, if necessary, so shells "sit" flat. Reserve pulp, and measure 4 cups. Thoroughly mix tuna, bread, parsley and mustard. Fill shells with mixture and set in baking pan. In nonstick pan, brown garlic and diced eggplant pulp. When brown, stir in tomato puree and hot pepper sauce. Bring to quick boil, pour over eggplant halves in pan. Bake at 375°F. 25 to 30 minutes or until eggplant shells are tender. Makes 4 servings.

CLAM SAUCE

For linguine or Celery Spaghetti (see page 222).

1 cup clam juice
¼ cup tomato paste
½ teaspoon coarsely ground
    black pepper
Salt to taste
1 pound drained canned
    minced clams

1 tablespoon chopped fresh
    chives
1 tablespoon chopped fresh
    parsley
¼ teaspoon oregano

In saucepan combine clam juice, tomato paste, pepper and salt. Simmer 30 minutes. Add a little water if sauce is too thick. Stir in clams, chives, parsley and oregano. Heat over low heat; mix well and serve over cooked enriched pasta. Makes 4 servings.

WHITE CLAM SAUCE

Use ⅓ cup cooked celery, processed in blender container, in place of ¼ cup tomato paste in preceding recipe. Makes 4 servings.

BAKED CLAMS IN SHELLS*

4 ounces onion, diced
1 garlic clove
8 ounces canned, drained minced
    clams (reserve 2 tablespoons
    juice)

½ teaspoon oregano
2 slices enriched white bread,
    made into crumbs
Salt and pepper to taste
2 teaspoons vegetable oil

Steam onions and garlic by covering with water in a shallow pan and cooking 5 to 8 minutes until water evaporates. Brown lightly. Press out juice of garlic with fork and discard garlic pulp. Stir in remaining ingredients except oil and 4 teaspoons crumbs. Divide mixture evenly into 4 portions and serve in shells. Sprinkle with remaining crumbs. Spoon oil (½ teaspoon each serving) onto clam stuffing. Bake in hot (400°F.) oven for 10 minutes. Makes 4 servings.

MUSSELS MARINARA

4 ounces diced onions
1 garlic clove, minced
½ cup beef bouillon
¾ cup tomato puree
¼ cup clam juice
2 tablespoons wine vinegar
2 tablespoons chopped fresh
parsley

¼ teaspoon salt
⅛ teaspoon pepper
8 ounces cooked mussels
(see note)
Grated lemon rind
2 slices enriched white bread
toasted, each cut into 4 triangles

In saucepan, cook onions and garlic in bouillon over low heat 20 minutes. Add tomato puree, clam juice, wine vinegar, parsley, salt and pepper. Bring to boil, then let simmer for 10 minutes. Turn off heat. Stir in mussels and lemon rind. Divide mixture into 2 equal portions. Serve with 4 toast points each. Makes 2 servings.

NOTE: Scrub mussels under cold running water and remove long beard; scrape away excess material clinging to shells. Cover mussels with cool water and allow to stand 2 to 3 hours. Discard any mussels that float or that have shells that are not tightly closed. Place cleaned mussels in a kettle with a small amount of water; cover and steam about 3 minutes, just until shells open. Discard any that do not open. Remove mussels from shells.

SCAMPI

Italian scampi do not exist in America. When listed on restaurant menus, large shrimp are invariably substituted, so, by long usage, scampi has come to mean simply garlic-flavored shrimp.

1 pound large (18 to 20) shelled
and cleaned raw shrimp
3 tablespoons water
2 tablespoons chopped fresh
parsley
2 teaspoons lemon juice

1 teaspoon sherry or sauterne
extract
2 garlic cloves, pressed
½ teaspoon salt
Freshly ground pepper to taste

Cut shrimp along the inside curve almost through to the outside curve, and gently open them so they lay flat. Combine water, parsley, lemon juice, extract, garlic, salt and pepper in large skillet or chafing dish. Bring to boil; add shrimp and cook, stirring constantly, until shrimp turn pink, 3 to 5 minutes. Serve shrimp with sauce. Makes 2 servings.

LOBSTER FRA DIAVOLO

1 pound uncooked meat of lobster (or lobster tails)
1 cup tomato puree
1 cup beef bouillon
1 garlic clove
2 tablespoons vinegar or lemon juice
1 tablespoon chopped fresh parsley
½ teaspoon oregano
Dash of cayenne pepper and salt

Cut lobster meat into 1-inch pieces and set aside. (If using rock lobster tails, thaw; cut away underside membrane and remove meat from shells and set it aside.) Combine remaining ingredients, bring to boil and cook rapidly until sauce is thick and bubbly, 15 minutes or so. Add lobster pieces, reduce heat to simmering temperature, and cook 5 to 8 minutes or until lobster is cooked. Makes 2 servings.

BARBECUED DEVILED CHICKEN (Pollo alla Diavola)

Go as heavy on the pepper as your palate dictates.

2½ pounds skinned chicken drumsticks and thighs
Barbecue Sauce (recipe follows)
2⅔ cups cooked enriched spaghetti or macaroni
Parsley or watercress sprigs

Barbecue Sauce

¾ cup tomato puree
1 tablespoon Worcestershire
¾ teaspoon salt
½ teaspoon black pepper
½ teaspoon chili powder
½ teaspoon basil
1 packet instant beef broth and seasoning mix

Broil chicken over red hot charcoal (or under broiler) until done on all sides, turning as necessary. Bring ingredients for Barbecue Sauce to boil. Keep hot on the grill. Serve well-done chicken pieces over cooked pasta; cover with Barbecue Sauce. Garnish with parsley sprigs. Makes 4 servings.

BAKED CHICKEN WITH LEMON (Pollo al Limone)

2½ to 3 pound chicken, skinned,
   cut up
Cut lemon
1 teaspoon salt

¼ teaspoon paprika
⅛ teaspoon black pepper
¼ cup chicken bouillon
1 lemon, sliced

Rub chicken pieces on all sides with cut lemon. Sprinkle with salt, paprika and pepper. Bake in shallow pan at 350°F. for 15 minutes. Pour in chicken bouillon and put lemon slices on top of chicken. Bake 45 minutes more, turning chicken several times. Serve hot. Makes 4 servings.

CHICKEN WITH PEPPERS AND TOMATOES

Follow recipe above. Fifteen minutes before chicken is done, add to pan 2 medium roasted green or red peppers, which have been peeled, seeded and cut in thin strips; 2 medium tomatoes, cut in half; and 1 mashed clove of garlic. Bake 15 minutes more. Makes 4 servings.

CHICKEN AND POLENTA—VENETIAN STYLE
(Pollo con Polenta Veneziana)

Chicken

2½-to 3-pound skinned broiling
   chicken, cut up
Salt and pepper to taste
4 ounces minced onions
1 garlic clove, minced
1½ cups tomato puree
¼ cup tomato paste

½ cup chicken bouillon
2 tablespoons minced fresh
   parsley
¾ teaspoon salt
½ teaspoon sage
¼ teaspoon rosemary

Polenta

4 ounces enriched dry yellow
   cornmeal
1 teaspoon salt

1 cup cold water
3 cups boiling water

Sprinkle chicken with salt and pepper; arrange in broiling pan, top with onion and garlic; brown nicely on all sides. Transfer chicken, onions and garlic to a large heatproof casserole with cover. Combine tomato puree, tomato paste, bouillon, parsley, salt, sage and rosemary. Pour over chicken. Bake covered in preheated 350°F. oven for

½ hour, or until chicken is very tender. While chicken is baking, prepare polenta. Follow package directions for making cornmeal mush or combine cornmeal, salt and cold water in a medium bowl. Gradually pour into boiling water, stirring constantly. Return to boil, stirring constantly. Reduce heat, cover. Continue cooking over low heat, about 5 minutes, stirring frequently. Divide polenta equally into 4 large soup bowls. Divide chicken mixture over polenta. Makes 4 servings.

CHICKEN PARMIGIANA

An easy-to-clean-up-after family lunch if you use shallow individual aluminum foil pans. Serve with tomato sauce, if desired.

For each serving:

3 ounces skinned and boned chicken, preferably cut from breast	Salt and pepper to taste ½ cup chicken bouillon 1 ounce mozzarella cheese

Season chicken with salt and pepper. Broil in shallow pan 4 inches from heat, basting frequently with bouillon; turn once. Don't over-cook; chicken should be moist. Top chicken with a slice of mozzarella cheese and place in hot oven (400°F.) for 8 to 10 minutes, or until cheese melts. Makes 1 serving.

CHICKEN CACCIATORE

A great Italian favorite frequently served with pickled sweet peppers.

2½ to 3 pound chicken, skinned and cut up 4 ounces sliced onion 2 garlic cloves 2 medium tomatoes	¾ cup tomato puree 1 teaspoon salt ½ teaspoon crushed oregano ¼ teaspoon pepper

Brown chicken on all sides in large preheated nonstick skillet. Remove from skillet and brown onion slices and garlic. Return browned chicken with remaining ingredients to skillet; cover and simmer for 45 minutes (*do not boil*), until chicken is tender and sauce is thick. To further reduce the sauce, remove the chicken and cook liquid at high heat until it evaporates and thickens. Makes 4 servings.

CHICKEN NAPOLITANO

1 pound boned and skinned chicken breasts
¼ teaspoon garlic powder
¼ teaspoon paprika
¼ teaspoon dried rosemary leaves, crumbled
Salt and ground black pepper to taste

1 cup canned drained mushroom stems and pieces
¼ cup red wine vinegar
2 tablespoons dehydrated parsley flakes

Season chicken with a combination of garlic powder, paprika, rosemary, salt and black pepper. Broil until brown; remove from broiler and place in casserole. Cover with mushrooms, vinegar and parsley. Bake covered, in 350°F. oven for about 15 minutes or until chicken is tender. Makes 2 servings.

TURKEY TETRAZZINI

A sensational Italian diva who sang with the Metropolitan and the Chicago Opera Companies inspired the original of this nice little dish. It is probably more American than Italian. You may omit the toast points and serve it, more traditionally, over ½ cup cooked enriched rice.

1 packet instant chicken broth and seasoning mix, or 1 bouillon cube
1 cup boiling water
2 teaspoons cornstarch dissolved in 2 tablespoons water
4 ounces cooked turkey, diced
¼ cup cooked or canned sliced mushrooms

¼ medium green pepper, blanched and diced
1 teaspoon diced pimento
⅓ cup evaporated skimmed milk
1 teaspoon chopped fresh parsley
1 slice enriched white bread, toasted and quartered

In a saucepan, dissolve bouillon in boiling water. Place over low heat; add cornstarch; heat until thick. Add turkey, mushrooms, green pepper and pimento. Simmer 5 minutes. Add milk; reheat (*do not boil*). Place in shallow serving dish, sprinkle with parsley and serve with toast points. Makes 1 serving.

VEAL CHOPS SORRENTO

1¼ pounds lean shoulder veal chops
1 cup small mushrooms
1 cup tomato juice
2 medium tomatoes, chopped
½ medium green pepper, cut into strips
2 ounces onion, diced
½ garlic clove, crushed
½ bay leaf
1 tablespoon lemon juice
⅛ teaspoon sage
Salt and pepper to taste

Broil chops on rack 4 inches from source of heat for 4 to 5 minutes on each side. Put in small baking pan; add mushrooms, tomato juice, tomatoes, pepper, onions, garlic, bay leaf, lemon juice and sage. Season to taste. Bake at 400°F., covered, for 20 minutes or until tender. Remove bay leaf. Makes 2 servings.

VEAL AND VEGETABLES IN ORANGE SAUCE

To use up meat left from the veal roast.

½ cup orange juice
6 ounces cooked veal, sliced
½ teaspoon sauterne or sherry extract
½ teaspoon grated orange rind
2 ounces cooked small onions
Salt, pepper and garlic powder to taste

In small saucepan, heat orange juice. Add remaining ingredients and simmer gently just long enough to heat. Makes 1 serving.

GROUND VEAL IN EGGPLANT SAUCE

½ cup tomato sauce, no sugar added
½ medium green pepper, cut into slivers about ⅛-inch wide
½ cup diced celery
½ teaspoon onion powder
½ teaspoon Pizza Pie Spice or Italian Seasoning
¼ teaspoon salt
1 packet instant beef broth and seasoning mix, divided
1 bay leaf
1 cup peeled and diced eggplant
8 ounces ground veal
½ cup cooked enriched rice (optional)

Combine tomato sauce, pepper, celery, onion powder, Pizza Pie Spice, salt, ½ packet broth mix and bay leaf in a saucepan. Bring to a boil; cover and reduce heat. Add eggplant and continue cooking about 30 minutes. Meanwhile, mix remaining broth mix with the veal and shape into a patty. Place in a nonstick pan and cook until well done. Remove from pan. Drain on a paper towel. Crumble veal, add to eggplant mixture and stir. Heat and serve over ½ cup cooked enriched rice if desired. Makes 1 serving.

BRAISED VEAL SHANKS (Osso Buco)

A piquant mixture of veal shank and a succulent sauce made with garlic, parsley, lemon juice and tomato. Osso Buco is usually served over risotto.

2 5-ounce veal shanks, each about 2½-inches thick
⅓ cup carrots, diced
½ cup chopped celery
½ garlic clove, crushed
1 medium tomato, peeled and chopped
1 cup tomato juice
2 cups chicken bouillon

2 teaspoons dehydrated onion flakes
¼ teaspoon rosemary
Salt and pepper to taste
1 tablespoon chopped fresh parsley
1 slice lemon or minced lemon rind

Brown veal under broiler 4 inches from source of heat for about 10 minutes, turning frequently; set aside. Lightly brown carrots and celery in nonstick saucepan; add garlic, tomato, tomato juice, bouillon, onion flakes and rosemary. Season to taste. Add veal, bring to a slow boil and simmer, covered, about 2 hours or until meat is tender. Just before serving, stir in parsley. Remove meat from bone and weigh portion. Serve with lemon. Makes 1 serving.

VEAL PICCATA MILANESE

1 pound thinly cut veal (cut for scallopini)
Juice of 1 lemon
1 cup diced mushrooms
1 cup chicken bouillon
1 tablespoon chopped fresh parsley

¾ teaspoon herbs (basil, rosemary, oregano)
½ teaspoon salt
Dash pepper

Place veal slices between 2 sheets of waxpaper and pound on both sides with cleaver or heavy plate for about 3 minutes. Veal should now be no more than ¼-inch thick. Cut in 1-inch squares. Brown on both sides in preheated nonstick skillet. Remove veal from skillet, squeeze lemon juice over veal squares and keep warm. Wipe out skillet. Brown mushrooms in skillet; add chicken bouillon, chopped parsley, herbs, salt and pepper. Bring to boil; let cook at high heat for 5 minutes, stirring often until liquid is reduced. Make a bed of the sauce on serving dish. Blanket it with veal. Makes 2 servings.

VEAL SCALLOPINI CALABRESE

1 pound boneless veal roast
  (rump) cut in 1½-inch cubes
1 medium green pepper
1 medium red pepper

1 cup sliced mushrooms
¾ cup tomato puree
½ teaspoon oregano
Salt and pepper to taste

Broil veal and peppers on rack in broiling pan until veal is brown on all sides and peppers are charred, turning as necessary. Transfer veal to shallow flameproof serving casserole. Cover veal with remaining ingredients except peppers; put lid on casserole and let cook over moderate heat 20 minutes. Cut broiled peppers into strips and add to meat. Cook 10 minutes more. Serve hot. Makes 2 servings.

MEAT-STUFFED MUSHROOMS FLORENTINE

¼ cup cooked spinach, finely
  chopped
2 ounces cooked ground meat
  (veal or chicken)
1 slice enriched white bread,
  made into crumbs
¼ cup skim milk
1 tablespoon chopped fresh
  parsley

2 teaspoons Worcestershire
1 teaspoon dehydrated onion
  flakes, reconstituted in
  1 tablespoon water
¼ teaspoon garlic powder
Salt and pepper to taste
1 cup large mushroom caps
1 ounce sharp cheddar cheese,
  grated

Combine spinach, meat and bread crumbs in mixing bowl. Add milk, parsley, Worcestershire, onion flakes and garlic powder. Mix thoroughly until all liquid is absorbed. Season with salt and pepper. Fill mushroom caps with mixture, and top with grated cheese. Bake on nonstick pan at 375°F. for approximately 25 minutes or until cheese is bubbly. Makes 1 serving.

BEEFSTEAK FLORENTINE (Bistecca alla Fiorentina)

The great steaks of Florence are prepared this way . . . Florentine without spinach.

8 ounces boneless well-trimmed steak (use a tender cut such as filet mignon, shell, club, porterhouse, T-bone, rib, etc.)

1 wedge lemon
Salt and freshly ground pepper

Broil steak over charcoal on rack in broiling pan set close to heat, turning once. Allow a total of 8 to 10 minutes. Do not overcook . . . its famous steak is always served rare in Florence, with a wedge of lemon. Add salt and pepper at the table. Makes 1 serving.

HAMBURGER ALLA PIZZAIOLA

2 8-ounce ground beef patties
2 garlic cloves
¾ cup tomato puree

2 teaspoons fresh oregano
(or ¼ teaspoon dried)

Broil patties on a rack, about 4 inches from source of heat; turn once. Meanwhile in nonstick skillet, lightly brown garlic; add tomato puree and oregano. Cook at high heat for 3 minutes. Add hamburgers to skillet and heat for 1 minute longer, turning once. Serve with sauce. Makes 2 servings.

MEATBALLS WITH SPAGHETTI

1½ pounds ground beef
½ teaspoon onion salt
1 garlic clove, minced fine
¼ teaspoon pepper
2 cups tomato puree
1 tablespoon chopped fresh parsley

2 teaspoons dehydrated onion flakes
½ teaspoon basil
¼ teaspoon fennel seeds (optional)
2⅔ cups cooked enriched spaghetti

Combine ground beef, onion salt, garlic and pepper. Mix well. Shape into 48 equal meatballs about 1½-inches in diameter. Broil on rack about 4 inches from source of heat for 5 minutes. Turn and broil 3 minutes more or until cooked throughout. In saucepan, combine tomato puree, parsley, onion flakes, basil and fennel seeds, if desired.

Simmer 10 minutes. Add meatballs and simmer 5 minutes or until meatballs are heated throughout. Arrange 11 meatballs in a circle around edge of serving plate. Place ⅔ cup spaghetti in center. Divide sauce evenly. Pour one portion of sauce over meat and spaghetti. Top spaghetti with one meatball. Repeat 3 more times with remaining meatballs, sauce and spaghetti. Makes 4 servings.

MEATBALLS IN SPICY SAUCE (Polpette Piccanti)

This is the type of richly flavored dish with meat, mushrooms, tomatoes and many kinds of seasonings and spices that most people think of as really Italian. *But its gutsy, hearty flavor is far more typical of Southern* cucina *than of the more refined, more delicate, less spicy Northern fare.*

1 pound pork
8 ounces frankfurters
½ teaspoon bitters or grated lemon rind
½ teaspoon Worcestershire
½ teaspoon salt
1½ cups tomato puree
¼ cup tomato paste
1 medium green pepper, chopped
1 tablespoon dehydrated onion flakes
2 garlic cloves, crushed
¼ teaspoon celery seed
¼ teaspoon crushed red pepper
Dash each of all or some of chili, cinnamon, nutmeg, fennel, oregano, marjoram, sage and basil
1 bay leaf
2 whole allspice, crushed
2 cups mushrooms, sliced
2 tablespoons shredded canned pimentos, rinsed
2⅔ cups cooked enriched macaroni

Put the pork and frankfurters through the food processor or meat grinder using finest blade. Add bitters, Worcestershire and salt, and mix very well. Shape into 24 equal meatballs each about 1½-inches in diameter. Broil on preheated rack about 4 inches from source of heat for 8 minutes, or until cooked throughout. Turn once during broiling. In saucepan, combine browned meatballs, tomato puree, tomato paste, green pepper, onion flakes, garlic, celery seed, red pepper, chili, cinnamon, nutmeg, fennel, oregano, marjoram, sage, basil, bay leaf and allspice. Cook uncovered at medium heat at least 4 hours, stirring frequently with a wooden spoon. If necessary, add a little hot water (if sauce thickens to a paste). Add mushrooms and pimentos, and cook 30 minutes more. Remove bay leaf. Serve each portion over ⅔ cup cooked enriched macaroni or extend the dish by mixing the macaroni with a heap of cooked Celery Spaghetti (see page 222). Makes 4 servings.

BABY LAMB STEAKS WITH ARTICHOKES
(Abbacchio con Carciofi)

2 leg of lamb steaks (10-ounces each)
Salt and pepper to taste
1 garlic clove, split
½ cup tomato puree
1 medium tomato, peeled and chopped
1 teaspoon dehydrated onion flakes

¼ teaspoon marjoram leaves, finely chopped
Salt to taste
Browning sauce
4 ounces canned, drained artichoke hearts

Season lamb steaks; rub with garlic. Broil or barbecue on a rack, 4 inches from source of heat, 5 minutes each side, or until well browned. In saucepan, combine tomato puree, tomato, onion flakes and marjoram; cook until sauce thickens; season; color as desired with browning sauce. Divide sauce and artichokes equally into two portions and serve with steaks. Makes 2 servings.

MELON AND HAM

½ medium cantaloupe, peeled and seeded
1½ ounces cooked ham, cut in 4 thin slices

Escarole leaves

Cut cantaloupe half into 4 wedges. Wrap a folded piece of ham around the middle of each wedge. Secure with toothpicks. Serve on a bed of escarole greens. Makes 1 serving.

PORK PERUGIA STYLE

1 well-trimmed 4-pound center cut pork loin roast
3 garlic cloves, cut into slivers
1 teaspoon fennel seed or rosemary

4 cloves
Salt
Pepper

For ease in carving, have butcher loosen the chine (back) bone by sawing across the rib bones. With the tip of a sharp pointed knife, cut small incisions in the meat and stick garlic slivers and fennel seeds into them. Insert the cloves along the top of the roast. Insert meat thermometer so bulb is in thickest part of roast, not touching bone. Place pork on a rack in a roasting pan. Pour water into pan. Roast pork 2 hours or until meat thermometer reaches 170°F. Baste with more water every half hour. Remove roast from oven and let stand 15 minutes so juices gather. Cut into thin slices and weigh 6-ounce portions. Serve salt and pepper at the table. Makes 4 servings.

RISOTTO WITH CHICKEN GIZZARDS (Risotto alla Fiorentina)

Short-grain (Piedmont) rice is usual in authentic risottos because it absorbs a great deal of liquid but, as it is not widely available in the United States, the uncooked long grain rice is substituted with no great harm to the dish. Cook rice following package directions, but substitute chicken bouillon for the water. Measure ½ cup cooked enriched rice for each serving, then continue with the following recipe:

2 medium green peppers, seeded and diced
2 cups sliced mushrooms
2 teaspoons dehydrated onion flakes
2 cups chicken bouillon or tomato juice
Pinch of saffron

½ teaspoon each basil and marjoram
1 pound cooked gizzards or chicken, diced fine, see note
2 cups cooked enriched rice (prepared in chicken bouillon)
Salt and freshly ground pepper to taste

Brown green peppers, mushrooms and onion flakes in nonstick pan. When lightly browned on all sides, add chicken bouillon, saffron, basil and marjoram. Cook for 10 minutes. Add diced gizzards (or chicken) and rice. Stir well. Serve as main dish. Season to taste with salt and pepper. Makes 4 servings.

NOTE: Remove all fat from gizzards and rinse in cool water. Place in saucepan and add enough cold water to cover. Cover pan and simmer until tender, 1 to 2 hours; add additional water during cooking if needed. Drain gizzards, reserve and chill liquid. It may then be skimmed of all fat and used as bouillon in recipes calling for chicken bouillon.

CHICKEN LIVER SPAGHETTI

A blanket of liver on a bed of spaghetti.

1 pound chicken livers, cut in half
2 garlic cloves, minced
2 ounces onion, chopped
½ cup chopped celery
1 teaspoon salt
¾ teaspoon oregano
¼ teaspoon basil
¼ teaspoon pepper

1 cup tomato puree
1 cup chopped canned
mushrooms
½ cup water
2 tablespoons snipped parsley
leaves
1⅓ cups cooked enriched
spaghetti

In large nonstick skillet, brown chicken livers on all sides, over moderate heat. Remove liver; dice and reserve. In same skillet, cook garlic, onion, celery, salt, oregano, basil and pepper until onion is tender. Add puree, mushrooms, water and parsley; cover and cook 15 minutes. Add reserved chopped chicken livers; heat. Divide evenly over equal amounts of cooked spaghetti. Makes 2 servings.

LIVER PUDDING (Sformato di Fegato)

4 ounces onion, sliced
1 garlic clove, minced
1 pound beef liver, sliced
¼-inch thick
1 cup cooked enriched rice
½ cup evaporated skimmed milk

2 teaspoons vegetable oil
Freshly ground pepper to taste
2 packets instant chicken broth
and seasoning mix
2 slices lemon

In a nonstick skillet, cook onions and garlic by covering them with small amount of water and cooking over medium heat until soft. Allow water to evaporate and onions to brown. Remove from skillet and set aside. Pour boiling water over liver. Drain and transfer to skillet. Cook liver over medium-high heat 4 to 5 minutes, turning constantly, until all sides are browned. Do not overcook. Let cool. Transfer liver and onions to a food processor or mill. Add rice, evaporated skimmed milk, oil, pepper and broth mix. Puree mixture. Transfer to a 7½ x 3½ x2-inch loaf pan; cover with foil and bake at 350°F. for 25 minutes. Remove cover and continue to bake 10 to 15 minutes or until pudding is browned. Garnish with lemon slices. Makes 2 servings.

SWEET AND SOUR CHICKEN LIVER VENETIAN STYLE

1 pound chicken livers, cut in half
1 cup canned pitted cherries, no sugar added
1 cup chicken bouillon
1 tablespoon minced fresh parsley

2 teaspoons vinegar or to taste
1 teaspoon fresh sage leaves
1 teaspoon brandy or wine extract
Salt and pepper to taste

Pour boiling water over liver in colander. Allow to drain immediately and dry. In nonstick skillet, brown livers on all sides over moderate heat. Add remaining ingredients and cook covered, 15 minutes. Makes 2 servings.

CALF'S LIVER TRIESTE STYLE (Fegato di Vitello alla Triestina)

1 pound calf's liver, sliced into bite-size pieces
6 ounces peeled potatoes, diced
4 ounces onions, sliced thin
1 cup sliced tender celery
1 cup carrots, cut in matchstick pieces

1 teaspoon chopped fresh parsley
1 clove, cracked to release fragrance
2 cups chicken bouillon

Pour boiling water over liver and drain immediately. Combine potatoes, onions, celery, carrots, parsley, clove and chicken bouillon in saucepan. Bring to boil; add liver, cover and simmer 45 minutes or until vegetables and liver are tender. Divide evenly in bowls. Makes 2 servings.

BROWN RICE PIEDMONT STYLE (Risotto alla Piemontese)

¼ cup beef bouillon
2 cups cooked brown rice (prepared in beef bouillon)
1 tablespoon dehydrated onion flakes, reconstituted in 2 tablespoons beef bouillon

1 small white truffle, diced (optional)
2 teaspoons sauterne or sherry extract
4 teaspoons margarine

Heat bouillon in saucepan. Add brown rice and onion flakes, and warm over moderate heat. Stir in truffle and wine extract. Remove from heat. Add margarine, mix well and serve immediately. Makes 4 servings.

LENTILS WITH RICE

1 cup chicken bouillon
1 cup sliced celery
⅓ cup sliced carrots
8 ounces cooked dried lentils
½ cup cooked enriched rice
1 teaspoon chopped chives

1 teaspoon imitation (or diet)
    margarine
Dash of salt, pepper and sage
    (or 1 teaspoon chopped fresh
    sage)

In saucepan, combine chicken bouillon, celery and carrots, and cook until vegetables are soft, 15 to 20 minutes. Remove from heat, stir in remaining ingredients, mix well, and serve hot as main dish. Makes 1 serving.

RICE AND PEA SALAD

An interesting variation on the risi e bisi *theme.*

1 tablespoon mayonnaise
½ teaspoon tarragon vinegar
¼ teaspoon onion salt
Salt and pepper to taste
½ cup cooked enriched rice

1 ounce cooked peas
2 tablespoons chopped celery
1 tablespoon chopped pimento
10 capers
Watercress

In medium bowl combine mayonnaise, vinegar, onion salt, salt and pepper. Add rice, peas, celery, pimento and capers. Toss. Chill. Serve with sprays of watercress. Makes 1 serving.

COOKING PASTA

Follow package directions using rapidly boiling water. Don't skimp on the water . . . use as many quarts as called for. Stir the pasta to keep it moving as it reaches the water, so it doesn't stick or cook unevenly.

Pasta is made in literally hundreds of shapes and it is usually possible to substitute one shape for another in a recipe. Most pasta products double in volume after cooking; egg noodles remain about the same.

In general, 8 ounces enriched pasta should be boiled in 3 quarts salted water (use 1 tablespoon salt). It will make about 6 servings of ⅔ cup each.

Cooking time varies, depending on the size and type of pasta. Average cooking time for *al dente* pasta is 8 to 10 minutes. Pasta cooked *al dente* is chewy to the taste, which is the Italian way. Drain the pasta as soon as it is cooked but don't rinse under cold water unless it is to be served cold.

Measure the pasta after it is cooked and do not exceed your portion: ½ cup cooked enriched noodles; ⅔ cup cooked enriched macaroni or spaghetti.

Pasta can be easily reheated. Put it in a colander or strainer and pour boiling water over it. Drain and serve.

FETTUCINI CARBONARA

For a more professional touch, cheese may be tossed with fettucini at table side. Serve with a mixed green salad for a fine lunch.

1 cup sliced mushrooms
½ cup chicken bouillon
¼ cup evaporated skimmed milk
1⅓ cups cooked enriched fettucini, drained

2 medium eggs, slightly beaten
2 teaspoons chopped fresh parsley
2 ounces freshly grated Parmesan cheese

Cook mushrooms in nonstick saucepan until they begin to brown. Add chicken bouillon, milk and cooked fettucini; reduce heat slightly. Slowly stir in eggs and parsley; stir constantly and continue cooking for about 2 to 3 minutes or until eggs are cooked. Remove from pan; toss with cheese. Makes 2 servings.

FETTUCINI AND CELERY SPAGHETTI

Follow preceding recipe, but add a handful or more of the cooked Celery Spaghetti (see page 222) to the cooked macaroni before tossing as directed above. The nice little lunch is now not so little. Makes 2 servings.

RIGATONI WITH RICOTTA SAUCE

1½ cups water
¾ cup tomato puree
2 teaspoons dehydrated onion
flakes
Salt to taste

1⅓ cups skim milk ricotta cheese
1⅓ cups cooked enriched rigatoni
or tube macaroni
Freshly ground black pepper to
taste

In a medium saucepan combine water, tomato puree, onion flakes and salt. Bring to a boil; reduce heat. Add ricotta cheese and simmer for one hour or until sauce thickens. Stir occasionally to avoid sticking and to break up ricotta. Add rigatoni and continue to simmer 15 minutes. Mixture should thicken even more. Serve hot. Season to taste with black pepper. Makes 2 servings.

MACARONI WITH ALL-VEGETABLE SAUCE, SICILIAN STYLE

Chocolate flavor, a surprise ingredient, is sometimes used in these dishes in this part of Italy.

2 cups diced eggplant
2 medium yellow or green
peppers, seeded and diced
½ cup diced celery
½ cup sliced fresh mushrooms
2 tablespoons dehydrated onion
flakes
3 garlic cloves, minced
1½ cups fresh or frozen
cauliflower or broccoli florets
1½ cups tomato puree
¼ cup tomato paste

¼ cup beef bouillon
1 tablespoon minced fresh
parsley
1 teaspoon basil
½ teaspoon oregano
½ teaspoon salt
¼ teaspoon rosemary
¼ teaspoon thyme
1 teaspoon burgundy, sherry or
chocolate extract
2⅔ cups cooked enriched mezzani
or other macaroni

In a large nonstick skillet, brown eggplant, green peppers, celery, mushrooms, onion flakes and garlic, stirring constantly until vegetables are browned. Transfer mixture to a large saucepan; add cauliflower, tomato puree, tomato paste, bouillon, parsley, basil, oregano, salt, rosemary and thyme. Bring to a boil, reduce heat, cover saucepan and simmer for at least ½ hour, or until sauce is thick and all vegetables are tender. Stir occasionally, bringing the vegetables on the bottom up. Add more bouillon, if necessary, to prevent scorching. Remove from heat. Put entire mixture through a food processor or strainer to puree, if desired. Stir in extract and mix well. Divide evenly into 4 portions.

Serve each portion over ⅔ cup macaroni. This sauce freezes well; divide into portions and label before freezing. Makes 4 servings.

CANNELLINI TUSCAN STYLE (Cannellini alla Toscana)

1 medium canned or fresh peeled tomato, chopped into small pieces
1 garlic clove, minced or pressed
¼ teaspoon sage (or 2 leaves fresh)

Salt and pepper to taste
2 tablespoons hot water
6 ounces cooked dried cannellini (small white beans)

In a small pan, combine tomato, garlic, sage, salt, pepper and hot water. Simmer for 5 minutes. Add drained beans and continue to simmer for 5 more minutes to let beans absorb flavor of sauce. Makes 1 serving.

CASSEROLE OF ZITI WITH CHEESE (Pasta al Formaggio)

½ cup tomato puree
½ cup chicken bouillon
1 tablespoon dehydrated onion flakes
Dash garlic powder
½ teaspoon Italian seasoning

Salt and pepper to taste
⅔ cup cooked enriched ziti
2 ounces fresh grated cheese (mozzarella, Emmentaler, fontina, stachino or Parmesan)

Place tomato puree, bouillon, onion flakes and garlic powder in saucepan. Add Italian seasoning. Simmer over low heat until thickened. Season with salt and pepper. Fold macaroni and cheese into sauce. Makes 1 serving.

ZITI AND ZUCCHINI OR BROCCOLI

Follow recipe above but fold 1 cup cooked, sliced zucchini or broccoli florets into the sauce with macaroni and cheese. Makes 1 serving.

PASTA AND LENTILS

8 ounces cooked dried lentils
1 cup water
⅓ cup chopped carrots
⅓ cup finely chopped celery
2 ounces chopped onion
1 medium tomato, peeled and chopped
1 packet instant beef broth and seasoning mix

1 small bay leaf
1 garlic clove, minced
½ teaspoon salt
⅛ teaspoon pepper
⅔ cup cooked enriched macaroni
1 tablespoon margarine

In medium saucepan combine all ingredients except macaroni and margarine. Bring to a boil; reduce heat; cover and cook 40 minutes. Remove bay leaf. Stir in macaroni; heat. Remove from heat; stir in margarine. Makes 1 serving.

LASAGNE NAPLES STYLE (Lasagne alla Napolitana)

A luscious combination of tomato sauce, vegetables and cheeses. The sauce may be made ahead and refrigerated for a day, or frozen for weeks; defrost before use.

2 cups peeled diced eggplant
2 medium green or yellow peppers, seeded and diced
½ garlic clove, minced
1½ cups tomato puree
1 teaspoon chopped fresh parsley

½ teaspoon salt
½ teaspoon cinnamon
2⅔ cups cooked enriched lasagne macaroni, well drained
4 ounces grated Parmesan cheese
4 ounces sliced mozzarella cheese

In a medium-size saucepan, lightly brown eggplant, green pepper and garlic, stirring to brown all sides (5 to 8 minutes). Add tomato puree and cook, uncovered, until sauce is very thick, about ½ hour or until eggplant is tender. Watch and stir as necessary so sauce does not brown. Stir in parsley, salt and cinnamon. Mix well. Spread a thin layer of the sauce in the bottom of rectangular baking dish. Put half of the strips of lasagne on top and half of each of the two cheeses. Repeat with sauce, remaining strips of lasagne and remaining cheese. End with a layer of sauce. Bake at 350°F. for 40 minutes. Let stand for 5 minutes before serving to make cutting easier. Makes 4 servings.

HERB FINGERS

2 teaspoons imitation (or diet) margarine
⅛ teaspoon marjoram
⅛ teaspoon oregano
1 slice enriched white bread, toasted

Combine first 3 ingredients. Spread on warm toast. Cut in quarters, lengthwise. Keep warm in oven. Makes 1 serving.

SALTY STICKS

1 slice enriched white bread
1 tablespoon concentrated chicken bouillon (¼ packet chicken broth and seasoning mix and 1 tablespoon boiling water)
¼ teaspoon coarse salt

Brush bread with bouillon, sprinkle salt on bread; bake at 375°F. (moderate oven) 15 minutes or until bread is lightly browned. Cut into 4 equal strips. Makes 1 serving.

GARLIC BREAD

1 slice enriched white bread, toasted
1 cut garlic clove
1 teaspoon vegetable oil
Salt and pepper to taste

While toast is hot, rub each side with cut clove of garlic and spread with oil. Cut into 1-inch strips. Sprinkle with salt and pepper and serve hot. Makes 1 serving.

LITTLE SHELLS WITH MUSHROOMS AND PEAS
(Maruzzine con Piselli)

1 cup mushrooms
½ garlic clove
2 ounces frozen peas
1 tablespoon water
1 teaspoon parsley
Salt and pepper to taste
⅔ cup cooked enriched macaroni shells (maruzzine)
2 ounces grated Parmesan cheese

Brown mushrooms and garlic in nonstick pan until mushrooms release their liquid. Add peas, water, parsley, salt and pepper. Cook until peas are tender. Pour over heated macaroni shells. Stir in Parmesan cheese and serve. Makes 1 serving.

PICKLED ARTICHOKES

Artichoke with parsley, garlic and oil.

8 ounces frozen artichoke hearts
2 tablespoons vegetable oil
4 teaspoons vinegar
2 teaspoons chopped fresh parsley
¼ teaspoon salt
¼ teaspoon oregano
¼ teaspoon prepared mustard
⅛ teaspoon pepper
1 garlic clove, crushed

Cook artichoke hearts according to package directions; drain. In a bowl combine oil with remaining ingredients. Stir in artichoke hearts. Cover tightly and refrigerate until thoroughly chilled, 1 hour or longer, turning artichoke hearts occasionally in marinade. Makes 6 antipasto servings.

ARTICHOKES NEAPOLITAN*

4 ounces cooked artichoke hearts (or combination of cooked artichokes and peas)
1 ounce hard cheese, grated
1 teaspoon vegetable oil
1 teaspoon dehydrated onion flakes
1 teaspoon chopped fresh parsley
½ teaspoon salt
¼ garlic clove, chopped
½ slice enriched white bread, made into crumbs

In small baking dish, make a bed of artichokes and other vegetables. Combine remaining ingredients and sprinkle on top. Bake at 400°F. until hot and brown. Serve at once. (If the dish has been frozen, defrost, bake with aluminum-foil cover.) Makes 1 serving.

BROCCOLI ALLA ROMANA

4 cups (about 2 pounds) fresh broccoli
½ cup boiling water
1 teaspoon salt
⅛ teaspoon pepper
1 garlic clove put through press
4 teaspoons vegetable oil
¼ teaspoon sauterne or sherry extract or lemon juice

Wash broccoli. Split ends of large stalks lengthwise into halves or quarters, depending on size. Place in large skillet. Sprinkle with water, salt and pepper. Cover tightly; cook over moderate heat 15 to 20 minutes, or only until stalks are tender, but florets still crisp and bright green. Divide broccoli into 4 serving bowls. Mix garlic with oil and wine extract. Stir mixture evenly into each bowl of broccoli. Makes 4 servings.

BROCCOLI MILANESE

Asparagus spears can be prepared this way too.

1 cup cooked broccoli florets
1 medium egg, beaten
1 slice enriched white bread, made into crumbs

1 ounce hard cheese, grated

In small baking dish, cover broccoli with egg; add crumbs and cheese. Bake in a 375°F. oven for 25 to 30 minutes, or until egg is set and crumbs are brown. Makes 1 serving.

ASPARAGUS AND CHEESE PIZZA

Pizza—pie—can be spicy and crusty in the familiar Sicilian style or soft and eggy, as here, in the Northern version.

3 medium eggs
1½ cups hot cooked enriched rice
3 ounces grated sharp cheddar cheese, divided
1 teaspoon salt, divided

1½ cups chopped asparagus
¾ cup cooked mushrooms, sliced
3 tablespoons tomato puree
⅛ teaspoon pepper

In small bowl, slightly beat 1 egg, stir in rice, half of cheese and half of salt. Mix well. Press firmly in even layer on bottom of a 9-inch pie pan. Cook asparagus in a minimum amount of water. Drain well in strainer. Beat remaining eggs slightly. Stir in mushrooms, tomato puree, pepper and remaining salt. Add asparagus. Mix well. Spoon over crust in pie pan. Bake in a preheated 375°F. oven for 20 minutes. Remove from oven. Sprinkle remaining cheese evenly over the top of vegetable mixture in pie pan. Return to oven. Bake 10 minutes more. Let cool 10 to 15 minutes and serve warm. Makes 3 servings.

"CREAMY" PESTO SAUCE*

Make this only when you have fresh basil, an herb you can grow in your window garden. Try a few drops of nut extract. Serve it over freshly cooked enriched pasta or Celery Spaghetti (see page 222).

6 tender sprigs basil
6 sprigs parsley
4 teaspoons vegetable oil
4 ounces grated Parmesan cheese

¼ cup evaporated skimmed milk
1 teaspoon salt
¼ teaspoon pepper
1 garlic clove

Combine in blender container and process at medium speed until smooth. Makes 4 servings.

BRUSSELS SPROUTS WITH BASIL

1 pound Brussels sprouts
¼ cup chicken bouillon
4 teaspoons margarine

Pinch basil
Pinch tarragon

Wash Brussels sprouts in cold salted water, remove wilted leaves if necessary. Cut a cross in stem ends. In saucepan cover with boiling water, add salt and bring to boil. Simmer uncovered for 10 to 12 minutes or until just tender. Drain. Combine hot bouillon, margarine, basil and tarragon and pour over Brussels sprouts. Makes 4 servings.

COOKED CHICORY AND ESCAROLE PIQUANTE

1 head chicory
1 head escarole
½ cup water
1 packet instant beef broth and seasoning mix

3 garlic cloves, minced
2 tablespoons chopped fresh parsley
Salt to taste
¾ teaspoon hot pepper sauce

Trim chicory and escarole, removing tough, wilted or discolored leaves. Wash thoroughly in cold water to remove sand; drain. Break leaves into 1-inch pieces. Combine remaining ingredients in large saucepan; add chicory and escarole. Cover tightly and cook 30 minutes or until escarole is tender. Serve hot. Makes 2 servings.

CELERY SPAGHETTI

You don't know it yet, but you'll love this spaghetti.

3 ribs celery	Salt
Boiling water	

Cut the celery ribs into long thin strands about the size of thick spaghetti. Lay the strands in a large kettle, pour on quarts of boiling water; stir in salt and cook until celery is limp (about 10 minutes) or to taste. Drain, serve with any of our pasta sauces. Makes 2 servings.

CELERY VINAIGRETTE

Cover Celery Spaghetti with Vinaigrette Dressing (see page 131 and prepare 2 servings), chill for several hours. Use a shallow oval serving dish, garnish with cross made of red pimento strips. Sprinkle with parsley or chopped capers for added color. Makes 2 servings.

CAPONATA

4 cups unpeeled eggplant, cut in 1-inch cubes	1½ tablespoons capers, rinsed
1½ teaspoons salt, divided	1 tablespoon chopped fresh chives
1 cup sliced celery	1 teaspoon basil, crushed
2 ripe medium tomatoes, chopped	¼ teaspoon pepper
¼ cup tomato paste	2 garlic cloves, minced
3 tablespoons lemon juice or vinegar	4 teaspoons vegetable oil

Sprinkle eggplant with 1 teaspoon salt and let stand for 15 minutes. Drain and dry. Brown in preheated nonstick skillet with celery. Add tomatoes and let cook for 10 minutes. Combine remaining ingredients (except oil). Add to skillet. Cook until vegetables are very soft, stirring occasionally, about 30 minutes; add a few tablespoons water if necessary to prevent sticking. Remove to a bowl; cover and chill in refrigerator a day or two before serving for fullest flavor. Stir in 1 teaspoon oil for each portion just before serving. Serve as antipasto, salad, vegetable or relish. Makes 4 servings.

STUFFED MUSHROOMS VENICE STYLE (Funghi alla Veneziana)*

2 cups fresh mushroom caps (select large uniform size)

2 ounces freshly grated Parmesan or Romano cheese

1½ tablespoons chopped fresh chives

1 tablespoon chopped fresh parsley

2 teaspoons imitation (or diet) margarine

2 teaspoons sherry extract

1 teaspoon prepared spicy mustard

½ teaspoon tarragon

Salt and pepper to taste

Peel the mushroom caps if they are discolored, otherwise wipe clean with damp towel. Combine remaining ingredients. Mash well. Fill mushroom caps with the stuffing. Makes 2 servings.

BAKED EGGPLANT PARMIGIANA

2 ounces chopped onion

¾ cup tomato puree

⅓ cup water

¾ teaspoon salt

½ teaspoon oregano leaves

Dash pepper

2 cups peeled and thinly sliced eggplant

4 ounces grated sharp cheddar cheese, divided

In nonstick skillet brown chopped onions. Add tomato puree, water, salt, oregano and pepper. Bring to a boil and simmer for 15 minutes. In 2-quart baking dish alternate layers of sliced eggplant, tomato sauce and half of the grated cheese; repeat layer of eggplant and layer of tomato sauce. Bake in moderate oven (350°F.) for 1 hour. A few minutes before done, sprinkle remaining grated cheese over top and continue heating until cheese melts. Makes 2 servings.

ZUCCHINI PARMESAN*

A hailstorm of hand-grated cheese on garlicky squash.

1 garlic clove

4 ounces coarsely chopped onion

1 tablespoon chopped fresh parsley

2 teaspoons salt

¼ teaspoon pepper

¼ teaspoon rosemary

⅛ teaspoon oregano

4 cups thinly sliced zucchini

2 medium tomatoes, peeled and chopped

4 ounces grated Parmesan cheese

In large nonstick skillet, brown garlic, onion, parsley, salt, pepper, rosemary and oregano. As it cooks, press the garlic against the pan with a fork to extract its juices. After 5 minutes, add zucchini and tomatoes, and cook 15 to 20 minutes, or until zucchini is tender. Turn mixture into a serving dish; sprinkle with Parmesan cheese. Makes 4 servings.

ZUCCHINI PIZZA

A tempting tart.

6 cups peeled zucchini, cut into ¼-inch slices
1 tablespoon salt
2 slices enriched white bread, made into crumbs
1 ounce grated Parmesan cheese

1 garlic clove, finely minced
1 cup tomato puree
¼ cup chicken bouillon
7 ounces mozzarella cheese, thinly sliced

Sprinkle salt over zucchini in a large bowl, and toss lightly. Let stand 20 to 30 minutes. Drain and discard liquid. Pat slices dry with paper towel. In a medium mixing bowl, combine bread crumbs, grated cheese and garlic. In cup with a spout, such as a liquid measuring cup, combine tomato puree with bouillon. Transfer half the slices to a 1½-quart casserole. Sprinkle with ½ bread crumb mixture, pour on ½ tomato puree mixture and cover with slices of mozzarella cheese. Repeat layers. Bake for 30 minutes or until zucchini are tender and cheese is melted. Remove from oven and allow to stand 15 to 20 minutes before serving. Divide evenly into 4 portions. Serve hot. Makes 4 servings.

ITALIAN RELISH

2 cups unpeeled eggplant, cut in 1-inch cubes
2 medium tomatoes, chopped
1 medium green pepper, cut in 1-inch pieces
4 ounces chopped onion

20 small seedless grapes
½ cup vinegar
½ cup water
½ teaspoon hot pepper sauce
¼ teaspoon bitters

Combine all ingredients in saucepan. Bring to boil; cover pan, reduce heat and simmer for 40 minutes, stirring frequently. Serve warm or chill. Makes 4 servings.

WHOLE GREEN BEAN SALAD

4 cups whole fresh green beans (see note)
¼ cup beef bouillon
2 tablespoons vinegar
4 teaspoons vegetable oil
1 tablespoon chopped fresh parsley

½ teaspoon salt
¼ teaspoon dehydrated onion flakes
⅛ teaspoon pepper

Cook and drain beans. While they're still hot, add bouillon, vinegar, oil, parsley, salt, onion and pepper. Toss well. Chill. Makes 4 servings.

NOTE: Remove tips at both ends. Cook beans in a large kettle containing several quarts of boiling salted water. Best way is to drop them into a strainer half a cup at a time, then immerse strainer into water, and keep there until done. Beans should be tender but cooked *al dente*, and with bright color. Refresh beans quickly under cold water. Drain and use immediately as above.

SALAD OF ESCAROLE, SORREL AND STRAWBERRIES

1 head escarole
½ cup sorrel (sour grass) leaves
½ cup very ripe strawberries

1 tablespoon vegetable oil
1 teaspoon lemon juice

Use only the white inside leaves of the escarole (save the outside leaves for soup). Wash escarole and sorrel leaves to remove all sand. Drain well and shake dry. Wrap in towels and refrigerate until ready to use. Arrange escarole leaves in salad bowl; with scissors cut sorrel leaves into julienne strips and sprinkle over escarole. Add strawberries. Combine oil and lemon juice. Pour over salad and toss. Makes 1 serving.

SPINACH SALAD WITH MUSTARD DRESSING

If the garlic taste lingers too long, chew a coffee bean.

2 cups bite-size fresh spinach leaves, thoroughly washed and dried (discard tough stems)
½ cup sliced mushrooms

1 tablespoon vegetable oil
2 teaspoons wine vinegar
1 teaspoon prepared mustard
1 garlic clove, minced

Place spinach leaves and mushrooms in medium bowl. Combine oil, vinegar, mustard and garlic; toss with vegetables. Makes 1 serving.

MIXED SALAD RUSTICA

The kind of everyday salad you're likely to find everywhere in Italy.

1 cup small fresh mushrooms, thinly sliced
½ head iceberg lettuce, chopped
½ head romaine, chopped
1 bunch watercress, chopped
10 cherry tomatoes, cut in halves
8 radishes, sliced
Mustard Dressing (see page 225; multiply amounts if necessary)

Place all ingredients in a large bowl, toss, and divide into 4 equal portions. Serve with Mustard Dressing. Makes 4 servings.

HEARTS OF PALM AND WATERCRESS VINAIGRETTE

Make a bed of escarole or Boston lettuce leaves on a round serving platter. Prepare 2 cups canned hearts of palm. Cut into spears lengthwise and then cut them in half. Arrange like spokes in a wheel on bed of lettuce. Place very crisp fresh watercress in center of spokes. Between spokes add pieces of red pimento. Spoon Lemony Vinaigrette Dressing (see page 186) over salad. Let stand 15 minutes before serving. Makes 4 servings.

ZUCCHINI FINGERS IN LEMONY VINAIGRETTE

2 cups peeled zucchini (about 1 pound) cut in 4-inch lengths
Salt
Boiling water
1 recipe Lemony Vinaigrette Dressing (see page 186)

Cut zucchini into julienne strips and sprinkle with salt; let stand 20 minutes. Press out moisture. Put in a large kettle and cover with two quarts of boiling salted water. Bring to boil and continue cooking until vegetable is just barely done (loses its opacity). Transfer to colander, pour cold water over zucchini, drain, dry with paper towels. Cover with Lemony Vinaigrette Dressing and chill until ready to use. Makes 4 servings.

ZUCCHINI FINGERS WITH GARLIC

Prepare zucchini as directed above, bringing to boil in kettle and cooking until vegetable is done to taste. Drain. Divide into each of four salad plates. Combine 4 teaspoons vegetable oil, 1 garlic (well-mashed) clove, 1 tablespoon each chopped fresh parsley and chives, salt and pepper (fresh turns from the pepper mill). Spread one-fourth of mixture over the vegetables in each of the salad plates, mix well, and serve hot. Makes 4 servings.

TOMATO AND ONION SALAD

Lettuce leaves
1 firm ripe medium tomato, sliced
2 ounces onion, thinly sliced
1½ teaspoons chopped fresh parsley
1 teaspoon vegetable oil
½ teaspoon Dijon mustard
¼ teaspoon dried basil, oregano or thyme
¼ teaspoon salt
Freshly ground pepper to taste

Arrange alternating rings of tomatoes and onions on lettuce leaves. Combine remaining ingredients and pour over tomatoes and onions. Let stand a few minutes before serving. Makes 1 serving.

CHEF'S SALAD (with egg and cheese)

1 cup shredded lettuce
½ cup sliced mushrooms
¼ medium green pepper, diced
1 ounce onion, sliced
1 pimento, cut into strips
1 hard-cooked medium egg, chopped
1 ounce mozzarella cheese, cubed
2 tablespoons evaporated skimmed milk
1 tablespoon mayonnaise
2 teaspoons lemon juice
1 teaspoon chopped capers
Salt and pepper to taste

Combine lettuce, mushrooms, green pepper, onion and pimento in a large individual salad bowl. Toss in egg and cheese. In a small mixing bowl combine remaining ingredients. Pour over salad and mix to combine. Makes 1 serving.

FRESH FRUIT CUP (Macedonia di Frutta Fresca)

1 small orange, peeled and diced (reserve juice)
¼ ripe medium pineapple, cut in wedges
1 medium apple, diced (peeled if desired)
20 small seedless grapes
4 fresh flowers, washed and refrigerated

Dice fruits into pieces of uniform size. Mix together. Serve in stemmed dessert glasses. Garnish with a fresh rinsed flower . . . violets, sweet peas, tiny rhododendron center, etc. Chill during dinner. Makes 4 servings.

RUM-CHERRY PUDDING*

4 medium eggs, separated
Artificial sweetener to equal
  10 teaspoons sugar
1 lemon
1 teaspoon rum extract
¼ teaspoon cherry extract

1 cup skim milk
4 slices enriched white bread,
  made into crumbs
2 cups canned pitted cherries,
  no sugar added

Use a small deep pudding mold or baking dish. In medium bowl beat egg yolks; add sweetener, juice of lemon, rum and cherry extracts and milk. Stir in bread crumbs and the cherries. Whip egg whites until stiff. Fold into cherry mixture; transfer to pudding mold. Set the mold into a larger pan and pour 1-inch hot water around mold. Bake pudding at 375°F. for 1 hour or until set and firm in center. Makes 4 servings.

STRAWBERRY-RICOTTA PANCAKE

1 slice enriched white bread,
  made into crumbs
1 medium egg
¼ cup skim milk

1 cup strawberries (hull and slice)
⅓ cup skim milk ricotta cheese
2 to 3 drops lemon juice

Beat bread crumbs, egg and milk in mixing bowl until smooth. Pour into a heated 8-inch nonstick pan. Cook over low heat until top of pancake is full of broken bubbles and underside is brown. Turn with spatula and brown the other side. Turn onto a platter. Mix strawberries, cheese and lemon juice. Place in center of pancake; fold over and serve. Makes 1 serving.

COFFEE ICE (Granita di Caffè)

2 cups double-strength coffee
1 teaspoon lemon juice

1 recipe Whipped Topping (see
  page x)
4 pieces of lemon rind, curled

Mix coffee and lemon juice. Pour into a shallow pan or metal ice cube tray (see note). Freeze, stirring occasionally to break up ice during freezing. Garnish with Whipped Topping and lemon rind, if desired. Makes 4 servings.

NOTE: If your metal ice cube tray has a stale odor, rinse it in a solution of warm water and baking soda.

STRAWBERRY ICE (Granita di Fragola)

4 cups fresh ripe strawberries
1 cup orange juice
Juice of ½ lemon
1 cup granulated sugar replacement
½ cup water

Wash and hull the berries just before use; process in blender until smooth; remove to bowl and add orange juice and lemon juice. Simmer sugar replacement and water in a saucepan for 5 minutes. Let cool and add it to the strawberry mixture. Pour the mixture into a refrigerator tray or 8x8-inch dish; let it freeze until firm, stirring well from time to time to prevent ice crystals from forming. Makes 6 servings.

COFFEE FRAPPE

1½ cups boiling water
1 tablespoon instant coffee
1 small cinnamon stick
Artificial sweetener to equal 4 teaspoons sugar, divided
2 tablespoons evaporated skimmed milk
Crushed ice
Grated orange rind

Combine water, coffee, cinnamon and artificial sweetener to equal 2 teaspoons sugar; cool. Whip remaining sweetener and milk until stiff. Remove cinnamon stick from coffee. Pour coffee over crushed ice in two glasses. Top with equal amounts of whipped milk; sprinkle with orange rind. Makes 2 servings.

COFFEE RUM STRATA

1¾ cups water, divided
1 envelope unflavored gelatin
2 tablespoons instant coffee
Artificial sweetener to equal 16 teaspoons sugar
⅛ teaspoon salt
⅛ teaspoon rum extract

Place ¼ cup water in a small saucepan. Sprinkle gelatin over water and place over low heat for 2 to 3 minutes, stirring constantly until

[229]

gelatin dissolves. Remove from heat. Stir in coffee, sweetener and salt. Add remaining water and stir to combine. Reserving ½ cup of the mixture, divide the remainder evenly into 4 dessert cups and chill until almost firm. Meanwhile, stir rum extract into the reserved liquid and chill until slightly thicker than unbeaten egg whites. Beat reserved gelatin mixture on the high speed of an electric mixer until mixture doubles in volume. Divide evenly and spoon over first layer. Chill until firm, at least 1 hour. This can be made a day ahead of time. Topping will firm slightly, but remain fluffy. Makes 4 servings.

RICOTTA CHEESE PIE (Torta di Formaggio)

A liaison of cheese, eggs and flavor extracts. Omit the crust if you've used up your daily bread quota.

1 recipe 7-inch pie crust (recipe follows)	¼ teaspoon cinnamon
⅔ cup skim milk ricotta cheese	¼ teaspoon grated lemon rind
½ teaspoon vanilla extract	¼ teaspoon grated orange rind
Artificial sweetener to equal 10 teaspoons sugar	2 medium eggs, separated

Prepare pie crust. Put ricotta cheese through a sieve or beat cheese with electric mixer until light and airy. Add vanilla extract, sweetener, cinnamon, lemon and orange rinds. Mix well. Beat in egg yolks, one at a time. Beat egg whites until stiff. Fold into cheese mixture, and gently transfer to pie crust. Bake at 350°F. for 50 to 60 minutes or until top is set and golden brown. Serve immediately or chill. Makes 2 servings.

Pie Crust

2 slices toasted raisin bread, made into crumbs	¼ teaspoon vanilla extract
	3 tablespoons water

Preheat oven to 350°F. Place bread crumbs in mixing bowl. Add extract and water. Mix to a smooth paste. Press into a 7- or 8-inch pie pan using the back of a teaspoon. If it is difficult to mold, wet the back of the spoon with a little water. Bake for 10 minutes. Makes 2 servings.

SHERRY FROST

½ cup cold water
⅓ cup nonfat dry milk
1 teaspoon sherry extract
⅛ teaspoon vanilla extract

Artificial sweetener to equal
   1 teaspoon sugar
2 ice cubes

Place all ingredients except ice cubes in blender container; cover and process at low speed to combine. Add ice cubes, one at a time, processing at high speed. Makes 1 serving.

WATERMELON ICE

This granular sherbet is served either mushy or frozen and scraped first. A few drops of red food coloring may be added if you wish.

4 cups seeded, cubed watermelon
2 tablespoons fresh lemon juice
Artificial sweetener to equal
   4 teaspoons sugar (or more if
   to taste)

Place all ingredients in blender container and process to puree. Pour into ice cube tray with insert and freeze for 1 to 2 hours or until cubes are crystalized. Return cubes to blender container; process to puree. Stir down with spatula if necessary. Divide evenly into sherbert glasses. Makes 4 servings.

CAFFE CAPPUCCINO

⅔ cup boiling water
1 tablespoon freeze-dried
   espresso coffee

⅔ cup skim milk, scalded
Ground cinnamon or nutmeg
2 cinnamon sticks (optional)

Pour boiling water into blender container. Add instant coffee, then hot milk. Process on high speed until frothy. Pour into cups and dust with cinnamon or nutmeg. May be served with cinnamon stick. Makes 2 servings.

Japan

The Japanese people, who are masters at technology, are equally skilled at the aesthetics of arranging flowers, designing perfect gardens, and preparing and serving food. A small people—though they are getting bigger as their menu pattern becomes more Westernized—they handle details with elegance and sophistication. In fact, they are artful at achieving "naturalness," and cunning at keeping things looking simple. Everything they do has meaning and tradition; even the tiny vegetable garnishing the soup is part of a design plan in which perfection is the goal. Perhaps it would be more accurate to say that the goal is "near perfection," because inherent in Japanese philosophy is the belief that perfection can never be achieved. To symbolize this inability to reach the ultimate, a Japanese craftsman will deliberately leave a thumbprint on his work, or drop a leaf on a meticulously groomed sand garden.

Although Japanese cooking has not achieved the popularity in our country of that of its Far East neighbor, China, you'll like our little sampling.

CLEAR SOUP (Suimono)

4 cups chicken bouillon
1 teaspoon Japanese shoyu (soy sauce)
Dash of salt
Radish roses

Combine first 3 ingredients and bring to a boil. In each of 4 bowls place a radish rose. Pour hot soup over and serve. (Japanese drink this from bowl and do not use spoons.) Makes 4 servings.

VARIATION:* Add 2 ounces cooked slivered chicken or pork to each bowl.

RICE CHOWDER

5 cups chicken bouillon
8 ounces cooked chicken, diced
2 tablespoons Japanese shoyu (soy sauce)
1 teaspoon freshly grated ginger root
1 teaspoon sherry extract
Salt and pepper to taste
1 cup cooked enriched rice
2 ounces chopped scallions

Combine chicken bouillon, chicken, shoyu, ginger, sherry extract, salt and pepper in a large saucepan. Bring to a boil. Add rice and scallions; lower heat and simmer 10 minutes or until rice is very tender. Pour into a strainer, reserving liquid. Divide chicken, scallions and rice mixture evenly into 2 soup bowls. Pour liquid over each portion. Makes 2 servings.

VARIATION: Serve piping hot soup in 4 covered casseroles. Carefully break an egg over rice chowder and cover. Eggs will poach in 3 to 4 minutes. Soup must be hot. Makes 4 servings.

PICKLED SHRIMP

12 ounces cooked, cleaned shrimp
4 ounces onion, minced
½ cup chopped fresh parsley
⅓ cup wine vinegar
2 tablespoons vegetable oil
1 garlic clove
1 teaspoon salt
Dash pepper
Lettuce leaves
Chinese Mustard (recipe follows)

Combine shrimp, onion and parsley in a bowl. Place remaining ingredients except lettuce and mustard in blender container and process.

Pour over shrimp. Chill at least 1 hour, or overnight if possible, before serving. Line a serving bowl with lettuce leaves. Arrange shrimp mixture on leaves. Serve shrimp with Chinese Mustard. Makes 2 servings.

Chinese Mustard

⅓ cup dry mustard
2 tablespoons water

½ teaspoon salt

Combine all ingredients to make a dip. Serve with Pickled Shrimp. Makes 2 servings.

SUKIYAKI

1 pound boned sirloin steak
2 ounces onion, thinly sliced
1 cup fresh mushrooms, sliced
1 cup diagonally sliced celery
½ medium green pepper, cut in
  ¼-inch wide strips
⅔ cup beef bouillon

1 cup bean sprouts
¼ cup bamboo shoots
2 tablespoons Japanese shoyu
  (soy sauce)
1 teaspoon salt
¼ teaspoon pepper
1 cup cooked enriched rice

Broil steak on rack in broiler pan, until medium-rare. Remove from broiler; cool; thinly slice; set aside. In large nonstick skillet cook onion, mushrooms, celery and green pepper, stirring, about 5 minutes. Add remaining ingredients except rice; add steak; heat. Serve, divided evenly, over equal portions of rice. Makes 2 servings.

STEAMED EGG PUDDING (Chawan Mushi)

3 cups chicken bouillon
4 medium eggs, beaten
4 ounces cooked diced chicken

4 ounces cooked baby shrimp
1 cup fresh spinach leaves,
chopped

In a large bowl, combine bouillon and eggs. Divide evenly into four individual 1¾-cup casseroles. Add 1 ounce chicken and 1 ounce shrimp to each casserole. Cover and place in steamer or on a rack in a large pot with boiling water halfway up the sides of casserole. Cover steamer and cook 20 minutes or until a knife inserted in the egg-bouillon mixture comes out clean. Remove cover from casseroles and add ¼ cup spinach to each. Replace cover and steam for 5 minutes more or until spinach is soft and wilted. Makes 4 servings.

VARIATION: Combine ¼ cup bamboo shoots cut in matchstick pieces, 1 ounce sliced scallions and 1 ounce green peas. Divide evenly into the 4 individual casseroles before steaming. Makes 4 servings.

CHICKEN SUKIYAKI

1½ pounds skinned and boned chicken breasts
1½ cups takenoko (bamboo shoots) sliced lengthwise ⅛-inch thick
1 cup sliced celery
1 cup fresh sliced mushrooms, ¼-inch thick
1 cup fresh spinach, washed and stemmed

2 cups cooked thin enriched noodles
½ cup Japanese shoyu (soy sauce)
½ cup water
2 teaspoons sherry extract
4 ounces scallions cut in 2-inch lengths

Chill chicken breasts to almost freezing and slice thin. This dish is ideally prepared in an electric nonstick skillet, but any nonstick skillet will do. Preheat skillet. Place sliced chicken in heated pan and allow to brown, turning occasionally until all pieces are a uniform color. Add takenoko, celery, mushrooms and spinach. Mix to combine. Stir in noodles. Cook 1 to 2 minutes. In a small bowl combine shoyu, water and extract. Pour mixture over chicken and vegetables. Add scallions. Bring to a boil and cook 4 to 5 minutes. Serve. Makes 4 servings.

CHICKEN LIVER TERIYAKI

1½ pounds chicken livers
Equal parts Japanese shoyu (soy sauce) and water
5 to 6 yoji (long bamboo toothpicks)

15 cherry tomatoes
Mustard Dip (recipe follows)

Marinate livers in shoyu and water for at least 1 hour. Remove livers from marinade, reserving liquid. Preheat hibachi or broiler. Divide livers into 3 equal parts. Truss on yoji. Truss tomatoes on separate yoji. Broil liver on hibachi or on a rack in the broiler about 10 minutes on one side and 3 to 4 minutes on second side. Baste occasionally with reserved marinade. Place skewered tomatoes on hibachi or on rack in broiler for last five minutes. Serve with shoyu and Mustard Dip. Makes 3 servings (1 liver yoji each and 5 cherry tomatoes).

Mustard Dip

½ teaspoon dry mustard   ½ teaspoon or more water

Combine ingredients and mix with a spoon until a heavy paste is formed. If softer paste is desired, add more water, a drop at a time, mixing after each addition. Serve with Chicken Liver Teriyaki.

MOTSU-GIZZARDS

1½ pounds gizzards, split and washed
2 cups water
1 cup Japanese shoyu (soy sauce)
Artificial sweetener to equal 12 teaspoons sugar

2 garlic cloves, minced or pressed
2 teaspoons freshly minced ginger root
2 cups cooked enriched rice

In a large saucepan, combine all ingredients except rice. Place over medium heat and cook 1½ to 2 hours or until gizzards are tender. Drain and discard liquid. Divide evenly into 4 portions. Serve each portion over ½ cup rice. Makes 4 servings.

TENDERLOIN OF PORK

1 pound pork tenderloin
Japanese shoyu (soy sauce)

Freshly ground black pepper to taste

Insert meat thermometer into thickest portion of meat. Place tenderloin on a rack in 350°F. oven and roast until meat thermometer registers 170°F. Remove from oven and sprinkle with shoyu and pepper. Slice across the grain into ¼-inch slices and serve with shoyu mixed with pepper as a dip. Makes 2 servings.

PORK CUCUMBER SALAD

8 ounces cooked pork, cut into julienne strips
2 medium cucumbers, sliced

3 tablespoons vinegar
1½ tablespoons dry mustard
1 tablespoon water

Place pork strips and cucumber in a large bowl. Combine vinegar, mustard and water. Pour over pork and cucumber. Turn carefully once or twice and serve. Makes 2 servings.

SALTED CUCUMBER

3 medium cucumbers, unpeeled
  and sliced into ½-inch slices
Salt to taste

Japanese shoyu (soy sauce)
Vinegar (optional)

Combine sliced cucumbers and salt in bowl. Place weighted dish on top. After about 1 hour drain and serve with dash shoyu over them or as a dip. Add a dash of vinegar if you like. Makes 3 servings.

SQUASHED RADISHES

½ cup red radishes
2 leaves iceberg lettuce
1 tablespoon lemon juice or
  vinegar

1 teaspoon Japanese shoyu
  (soy sauce)
½ teaspoon sesame oil or
  vegetable oil

Wash radishes and trim away ends. Lay radishes on their sides and squash with flat side of cleaver or bottom of a flat skillet or saucepan to produce colorful irregular shapes. Serve on lettuce leaves as a salad with dressing, made by combining remaining ingredients, poured over it. Makes 1 serving.

SOY WITH RADISH (Shoyu No Daikon)

2 to 3 large daikon (radishes),
  about 2 pounds

1 teaspoon Japanese shoyu (soy
  sauce)

Peel daikon and slice crosswise in about ¼-inch slices. Place in crock; pour shoyu over and turn a few times. Cover and store in cool place or refrigerator for at least 24 hours. Will keep a few days, but be sure to turn them daily. Serve as a side dish with meat or fish. Makes 8 servings.

BOILED TURNIPS

4 cups peeled and diced small
  turnips

1½ cups bouillon
Japanese shoyu (soy sauce)

Boil turnips in bouillon until tender, 8 to 10 minutes. Serve and sprinkle shoyu over them. Makes 4 servings.

SUNOMONO DRESSINGS (For Japanese Vegetables)

I

3 tablespoons vegetable oil (or half vegetable and half sesame oil)
2 tablespoons vinegar

2 tablespoons lemon juice
1 tablespoon Japanese shoyu (soy sauce)
2 teaspoons sherry extract

Combine all ingredients in a jar with a lid. Shake well and pour over vegetables, fish or meat. If prepared prior to serving, shake again just before serving. Makes 3 servings.

II

6 tablespoons vinegar
Artificial sweetener to equal 2 tablespoons sugar

1 teaspoon Japanese shoyu (soy sauce)

Combine all ingredients in a small bowl. Pour over vegetables, fish or meat. Makes 3 servings.

SUKIYAKI ORANGE SLICES

2 small oranges
½ cup orange juice
2 tablespoons Japanese shoyu (soy sauce)

1 tablespoon lemon juice
2 ounces sliced onion

Peel oranges; slice each orange into four slices. In a large skillet, heat orange juice, soy sauce, lemon juice and onions to boiling. Reduce heat. Add orange slices; heat. Divide portions equally. Makes 2 servings.

Latin America

No handful of dishes can do more than suggest the wonderful foods of our neighbors to the south. From country to country, different influences have been at work. In Mexico alone, where the background is not only Spanish but also Indian (from the primitive Soris to the civilized Mayas and Aztecs), there is a tremendous variety of taste-tempting dishes. In Argentina and Paraguay, the cuisines show strong Italian accents; in Colombia and Venezuela, certainly in wealthier homes, French foods are popular, as they are in Brazil, where the cuisine and life-styles mostly reflect the Portuguese colonization.

But Latin America also has some common denominators, not only in the Spanish language (except in Brazil) but also in its food tastes. Recipes which include garlic, onion, peppers and tomatoes, plus spices derived from hot red peppers, all recall their Iberian origins, as do the *pucheros* (stews), *arroz con pollo* (chicken with rice) and bean and cornmeal dishes.

So here then is our glimpse of the foods of Mexico, Central America and South America—a gourmet's tour for people who are hooked on staying thin even as they cook their way down the Americas.

"CREAM" OF ARTICHOKE SOUP

This soup may also be chilled.

10 ounces frozen artichoke hearts	Garlic powder to taste (optional)
2 ounces minced scallions (white part) or onion	Salt and pepper to taste
	½ cup evaporated skimmed milk
3 cups chicken bouillon	3 thin slices lemon

Cook artichoke hearts following package directions. Add scallions and continue cooking until tender. Add more water, if necessary. Reserve 2 artichoke hearts. Puree remaining artichoke/scallion mixture in blender or food processor using the liquid from the cooking. Return pureed vegetable to saucepan. Add bouillon, garlic powder, salt and pepper. Simmer 10 to 15 minutes. Pour in skimmed milk; stir well and heat without boiling. Serve in bowls with dice of remaining 2 artichoke hearts. Top each serving with lemon slice. Makes 3 servings.

"CREAM" OF VEGETABLE SOUP, RANCH STYLE
(Sopa Ranchera)

½ cup diced carrots	Dash of nutmeg
4 ounces banana squash, diced	Salt and pepper to taste
1 cup diced celery	Garnish: watercress or chopped fresh parsley
1 tablespoon dehydrated onion flakes	
1 cup skim milk plus 1 cup vegetable liquid or water	

In saucepan, cook together diced carrots, squash, celery and onion flakes in 1½ cups water until tender. Drain off liquid, measure and add to milk. Return to saucepan with vegetables. Sprinkle with nutmeg, salt and pepper. Heat without boiling. If watercress is available, shred ¼ cup and add to soup just before removing from heat. Or use parsley. Makes 2 servings.

ASPARAGUS GUACAMOLE

Cut off the scales which hold sand and break the asparagus spears to remove the tough ends. (These ends can be peeled and cooked to make soup.) Cover spears with boiling salted water and cook 8 to 10 minutes or until tender. Drain. Puree in food mill, blender or food processor.

2 cups cooked asparagus, pureed
2 ounces grated onion
1 tablespoon lemon juice
1 garlic clove, minced

12 drops hot pepper sauce
½ teaspoon salt
¼ teaspoon chili powder
Freshly ground pepper to taste

Combine ingredients in bowl. Mix well. Serve in a bowl just as you would Guacamole. Makes 2 servings.

CHEESE AND CHILI DIP (Chile con Queso)

4 ounces processed American cheese
2 ounces cheddar cheese
½ cup evaporated skimmed milk
1 medium tomato, finely chopped
1 frozen or canned green chile, seeded and chopped

3 ounces scallions, finely chopped
⅛ teaspoon garlic powder or small piece of garlic
Dash cayenne pepper (optional)

Dice cheeses and melt in double boiler or in saucepan, over low heat. When cheese melts, stir in milk; continue stirring until it is thoroughly mixed. Add tomato, chile, scallions, garlic powder and cayenne. Heat thoroughly, stirring for about 15 minutes. Serve in fondue pot or in small covered dishes. Reheat if necessary. Use as dip for raw vegetables. Makes 3 servings.

TOMATO OMELET

1 medium tomato, peeled and diced
2 medium eggs, lightly beaten

¼ teaspoon salt
Dash of pepper
1 teaspoon chopped fresh chives

In small preheated nonstick skillet, cook tomato until it loses most of its moisture, stirring constantly. Add eggs and allow to set. Sprinkle with salt and pepper. Cook over moderately high heat. As mixture sets, lift up edges with fork, tilting the pan so that uncooked portions flow evenly to bottom. Serve soft set or turn with spatula to brown other side. Fold over and serve at once, sprinkled with chives. Makes 1 serving.

BAKED WHITEFISH WITH TOMATO SAUCE

6 ounces onion, finely chopped
1½ medium green peppers, diced
3 packets instant chicken broth
 and seasoning mix
3 canned medium tomatoes,
 crushed
1½ cups tomato puree

½ small bay leaf
½ teaspoon thyme
¼ teaspoon garlic powder
Dash cayenne pepper
Dash salt
3 pounds boned whitefish

In a nonstick skillet, cook onions until transparent. Add green pepper and sprinkle on broth mix; cook for 3 minutes. Stir in remaining ingredients except fish; simmer for 20 minutes. Place fish in baking dish; top with sauce. Bake in 350°F. oven for 40 to 45 minutes or until fish flakes with a fork. Makes 6 servings.

CHICKEN WITH SWISS CHARD

2 8-ounce skinned and boned
 chicken breasts
3 cups water
2 ounces onion, chopped

⅓ cup diced carrots
3 cups Swiss chard (or spinach)
Salt and pepper to taste

Brown chicken on both sides in nonstick skillet, then transfer to saucepan and add water, onion and carrots. Cover and cook 20 minutes. Put stemmed Swiss chard on top of chicken, cover tightly and cook until chard is tender (5 to 6 minutes); do not overcook chard as it gets bitter. Serve as stew. Makes 2 servings.

BAKED ORANGE CHICKEN WITH MUSHROOM STUFFING

2½- to 3-pound chicken, skinned
Mushroom Stuffing (recipe
 follows), optional
½ teaspoon salt

¼ teaspoon cinnamon
½ cup orange juice
1 small orange, unpeeled, sliced

Broil the chicken on all sides, turning to brown. Meanwhile prepare Mushroom Stuffing. Put stuffing in 12x8-inch baking dish. Add broiled chicken. Mix salt and cinnamon with orange juice, and pour over chicken. Top with orange slices. Bake in moderately hot oven (375°F.) 20 to 25 minutes until chicken is tender. Weigh chicken portions and divide stuffing evenly. Makes 4 servings.

NOTE: If too much browning occurs, cover with foil for last part of baking time.

Mushroom Stuffing for Chicken

1 tablespoon dehydrated onion flakes, reconstituted
1 tablespoon chopped fresh parsley
1 garlic clove, minced or pressed
4 cups fresh mushrooms, finely chopped

Combine onion, parsley and garlic. Mix with mushrooms and place in casserole. Bake as above. Makes 4 servings.

CHICKEN NICARAGUENSE

2 8-ounce skinned and boned chicken breasts
1 medium green pepper, chopped
½ cup diced celery
2 ounces onion, chopped
⅓ cup diced carrots
1 garlic clove, finely minced
1 cup tomato juice
2 cups sliced summer squash
1 teaspoon cumin
Salt and freshly ground black pepper to taste
2 ounces fresh or frozen peas

Brown chicken on both sides in nonstick skillet, then transfer to a casserole or Dutch oven. Add green pepper, celery, onion, carrots and garlic to the skillet in which the chicken cooked. Cook briefly, stirring until vegetables are cooked but crisp. Spoon the vegetables over the chicken and add the tomato juice, squash, cumin, salt and pepper. Cover the casserole and bake 50 minutes or until the chicken is tender when pierced with a fork. Add the peas, and return casserole to oven, covered, for 10 more minutes. Makes 2 servings.

CHICKEN WITH RICE (Arroz con Pollo)

8 ounces boned chicken breast
2 ounces onion, finely chopped
¼ cup sliced mushrooms
½ medium tomato, peeled and chopped
1 ounce cooked peas

½ cup cooked enriched rice
1 tablespoon chopped pimento
½ cup tomato juice
½ cup chicken bouillon
Salt and pepper to taste

Place chicken under broiler 4 inches from heat. Cook for 8 to 10 minutes until brown, turning frequently. Remove skin and set chicken aside. Lightly brown onions and mushrooms in nonstick pan. Transfer to a small casserole; add tomato, peas, rice and pimento. Cut chicken into small pieces and add to rice mixture. Add tomato juice and bouillon; season to taste. Bake, covered, at 375°F. for 15 to 20 minutes, until liquid is absorbed. Makes 1 serving.

TRIPE WITH TOMATOES

2¼ pounds precooked tripe
Salted water
½ lemon
1¼ cups chicken bouillon, divided
6 ounces sliced onions
1 medium green pepper, chopped
1½ hot green chili peppers, finely chopped

2 garlic cloves, pressed
5 medium canned tomatoes
2 tablespoons Worcestershire
2 tablespoons chopped capers
1 tablespoon chopped fresh coriander
1 teaspoon oregano
Salt and pepper to taste
½ cup tomato paste

In a large stainless steel pot, cover tripe with salted water. Squeeze in juice from lemon and include whole rind. Simmer until tender, about 2 hours. Drain and discard lemon rind. Cut tripe into 1-inch squares. Return to pot; set aside. In a large nonstick skillet, place ¼ cup bouillon with onion, green pepper, chili pepper and garlic. Cook, stirring occasionally, until onions become translucent. Add to pot with tripe. Add tomatoes, Worcestershire, capers, coriander, oregano, salt and pepper and remaining bouillon. Simmer 15 minutes. Add tomato paste and stir to combine. Cover. Simmer 30 to 45 minutes or until tripe is very tender. Divide evenly and serve. Makes 6 servings.

CARBONADO BOLIVIA

Usually served with rice.

1½ pounds freshly broiled beef, cut in cubes
3 cups water
1 teaspoon cider vinegar
½ teaspoon salt
1 bay leaf
½ teaspoon ground cumin
6 peppercorns
1 garlic clove, crushed
4 ribs celery, sliced
1 medium tomato, diced
½ cup peeled and cubed carrots
1 ounce onion, chopped
½ teaspoon oregano
4 medium apricots, cut into halves and pitted (optional)
4 medium plums or 2 medium peaches, quartered and pitted

Place meat in saucepan with water, vinegar, salt, bay leaf, cumin, peppercorns and garlic. Cover and simmer slowly for about one hour. Add celery, tomato, carrots, onion and oregano. Stir to combine. Add fruit. Cover and cook until fruits are tender. Makes 4 servings.

"TACOS"

Our version of Tacos.

4 ounces cooked ground veal
1 teaspoon chili powder
1 teaspoon dehydrated onion flakes
¼ teaspoon salt
¼ teaspoon onion powder
¼ teaspoon paprika
Dash hot pepper sauce
1 slice enriched white bread
Toothpicks
½ cup shredded lettuce
"Creamy" Pimento Dressing (see page 249)

Place veal in nonstick pan. Add seasonings and cook 5 minutes. Toast bread lightly. Spread meat mixture over one half of the toast; fold and hold in place with toothpicks. Combine lettuce and 1 tablespoon "Creamy" Pimento Dressing; cover taco. Makes 1 serving.

HOMEMADE CHORIZO*

12 ounces roasted pork
1 garlic clove
2 tablespoons vinegar or lemon juice
1 tablespoon chili powder
1 teaspoon salt
Dash of grated nutmeg, marjoram or cumin (optional)

Put roasted pork and garlic through the food chopper or processor. Transfer to a medium mixing bowl. Add remaining ingredients, mix well and pack into a pint crockery pot or glass jar, pressing it down with the back of a spoon. Cover tightly and refrigerate. Makes 4 servings.

EGGPLANT WITH "CREAMY" PIMENTO DRESSING

2 cups diced eggplant
½ garlic clove, minced
1 tablespoon lemon juice
1 teaspoon salt

2 ounces onion, chopped
¼ cup chopped celery
Romaine lettuce

Cover eggplant with water and bring to a boil. Add garlic, lemon juice and salt and simmer about 5 minutes until just tender. Drain and cool. Mix with onion and celery. Serve on romaine lettuce with "Creamy" Pimento Dressing (recipe follows). Makes 1 serving.

"Creamy" Pimento Dressing

3-ounce jar pimentos, drained
1 tablespoon white vinegar
1 teaspoon prepared mustard

¼ cup + 2 tablespoons buttermilk

Place all ingredients in blender container. Process until smooth. Makes 1 serving.

EGGPLANT CASSEROLE (Berenjenas en Cacerola)

4 cups raw eggplant, cut into ½-inch slices
1½ cups tomato puree
2 tablespoons canned pimento, drained and diced
2 tablespoons canned green chiles, seeded and chopped

1 tablespoon dehydrated onion flakes
½ teaspoon ground cumin
½ teaspoon garlic salt
8 ounces shredded cheddar cheese

Place unpeeled eggplant in a single layer on a nonstick baking sheet; bake uncovered in hot oven (450°F.) until soft, about 20 minutes. In a saucepan, combine next 6 ingredients; bring to a boil. Lower heat and simmer, uncovered, for 10 minutes. Lower oven temperature to 350°F. Line bottom of a shallow 1½-quart casserole with a single layer of eggplant, spoon on half the sauce, and sprinkle with half of the cheese; repeat, ending with cheese on top. Bake, uncovered, until hot and bubbly, about 25 minutes. Makes 4 servings.

EGGPLANT WITH CHEESE (Berenjenas con Queso)

2 cups peeled and cubed eggplant
Salt
2 ounces American cheese, grated, divided
½ medium apple, pared, chopped
1 slice enriched white bread, made into crumbs
¼ cup chopped fresh parsley
1 teaspoon vegetable oil

In medium bowl, sprinkle eggplant with salt; let stand 30 minutes; rinse well. Parboil eggplant in boiling water for 5 minutes; drain. Combine the eggplant, half the cheese and apple in a medium casserole. Mix the bread crumbs, remaining cheese, parsley, ¼ teaspoon salt and oil; sprinkle over eggplant mixture. Bake in 350°F. oven for 30 to 35 minutes. Makes 1 serving.

CHILI CON CARNE

More Tex than Mex? Omit tomatoes? Use beef instead of pork? The arguments on these subjects are as fiery as the dish itself.

1 pound red (kidney or pinto) cooked dried beans, drained (save liquid)
12 ounces roasted pork, cut into fine pieces
1 cup liquid (beef bouillon plus bean liquid)
4 medium canned tomatoes
1 medium green pepper, diced
¾ cup tomato puree
1 tablespoon dehydrated onion flakes
1 teaspoon chili powder
½ teaspoon oregano
¼ teaspoon chocolate extract (optional)
⅛ teaspoon ground cumin
2 garlic cloves, crushed

In kettle combine ingredients. Break up the tomatoes with the back of a wooden spoon. Simmer about 40 minutes or until thick. Makes 4 servings.

FRESH CHILI RELISH (Salsa)

1 medium tomato
4 ounces onion
½ garlic clove
4-ounce can of chopped green chile or jalapeños

Chop tomato, onion, garlic and chile very fine. Let stand up to one week (refrigerated in closed container). Makes 4 servings. Use as sauce for roasted meat or poached fish.

CHILI SAUCE

5¾ cups (46 fluid ounces) mixed vegetable juice
½ cup wine vinegar
3 ribs celery, diced
3 tablespoons dehydrated onion flakes
1 tablespoon prepared horseradish
1 tablespoon steak sauce
1¾ teaspoons chili powder
½ garlic clove, mash to extract juices
1 teaspoon browning sauce
3 to 4 drops hot pepper sauce
Artificial sweetener to equal 6 teaspoons sugar
Salt and pepper to taste
1 chili pepper, diced
1 bay leaf

Combine all ingredients in large saucepan; bring to a boil. Cover and simmer, stirring occasionally, until reduced to half. Remove bay leaf. Serves: one tablespoon equates to two tablespoons (one fluid ounce) mixed vegetable juice.

BLACK BEAN AND RICE STEW (Feijoada)

Black beans are a staple of the Brazilian diet but soybeans are catching on too—and are now a huge crop in this country.

1 medium green pepper, diced
1 small garlic clove, crushed
½ teaspoon oregano
¼ teaspoon cumin
¼ cup beef bouillon
8 ounces cooked dried black (turtle) beans
½ cup cooked brown rice
1 ounce slice red onion

In saucepan combine green pepper, garlic, oregano and cumin with ¼ cup beef bouillon. Simmer 10 minutes; stir in black beans and rice and more bouillon if desired. Serve in bowl with slice of raw onion. Makes 1 serving.

SWEET PEPPER AND MUSHROOM SALAD

2 medium green peppers
2 medium red peppers
2 cups mushrooms
2 tablespoons lemon juice, divided
2 garlic cloves, chopped fine
¼ cup vegetable oil

Broil peppers over an open gas flame close to broiler unit until skins are wrinkled and browned, turning as necessary. Pop them into a paper bag and let stand 10 minutes; then peel off skins under cold running water and remove seeds. Cut peppers into 1-inch strips. Cut mushrooms into thin slices from cap through stem. Sprinkle them with 1 tablespoon of the lemon juice to preserve color. Combine with pepper strips. Combine garlic, oil and remaining 1 tablespoon lemon juice and let stand. Just before serving, pour salad dressing over mushrooms and peppers and serve at once. Makes 4 servings.

SHREDDED BEEF AND ORANGE SALAD
(Ensalada de Carne y Naranjas)

Cooked green beans or tender raw florets of cauliflower are good with this combination too.

6 ounces cooked shredded beef	1 teaspoon vinegar
1 ounce thinly sliced onions	¼ teaspoon salt
1 small orange, peeled and diced	Dash pepper
1 tablespoon vegetable oil	Lettuce leaves

In bowl combine meat, onions and oranges; toss lightly until well mixed. Combine vegetable oil, vinegar, salt and pepper; shake well. Pour over meat-orange mixture; toss lightly until well mixed. Refrigerate covered at least 2 hours. Before serving, toss lightly again until well mixed. Serve on lettuce leaves. Makes 1 serving.

MEXICAN RICE (Arroz Mexicano)

1 medium tomato, diced	1 teaspoon minced fresh chives
⅓ cup diced carrots	1 teaspoon minced fresh parsley
2 ounces peas	¾ teaspoon marjoram
¼ cup diced mushrooms	⅛ teaspoon crushed red pepper or
¼ cup diced celery	dash of cayenne pepper or
2 teaspoons dehydrated onion	hot pepper sauce
flakes	½ cup chicken bouillon
1 small garlic clove, crushed	1 cup cooked enriched rice

Cook tomato, carrots, peas, mushrooms, celery, onion flakes, garlic, chives, parsley, marjoram and pepper in bouillon until celery is tender. Combine with rice. Cook until most of the liquid is evaporated or bake uncovered in moderate oven (350°F.) until liquid evaporates. Makes 2 servings.

SAFFRON RICE (Arroz Amarillo)

2 cups cooked enriched rice
½ cup chicken bouillon
½ teaspoon dehydrated onion
flakes

Pinch saffron
1 tablespoon finely diced pimento,
rinsed

Combine all ingredients, except pimento, in saucepan. Cook over low heat until all liquid is absorbed. Add pimento and mix well. Makes 4 servings.

CUMIN RICE

Omit saffron from preceding recipe and substitute ½ teaspoon cumin. Makes 4 servings.

CHICK PEA CAKE (Torta de Garbanzos)

½ cup evaporated skimmed milk
12 ounces cooked dried garbanzos
4 medium eggs, separated
Artificial sweetener to equal ½
cup sugar

2 teaspoons brandy or wine
extract
1 teaspoon cinnamon

Pour milk in blender container or food processor; add garbanzos and process. In a separate bowl, beat egg yolks until light in color. Add sweetener, extract and cinnamon; add garbanzos and mix well. Beat egg whites until stiff but not dry. Fold into garbanzo mixture. Pour into an 8x8x3-inch nonstick baking pan or pan sprayed with release agent. Bake in moderate oven (350°F.) until center is done, or about 1 hour. Chill and serve cold. Makes 4 servings.

PINEAPPLE "CHEESECAKE"

1 cup skim milk ricotta cheese
3 medium eggs, separated
1 tablespoon lemon juice
½ teaspoon vanilla extract
Artificial sweetener to equal 4
teaspoons sugar

¼ teaspoon salt
1½ cups canned crushed
pineapple, no sugar added,
drained, reserving liquid
2 envelopes unflavored gelatin

In a medium-size mixing bowl, place ricotta cheese and beat with an electric mixer on high speed until smooth and fluffy, 3 to 4 minutes.

[253]

Beat in egg yolks, one at a time, blending well after each addition. Add lemon juice, vanilla extract, sweetener and salt. Beat well. Stir pineapple into cheese-egg mixture. Pour pineapple juice in a small saucepan and sprinkle gelatin over. Heat to dissolve gelatin. Allow to cool. Beat egg whites until stiff but not dry. Pour pineapple juice-gelatin mixture into cheese-egg mixture. Mix well with a spatula. Fold in egg whites. Transfer to a 9-inch nonstick cake pan. Place pan in a water bath, with water coming up the sides of cake pan as high as batter mixture. Bake for 1 hour at 350°F. or until cake is brown and dry on top. Cool. Refrigerate when cake reaches room temperature. Serve cold. Makes 3 servings.

SPICED GRAPES

1 cup red wine vinegar
¾ cup white sugar replacement
¾ cup brown sugar replacement
3 sticks cinnamon
3 cloves
1 tablespoon dehydrated onion flakes
½ teaspoon burgundy extract
60 small seedless grapes

In kettle combine vinegar, sugar replacements, cinnamon, cloves, onion flakes and extract. Bring to boil; lower heat and simmer 10 minutes. Pour over grapes. Cover and let stand until cool, then chill. Drain and discard liquid, cloves and cinnamon. Makes 6 servings.

MEXICAN CARROT CAKE (Torta de Zanahoria)*

4 cups finely grated carrots
4 teaspoons lemon rind, grated
4 teaspoons lemon juice
1 teaspoon vanilla extract
Artificial sweetener to equal 6 tablespoons sugar (or to taste)
¼ cup margarine, melted, or vegetable oil
4 medium eggs, beaten
2 slices enriched white bread, made into crumbs

Combine carrots, lemon rind, lemon juice and vanilla extract; set aside. Combine sweetener with margarine; stir in eggs. Add crumb and carrot mixture. Bake in nine-inch spring form pan in moderate oven (350°F.) for 1 hour or until top is browned and eggs set. Makes 4 servings.

PAPAYA WITH LIME JUICE

1 medium papaya cut into ½-inch cubes   2 tablespoons lime juice

In medium bowl sprinkle lime juice over cubes and chill for at least 30 minutes before serving. Makes 2 servings.

HONDURAS MILK SHAKE

This frosty milk shake needs no added sweetener if you use a very ripe banana.

1 very ripe medium banana   ½ teaspoon vanilla extract
½ cup water   4 ice cubes
⅓ cup nonfat dry milk

Use a banana with brown mottled skin. Put in plastic bag and freeze. Before use, slightly defrost banana, peel, cut into slices, and put in blender container with water, milk, vanilla extract and an ice cube. Process at low speed, adding one cube at a time. Serve in tall glass. A deliciously sweet and frothy summer milk shake. Makes 2 servings.

Middle East

If Scheherazade had been entertaining a gourmet sultan, regaling him with fabulous recipes rather than Arabian fables, she could have spent a thousand and one nights just telling tales about eggplant, so exceedingly popular is that vegetable in Arabic countries. We, too, have culinary stories to recite, not only of eggplant but also of marvelous mint-scented soups and stews, of fabled pilavs rich with cinnamon, of chunks of meat skewered on vicious swords and roasted to perfect succulency, of vegetables so deliciously stuffed that even a ruling sovereign will find them irresistible. And now, we hope you are as curious as the sultan was, and are prepared to listen to our Arabian tales.

SWEET YOGURT SOUP

Middle Easterners use an enormous amount of yogurt, especially in soup, and there are almost as many recipes for yogurt soup as there are cooks, with every cook adding his own personal touch. Here's one authentic soup that will provide a new taste sensation for most of us.

2 cups plain yogurt
1 cup water
4 pitted, medium dried prunes quartered
1 medium cucumber, peeled and cut in pieces

Salt and pepper to taste
1 tablespoon chopped fresh chives and/or dill
Parsley to garnish

Combine first five ingredients in blender container; process until smooth. Stir in chives or dill. Chill and garnish with parsley before serving. Serve in bowls. Divide evenly into 4 servings.

MINTED CONSOMME

3 tablespoons boiling water
2 tablespoons chopped fresh mint leaves

¾ cup hot chicken bouillon

Pour boiling water over mint leaves and let stand 25 minutes. Combine with hot chicken bouillon and serve at once. A pick-me-up that doesn't put you down at weigh-in time. Makes 1 serving.

LENTIL AND SPINACH SOUP*

12 ounces freshly cooked dried lentils (reserve liquid)
Lentil liquid, plus water, to equal 3 cups liquid
1½ cups frozen chopped spinach, thawed and well drained

3 packets instant beef broth and seasoning mix
3 ounces sliced onion
1 tablespoon lemon juice
Freshly ground pepper to taste

In a large saucepan, combine lentils, liquid, spinach, broth mix and onion. Cover and simmer 20 minutes. Stir in lemon juice and serve hot with sprinkling of pepper. Makes 3 servings.

POACHED EGGS WITH GARLIC

A good breakfast dish if you are planning to ride the New York subway. It won't help in Turkey, because there almost everything is flavored with garlic.

½ cup buttermilk
1 teaspoon vinegar
1 garlic clove, mashed
Dash salt, paprika, pepper

Hot pepper sauce to taste
2 medium eggs, poached
Parsley to garnish

In small saucepan, combine buttermilk, vinegar, garlic, salt, paprika, pepper and hot pepper sauce. Beat together. Heat and divide into 2 small bowls. Slide 1 poached egg (careful not to break it) into each bowl. Garnish with parsley and serve at once. Makes 2 servings.

EGGS AND CHEESE

4 ounces grated hard cheese
4 medium eggs

Salt and pepper to taste

Use 4 custard cups. Into each of the cups, sprinkle ½ ounce layer of cheese; break an egg over each cheese layer; cover with another ½ ounce of grated cheese. Sprinkle with salt and pepper and bake in preheated hot oven (400°F.) until eggs are done, about 6 minutes. Serve piping hot. Makes 4 servings.

SWEET AND SOUR BAKED FISH

2 pounds whitefish fillet or striped bass fillet, cut into serving pieces
8 ounces onions, peeled and sliced
1 garlic clove
¼ cup chicken bouillon
1 teaspoon curry powder

¼ teaspoon cumin
Salt and pepper to taste
Dash of turmeric
2 medium tomatoes, sliced into ¼-inch slices
½ cup lemon juice
Artificial sweetener to equal ¼ cup sugar

Wash fish in cold water and dry with paper towels. Place in nonstick baking dish. Steam onions and garlic in ¼ cup chicken bouillon until soft, 5 to 6 minutes. Add curry, cumin, salt, pepper and turmeric and cook 2 minutes more. Spread over fish. Put tomato slices on top.

Sprinkle with lemon juice and salt. Cover dish with aluminum foil and bake in moderate oven (350°F.) for 25 minutes. Remove from oven. Spoon off some liquid from pan and mix it with artificial sweetener. Put sweetened liquid back in pan, basting fish with it. Makes 4 servings.

MEAT PATTIES WITH EGGPLANT

"Delicious" was the test-kitchen report when this was prepared.

4 cups peeled eggplant, sliced ¼-inch thick
1 pound ground beef
1 tablespoon dehydrated onion flakes
1 tablespoon chopped fresh parsley
1 small garlic clove, minced fine
1 teaspoon salt
Pepper to taste
¾ cup tomato puree

Soak eggplant in cold water to cover for 10 minutes. Drain and dry. Set aside. Meanwhile, combine beef, onion flakes, parsley, garlic, salt and pepper. Mix well, shape into 2 even, large patties and broil on preheated rack, turning once. In baking dish make a layer of eggplant slices, add the broiled beef patties and top with remaining eggplant. Pour in tomato puree; cover and bake in moderate oven (350°F.) for 1 hour. Serve hot. Makes 2 servings.

SWEET AND SOUR BEEF WITH BEETS

1 pound lean round steak, ground
¾ cup chopped fresh parsley
¼ cup lemon juice, divided
Dash pepper and paprika
8 ounces canned beets (reserve liquid)
Artificial sweetener to equal 3 tablespoons sugar
Pinch of salt

Combine beef, parsley, 2 tablespoons lemon juice, pepper and paprika. Mix well. Shape into 4 even patties and broil 4 inches from heat, on rack, turning once. In saucepan combine beets with reserved liquid and water to equal 1½ cups, remaining lemon juice, artificial sweetener and salt. Bring to boil; add beef and let simmer 15 to 20 minutes. Serve hot. Makes 2 servings.

ARABIAN CHICKEN GIBLETS AND VERMICELLI

1½ pounds gizzards, cut in
   quarters
3 cups chicken bouillon
¼ cup chopped fresh parsley
¼ teaspoon each thyme,
   marjoram and mint

4 garlic cloves, minced or pressed
Salt and pepper to taste
Dash hot pepper sauce
2⅔ cups cooked enriched thin
   vermicelli

Combine all ingredients except vermicelli in a medium saucepan. Bring to a boil, reduce heat and let simmer for 1 hour or until gizzards are tender. Drain and discard liquid. Divide evenly into 4 portions. Serve each with ⅔ cup vermicelli. Makes 4 servings.

LAMB AND VEGETABLE STEW (Türlü Givech)

1 pound trimmed boneless lamb
2 ounces onion, diced
1 medium green pepper, cut in
   squares
1 medium tomato, sliced
1 cup green beans, sliced
1 cup peeled eggplant, cut in
   1½-inch cubes

1 cup zucchini, cut in 1½-inch
   cubes
3 ounces okra, sliced
Salt and pepper to taste
Paprika
1 cup water

Broil meat on rack in broiler, turning to brown all sides (about 15 minutes). Transfer to 2-quart shallow casserole. Combine remaining ingredients except water, mix well, and pour over lamb in casserole. Add water. Cover casserole and bake in moderate oven (350°F.) for 45 minutes to 1 hour, or until meat and vegetables are tender. Makes 2 servings.

LOOLA KABOB

1½ pounds lean boneless lamb,
   cut from leg
8 ounces top round steak
¼ cup chopped fresh
   parsley, divided
1 tablespoon chopped fresh
   chives
½ teaspoon black pepper

½ teaspoon allspice
Salt to taste
Cayenne pepper to taste
   (optional)
4 wooden sticks or skewers
   (12 inches long)
4 ounces diced red onion
2 cups cooked enriched rice

Grind lamb and beef together in a meat grinder or food processor. Add 2 tablespoons of the parsley, chives, black pepper, allspice, salt and cayenne pepper. Mix with hands until mixture is uniform. Roll into 8 rolls each about 3 inches long (like sausages). Place 2 "sausages" on each skewer. Place on rack and grill over hot charcoal or indoors on a rack in broiler about 4 inches from source of heat and broil until done on all sides, turning to brown evenly. With side of knife, gently push rolls off skewers onto serving plates and serve hot over rice. Diced onions and the remaining parsley are the accompaniments. Makes 4 servings.

LIVER PILAF (Tockov Pilav)

1 pound chicken livers
½ cup boiling salted water
1 cup cooked enriched rice
¾ cup tomato puree

1 tablespoon dehydrated onion flakes
Parsley sprigs for garnish

Cook liver in ½ cup boiling salted water until done; do not overcook; liver should stay soft and moist. Drain, taste liquid: if it is bitter, discard and substitute chicken bouillon, otherwise reserve liquid. Chop ¼ of cooled liver using coarse blade of food chopper, by hand or food processor. Return to pan with ¼ cup reserved liquid or bouillon. Add rice, tomato puree and onion flakes. Stir to combine. Add whole livers and simmer gently for 15 minutes. Serve in bowls with parsley to garnish. Makes 2 servings.

STUFFED TOMATO

2 medium tomatoes
2 ounces onion, chopped
8 ounces cooked ground lamb, crumbled

1 cup cooked enriched rice
½ teaspoon chopped fresh mint
½ teaspoon chopped fresh dill
Salt and pepper to taste

Slice tops off tomatoes and remove and reserve pulp and seeds. Cook onion in nonstick pan; add lamb and heat through. Add tomato pulp, rice, mint, dill, salt and pepper. Fill tomato shells with mixture and replace tops. Place in casserole with ¼ cup water and any filling that doesn't fit in tomatoes. Cover and bake in 325°F. oven for 30 minutes. Serve hot. Makes 2 servings.

EGGPLANT PUREE

Eggplant broiled over an open gas fire has a delicious smoked taste. Put it under cold running water and you can easily peel off charred skin.

1 large eggplant (about 6 cups)
4 ounces onion, finely diced
½ to 1 cup finely diced (inside ribs) celery
1 garlic clove
1 tablespoon chopped fresh parsley

1 tablespoon lemon juice
Salt and pepper to taste
Lettuce leaves
4 teaspoons sesame or vegetable oil

Bake eggplant whole or broil on rack over open flame until it is very soft and collapsed on all sides. Peel off skin and remove any large seeds. Mash eggplant. Stir in onions, celery, garlic, parsley, lemon juice, salt and pepper. Serve on lettuce leaves. Make a well in each serving and, at the table, stir 1 teaspoon oil into each well. Mix. Makes 4 servings.

MINTED PEAS AND CARROTS

1 tablespoon margarine
1 teaspoon chopped fresh mint leaves
⅛ teaspoon salt

⅛ teaspoon white pepper
4 ounces cooked peas
¾ cup cooked sliced carrots

In top of double boiler over boiling water heat margarine, mint leaves, salt and pepper until margarine melts. Mix in peas and carrots; heat. Makes 2 servings.

"CREAMED" GARLIC SPINACH

2 cups fresh spinach
Boiling water
1 cup skim milk

1 garlic clove, crushed
1 teaspoon imitation (or diet) margarine (optional)

Place spinach in a colander. Blanch by pouring boiling water over it. Drain and squeeze out moisture. Chop spinach and combine in a small saucepan with milk and garlic. Simmer until milk evaporates. Remove from heat. Remove garlic. If desired, stir in margarine until it melts. Serve immediately. Makes 1 serving.

"CREAMED" EGGPLANT

Short chunky eggplants make decorative containers for "Creamed" Eggplant. To prepare, slice and reserve top; cut out the eggplant meat, leaving a thick shell. Cook the eggplant following this recipe below. Stuff "Creamed" Eggplant into case and garnish as in our color plate.

1 cup cooked, mashed eggplant	Salt and pepper to taste
¼ cup skim milk	

Combine ingredients in small saucepan. Heat gently; beat mixture until it is the consistency of fluffy potatoes. Serve as meat accompaniment. Makes 2 servings.

PICKLED TURNIPS

3½ cups sliced small white turnips	Vinegar to cover
2 ounces beets, sliced	1 teaspoon salt
Water to cover	3 garlic cloves, crushed

Soak turnips and beets in water overnight. Drain and rinse. Place in jar or jars with all other ingredients for at least 3 days. These pickled rose-colored turnips are very popular as meze (appetizer). Makes 4 servings.

TOOTH OF LOVE STRING BEANS*

4 ounces sliced onion	6 tablespoons chopped fresh
1½ medium green peppers, diced	parsley
1 cup beef bouillon	¾ teaspoon salt
1½ medium tomatoes, sliced	¼ teaspoon pepper
1 cup diced celery	4 medium eggs
3 cups frozen cut green beans	

In wide shallow flameproof casserole, cook onions and green peppers in bouillon until soft. Add tomatoes, celery, beans, parsley, salt and pepper. Cover and simmer gently about 15 minutes or until tender. Just before serving, break each of the 4 eggs into a cup, then slide onto the vegetable mixture. Set the casserole in a hot oven (400°F.) and cook uncovered until the eggs are firm. Makes 4 servings.

LEBANESE SALAD

1 garlic clove
½ teaspoon salt
1 teaspoon mint (or 1 tablespoon chopped fresh mint leaves)

1½ cups buttermilk
2 medium cucumbers, peeled and sliced
1 cup cooked green beans

Mash garlic with salt and mint to a paste. Stir into buttermilk. Add cucumber slices and green beans. Chill. Makes 4 servings.

RICE "CREAM"

¼ cup cold water
1½ teaspoons unflavored gelatin
¼ cup skim milk
Rind of ½ lemon, grated
Artificial sweetener to equal
    ¼ cup sugar

Dash salt
½ cup cooked enriched rice
½ cup canned crushed pineapple, no sugar added, divided

Pour water into blender container. Sprinkle gelatin over water to soften. In a small saucepan, combine milk, lemon rind, sweetener and salt, and bring to a boil. Add rice and simmer for 15 to 20 minutes or until no more of the liquid is visible. Transfer rice mixture to blender container with softened gelatin. Add all, except 2 tablespoons pineapple, and process until smooth. Pour into a medium mixing bowl and add remaining pineapple, stirring to combine. Pour into 2-cup mold and refrigerate until set. Makes 1 serving.

YOGURT AND PRUNE "PIE"*

This dessert treat comes from Yugoslavia, famous for its prunes, yogurt and the "sweet tooth" of its people.

2 medium eggs, separated
1 cup plain yogurt
Artificial sweetener to equal 6 teaspoons sugar

½ teaspoon cinnamon
½ teaspoon nutmeg
8 pitted medium dried prunes, diced

Beat egg yolks. Add yogurt, sweetener and spices. Fold in prunes and stiffly beaten egg white. Turn into 8-inch pie pan. Bake at 450°F. for 10 minutes; lower oven to 300°F. and bake 15 to 20 minutes longer, or until browned. Makes 2 servings.

YOGURT FROTH

1 cup plain yogurt ½ cup ice water
¼ teaspoon salt Fresh mint leaves

Beat yogurt until frothy, about 5 minutes. Add salt and ice water and beat another 2 minutes. Serve in tall glasses garnished with mint sprigs. Makes 2 servings.

TURKISH WATERMELON DRINK

4 cups seeded, cubed watermelon ½ cup buttermilk
Artificial sweetener to equal 4
teaspoons sugar

Combine all ingredients in blender container. Process until smooth. Chill. Divide evenly. Makes 4 servings.

Poland and Russia

These two Slavic countries share not only a border and a political system, but also a predilection for using dill and a taste for that great soup: borscht. It's a one-pot dinner meal for hearty eaters when prepared with chunky pieces of beef, or it can be served for lunch with a hard-cooked egg, a snowy peak of creamy cheese and an invigorating squirt of lemon. You'll find a number of other less-familiar dishes from this part of the world, and we are sure you'll enjoy them, too.

HEARTY UKRAINIAN BORSCHT

For a dinner serving, increase the beef to 2 pounds.

1½ pounds lean stew beef, cut in ¾-inch cubes
8 ounces cooked beets (reserve liquid), cut in slivers
1 quart beef bouillon (more if necessary)
1 bay leaf
4 3-ounce peeled potatoes

2 cups shredded green cabbage
1 cup sliced carrots
4 ounces diced onion
¾ cup tomato puree
¼ cup chopped fresh parsley
¼ cup red wine vinegar
Freshly grated black pepper

Broil beef on a rack until done. Transfer to soup kettle. Add beets and beet liquid, beef bouillon and bay leaf. Bring to boil; let cook for 10 minutes. Add potatoes, cabbage, carrots, onion, tomato puree, parsley and vinegar. Cover pot and simmer very slowly for 1½ to 2 hours. Divide evenly and serve with a sprinkling of freshly grated black pepper. Makes 4 servings.

QUICK AND EASY RUSSIAN BEET BORSCHT

6 ounces canned whole beets, finely grated (reserve liquid)
2 cups water
¼ cup celery, chopped
2 ounces onion, chopped
2 packets instant beef broth and seasoning mix, or 2 beef bouillon cubes

Salt to taste
1 tablespoon lemon juice
Artificial sweetener to equal 2 teaspoons sugar

Measure 1½ cups of liquid from beets into a saucepan and add grated beets. Place water, celery, onion and broth mix in blender container; process until smooth. Add to beets. Bring to a boil; lightly season. Simmer 15 minutes. Add lemon juice and sweetener. Makes 2 servings.

POLISH BEET SOUP (Barszcz)

Barszcz is made in dozens of different ways but always with beets and lemon juice, which gives this soup its typical slightly acid flavor.

7 ounces canned beets, finely chopped (reserve 1 cup liquid)
1 ounce chopped scallions
1 medium cucumber, peeled and finely diced
1 medium dill pickle, finely diced
⅔ cup cottage cheese
6 radishes, thinly sliced
2 teaspoons lemon juice
1 tablespoon chopped fresh dill
2 hard-cooked medium eggs, finely chopped
½ teaspoon prepared horseradish

Combine beets, scallions, cucumber and dill pickle. Remove one cup and set aside. Place remaining beet mixture in blender container; add beet juice and cottage cheese; process until smooth. Place in bowl and add remaining ingredients. Mix thoroughly. Makes 2 servings.

"CREAM" OF MUSHROOM SOUP

Almost as popular as borscht is a soup made from the famous Russian mushroom. We have given it the highly seasoned flavor, including dill, which the soup is supposed to have.

3 cups water
4 packets instant chicken broth and seasoning mix
2 cups mushrooms, finely chopped, divided
1 tablespoon dehydrated onion flakes
¼ teaspoon chopped fresh dill
1 cup evaporated skimmed milk
1 teaspoon Worcestershire (or to taste)
Salt and white pepper to taste

Combine water, broth mix, 1½ cups of the mushrooms, onion flakes and dill in a saucepan. Simmer for 10 minutes. Transfer to blender container; process until smooth. Return to saucepan; add remaining ingredients. Heat thoroughly. Do not boil. Makes 4 servings.

"CREAMY" GREEN TURNIP-TOP SOUP

In farmhouses around the world, the first meal of the day is often a hearty soup. This one is favored by Lithuanians.

½ cup turnip (or collard) greens, chopped fine
1½ cups chicken bouillon

1 ounce uncooked oatmeal
¼ cup evaporated skimmed milk
Salt and pepper to taste

In strainer, pour boiling water over greens; then rinse several times in cold water and drain. Place greens in medium saucepan. Cover with bouillon and cook until almost tender; add oatmeal and continue cooking until oatmeal is done and liquid almost evaporated. Cool slightly. Stir in milk, salt and pepper and simmer gently just long enough to heat; do not boil. Makes 1 serving.

MUSHROOM-FILLED PANCAKES WITH "SOUR CREAM" SAUCE

Pancakes

2 medium eggs
2 tablespoons water
2 slices enriched white bread, cubed

Salt and pepper to taste
1 tablespoon chopped fresh parsley

Filling

½ cup chicken bouillon
1 cup drained and finely chopped canned mushrooms

2 ounces chopped scallions
1 tablespoon chopped fresh dill
Salt and pepper to taste

Topping

⅔ cup cottage cheese
2 tablespoons water

½ teaspoon lemon juice

Process eggs, water, bread, salt and pepper in blender container until smooth; add parsley. Divide into 2 equal portions. Pour 1 portion, all at once, into a 9-inch nonstick skillet which has been sprayed with a release agent. Tip pan quickly to spread batter evenly. Cook until underside is done and bubbles form on top. Turn over with a spatula and cook on the other side. Repeat with remaining batter. Set pancakes aside. Combine chicken bouillon, mushrooms and scallions in a small saucepan. Cook until scallions are tender. Remove from heat and drain. Add dill and season to taste with salt and pepper. Set aside. Place cottage cheese, water and lemon juice in blender container. Process until smooth. Remove from blender. Place ½ of the mushroom filling lengthwise along each pancake; roll up. Serve at once with topping which has been divided evenly. Makes 2 servings, 1 pancake each.

EGGPLANT CAVIAR RUSSIAN STYLE

One roasted seeded green pepper may be chopped and added along with 2 teaspoons of vegetable oil.

1 medium eggplant (4 cups)	1½ teaspoons vinegar
2 ounces onion, finely chopped	½ teaspoon salt
3 garlic cloves, minced	Dash hot pepper sauce
1 medium tomato, peeled, chopped	

Pierce eggplant with fork in several places. Bake in moderate oven (350°F.) for 30 minutes, or until tender. Remove from oven and place in bowl of cold water to cool. Peel eggplant; chop. Combine 2 cups chopped eggplant with remaining ingredients in a medium bowl. Chill. Makes 2 servings.

BEEF STROGANOFF AND NOODLES

8 ounces boneless steak	¼ cup evaporated skimmed milk
4 ounces onion, diced	Salt and pepper to taste
½ cup sliced mushrooms	½ cup cooked enriched noodles
1 cup tomato juice	½ teaspoon chopped chives
1 tablespoon white wine vinegar	
1 packet instant beef broth and seasoning mix	

Broil steak on a rack until rare. Cut it in 2-inch strips; set aside. In nonstick skillet lightly brown onions. Add mushrooms, tomato juice and vinegar; add broth mix. Cook over the heat until mixture thickens, about 10 minutes. Add steak; pour in milk and season with salt and pepper. Heat thoroughly. *Do not boil.* Serve over noodles; sprinkle with chives. Makes 1 serving.

HUNTER'S STEW (Bigos)

Sweet dishes are favored in Poland—apple thickens and sweetens this stew.

2 cups reconstituted dried mushrooms, sliced
8 ounces onions, sliced
4 canned medium tomatoes, chopped
2 medium apples, cored, peeled and sliced
3 packets instant chicken broth and seasoning mix
1 teaspoon browning sauce
½ teaspoon garlic powder
2 cups water
2 cups sauerkraut, rinsed
½ bay leaf
Salt and pepper to taste
2 pounds skinned broiled chicken pieces
4 3-ounce boiled potatoes (optional)

Combine mushrooms, onions, tomatoes, apples, broth mix, browning sauce and garlic powder in a large saucepan or Dutch oven. Cook until onions are transparent. Add water, sauerkraut, bay leaf, salt and pepper; mix thoroughly. Place chicken pieces on top and cover. Simmer for 1 hour. Serve with boiled potatoes, if desired. Makes 4 servings.

VEGETABLE POLONAISE*

2 tablespoons imitation (or diet) margarine, melted
1 teaspoon lemon juice
Dash garlic powder
1 slice enriched white bread, made into crumbs
2 hard-cooked medium eggs, finely chopped
1 tablespoon chopped fresh parsley
Salt and white pepper to taste
2 cups cooked broccoli or cauliflower

Combine margarine, juice and garlic powder and add to remaining ingredients, except vegetables. Toss lightly. Place vegetables in a small baking dish, and cover with crumb mixture. Bake at 375°F. for about 15 minutes or until thoroughly heated. Makes 2 servings.

BAKED APPLE AND STRAWBERRY COMPOTE

4 cups strawberries, sliced, divided
1½ teaspoons sherry extract
Artificial sweetener to equal 8 teaspoons sugar

½ teaspoon cinnamon
4 medium apples, cored, peeled and sliced

Place 1 cup strawberries in blender container. Add extract, sweetener and cinnamon; process until smooth. Combine remaining berries and apples in a medium-size baking dish. Cover with pureed strawberries and toss lightly. Bake at 375°F. for about ½ hour or until apples are tender. Makes 4 servings.

Portugal

Portuguese cookery, rich and varied though it is, is not well publicized in our country, perhaps because it has been overshadowed by the Spanish. Both the Portuguese and Spanish are fond of garlic, onions, tomatoes, green peppers and parsley. But Portuguese cooking is more virile and more highly seasoned, since the Portuguese were explorers who introduced Indian, South African and South American spices, tastes and ancestry to their country centuries ago, as a natural result of their travels around the world and back.

Geography plays the major role, of course, in developing kitchen customs. Along the seacoasts, which is the biggest border in Portugal, fish, especially cod (dried and sold as *bacalhau*) is a staple. In the mountains, partiality is shown to thick, hearty soups made of inexpensive ingredients. Eggs are popular throughout Portugal and are used in many different ways: poached in tomato sauce, over meat and in dessert puddings (though the favorite Portuguese dessert is just a peeled orange).

We've given you a sprinkling of everything so you can eat native Portuguese style wherever you are.

BEAN AND PUMPKIN SOUP, BEIRA STYLE

6 ounces cooked dried black-eyed peas
2 teaspoons dehydrated onion flakes or 1 ounce diced onion
2 ounces diced pumpkin
¼ cup finely diced celery
1½ cups chicken bouillon

Combine all ingredients in saucepan. Simmer 40 minutes or until vegetables are tender and soup is thick. Makes 1 serving.

POTATO AND KALE SOUP (Caldo Verde)

Most Portuguese cooks have their own way of making this soup. Typically, the greens are cut into fine grasslike pieces with a special shredding gadget sold for this purpose. A teaspoon of dehydrated onion flakes could be added for flavor if desired. The potatoes are often cooked in chicken bouillon rather than water. Because chicken bouillon is quite salty, we do not add salt to our ingredients.

4 cups dark green kale or collard greens, or cabbage
12 ounces cooked potatoes, diced
4 cups chicken bouillon
¼ teaspoon black pepper

Wash the greens thoroughly, discard tough stems and discolored leaves. Pile greens (or roll cabbage leaves) and cut into strips; this can also be done in food processor. Add to potatoes with bouillon; bring to boil, and fast-simmer for about 10 minutes; do not overcook greens. Stir in pepper and serve at once. Makes 4 servings.

EGG, POTATO AND CHEESE AZORES

⅓ cup cottage cheese
2 teaspoons vegetable oil, divided
½ teaspoon vinegar
½ garlic clove, mashed
¼ teaspoon prepared mustard
¼ teaspoon chopped fresh parsley
⅛ teaspoon dried coriander leaves
Salt and freshly ground pepper to taste
1 hard-cooked medium egg, finely chopped
3 ounces boiled potato, sliced
Lettuce leaves
Parsley sprigs

Combine cottage cheese with 1 teaspoon oil, vinegar, garlic, mustard, parsley, coriander, salt and pepper. Combine egg with remaining oil.

Arrange potatoes on a bed of lettuce. Spread cottage cheese mixture over potatoes. Top with egg mixture. Garnish with parsley sprigs. Makes 1 serving.

FLOUNDER FILLETS WITH MUSHROOMS AND BREAD STUFFING

4 slices enriched white bread
1 garlic clove, cut
4 6-ounce sole or flounder fillets
Salt and freshly ground pepper to taste
¾ cup clam juice
1 medium canned tomato, chopped

2 cups mushrooms, sliced
2 tablespoons chopped fresh parsley
1 tablespoon dehydrated onion flakes

Rub garlic over bread slices on both sides. Soak bread in hot water. Squeeze out excess liquid. Wash fillets and wipe them dry with paper towels. Top with bread. Roll from the short end; secure with toothpicks. Sprinkle lightly with salt and pepper. Place in a baking dish. Add clam juice, tomato, mushrooms, parsley and onion flakes. Cover baking dish tightly. Bake in moderately hot oven (375°F.) until fish is done, or flakes easily with fork, about 30 minutes. If sauce is thin, drain it off into small saucepan and heat until it is reduced. Season the sauce with salt and pepper if desired. Pour over the fish. Makes 4 servings.

MARINATED FISH (Escabeche)

12 ounces cooked fish
2 ounces sliced onions
½ cup white vinegar
½ cup water
½ medium green pepper, coarsely chopped
⅓ cup cooked sliced carrots
¼ cup coarsely chopped celery

½ teaspoon pickling spice
¼ teaspoon crushed dried hot pepper
½ garlic clove, crushed
Dash salt and pepper
1 tablespoon chopped fresh parsley

Arrange fish in a shallow casserole. Lightly brown onions in non-stick skillet. Add vinegar, water, pepper, carrots, celery, spice, crushed hot pepper and garlic. Simmer 2 to 3 minutes; add salt and pepper. Pour liquid over fish, let cool. Sprinkle with parsley, refrigerate overnight. Makes 2 servings.

PORTUGUESE COD WITH CORNMEAL

2 pounds cod, cusk, or hake fillets, fresh or frozen
4 ounces chopped onion
2 garlic cloves, minced
¾ cup tomato puree
1 clove
1 tablespoon chopped fresh parsley
1 teaspoon salt
⅛ teaspoon paprika
Pinch of pepper
Pinch of cumin
4 ounces enriched dry cornmeal (cooked according to package directions)

Thaw frozen fish. Cut into 1½-inch slices. Cook onion and garlic in nonstick pan until softened. Add tomato puree, clove, parsley, salt, paprika, pepper and cumin. Add fish; cover and cook until fish flakes easily when tested with a fork, about 10 minutes. Do not add water as the fish produces its own juices. Serve over cornmeal. Makes 4 servings.

CURRIED FISH MINHO STYLE

The Portuguese were great navigators as well as imaginative cooks, and when they found the sea route to India more than 500 years ago, they lost no time in importing the spicy curry powder mixture popular in that exotic country.

½ cup chicken bouillon
½ medium apple, peeled and diced
1 tablespoon dehydrated onion flakes
½ teaspoon curry powder
Salt and pepper to taste
6 ounces cooked flaked fish

In medium saucepan combine bouillon, apple, onion flakes, curry, salt and pepper. Heat for 1 minute. Stir in fish. Serve hot. Makes 1 serving.

PORTUGUESE SHRIMP

6 ounces cleaned large shrimp
1 teaspoon sauterne or sherry
  extract
¼ teaspoon minced fresh ginger
  root
¼ teaspoon salt
Dash pepper
½ cup tomato puree
1 teaspoon Worcestershire

½ medium green pepper, diced
½ medium red pepper, diced
1 ounce scallion, sliced
1 tablespoon dehydrated onion
  flakes
1 teaspoon fennel leaves,
  chopped (if available) or dash
  anise extract

Season shrimp with sauterne extract, ginger, salt and pepper. Let stand 20 minutes. Put into a saucepan with tomato puree, Worcestershire, green and red pepper, scallion, onion flakes and fennel leaves. Cover and simmer until shrimp are done, about 10 minutes. Do not overcook or they get tough. Shrimp are done when they turn pink. Makes 1 serving.

BEIRA CHICKEN

3 ounces skinned and boned
  chicken breast
1 teaspoon margarine

⅓ cup cottage cheese
Salt and freshly ground pepper
  to taste

Pound chicken breast thin. Spread with margarine and put cottage cheese in center. Roll; secure with toothpick. Place in individual heat-proof serving dish and bake in moderate oven (350°F.) until chicken is done, about 30 minutes. Sprinkle with salt and pepper and serve hot. Makes 1 serving.

CHICKEN BREASTS PORTUGUESE STYLE

2 8-ounce skinned and boned
  chicken breasts
¼ teaspoon freshly grated or
  ground nutmeg
Salt and freshly ground pepper
  to taste

1 cup evaporated skimmed milk
1 teaspoon sherry extract
2 cups sliced mushrooms

Place the chicken breasts between pieces of wax paper and pound lightly with a wooden mallet or the bottom of a skillet on both sides to flatten. Combine nutmeg, salt and pepper; rub on chicken and pound on both sides; brown in nonstick skillet on both sides; remove from the skillet and add evaporated skimmed milk, stirring. Heat, but do not boil; simmer 2 minutes. Add sherry extract to milk and return the chicken pieces to the skillet. Cover and simmer about 10 minutes; turn chicken, simmer another 10 minutes. Meanwhile in another skillet, cook the mushrooms, stirring, until they are softened. Pour over the chicken and season with salt and pepper, if desired. Cover again and simmer a few minutes longer. Serve hot. Makes 2 servings.

PORTUGUESE BAKED CHICKEN IN CASSEROLE
(Frango na Pucara)

1 skinned broiler-fryer (about 2½-pounds), cut in serving pieces	½ cup tomato puree
	1 medium green pepper, diced
	2 tablespoons soy sauce
½ garlic clove, crushed	2 to 3 teaspoons prepared mustard
Salt, paprika and pepper to taste	2 small oranges, peeled and
1 cup orange juice	sectioned

Rub garlic over chicken and sprinkle all over with salt, paprika and pepper. Put in earthenware casserole. Combine remaining ingredients except oranges; pour over chicken. Bake, covered, at 350°F. for 50 minutes. Add oranges; bake 5 to 10 minutes longer. Makes 4 servings.

VARIATION: Omit orange juice, oranges and soy sauce. Add 2 medium tomatoes, chopped, 8 ounces diced onion and 1 teaspoon brandy or sherry extract. Combine with remaining ingredients before baking as directed above.

PORTUGUESE VEAL ROASTED ON A SPIT
(Vitela Assada no Espeto)

3 pounds boned well-trimmed veal roast (from leg)	1 teaspoon salt
	1 teaspoon chopped fresh parsley
1 to 2 garlic cloves, pressed	
½ bay leaf, crushed	2 teaspoons vinegar
1 small piece hot chili pepper, crushed	3 tablespoons bouillon

Wipe veal. Make a paste of remaining ingredients and rub on veal roast. Let stand 1 hour or longer. Roast in slow oven (300°F.) or secure on spit and cook on rotisserie until done, allowing 1½ to 2 hours. Makes 6 servings.

PORTUGUESE TOMATO STEW (Guisado de Tomate)

This is served to border scrambled eggs, over rice, with fish, etc. Minced garlic may be added.

1 cup cooked diced green vegetables (asparagus tips, green beans, broccoli, zucchini)
1 cup cooked diced carrots, cauliflower or turnips
4 ounces cooked peas or diced artichoke hearts

½ cup cooked sliced mushrooms
4 ounces cooked onion, pureed
1 cup tomato puree
Salt and pepper to taste

Select 3 or 4 vegetables from the list. In saucepan bring tomato puree to quick boil; add cooked vegetables and heat, stirring. Serve at once bordering scrambled eggs. Makes 4 servings.

BEIRA GREEN BEAN STEW

12 ounces potatoes, cut in pieces
3 cups chicken bouillon
4 ounces onion, sliced
2 medium tomatoes, peeled, seeded and sliced

4 cups runner or green beans, cut French style (thin diagonal slices)

Cover potatoes with chicken bouillon; add onion and tomatoes. Cook until potatoes are soft. Place vegetable mixture in blender container. Process until smooth. Return to saucepan and bring to boil; add beans. Lower heat and simmer until beans are tender, and sauce is reduced to desired consistency. Makes 4 servings.

RICE WITH EGGPLANT

2 cups eggplant, peeled and cut into 1-inch cubes
1 teaspoon salt

½ cup chicken bouillon, divided
4 ounces onion, chopped
1 cup cooked enriched rice

In a medium bowl, sprinkle eggplant with salt and let stand for 1 hour. Drain off liquid. In a covered skillet, cook onions, in ¼ cup bouillon, until tender, stirring occasionally. Add eggplant and continue to cook until eggplant is done. Add rice and remaining bouillon. Heat. Makes 2 servings.

SOFT ONION PUREE (Cebolada)

To serve as a side dish for roast meat or chicken, usually with a 3-ounce boiled potato for each serving.

Slice 1 pound peeled onions. In a one-quart casserole, combine sliced onions with 1 cup chicken bouillon; cover casserole and cook at 300°F. 1 to 2 hours. Place in blender container and process until smooth. Stir in ½ teaspoon sherry extract, if desired. Serve hot. Makes 4 servings.

ORANGE AND ONION SALAD

1 small orange peeled and sliced thin
2 ounces red onion, sliced thin
¼ cup orange juice
½ teaspoon brandy extract
1 slice lime

Arrange orange slices in center of salad plate in overlapping rings. Leave space for dip in middle. Make a border of onion slices separated into rings. Combine orange juice and brandy extract in a small bowl; add a slice of lime and center on salad plate. Makes 1 serving.

KIDNEY BEAN SALAD*

The Portuguese are as fond of beans as the Italians of pasta, and they've devised almost as many ways of serving them. The plentiful use of garlic is typical of Iberian cooking.

½ garlic clove
1 cup assorted lettuce leaves, cut
4 ounces cooked dried red kidney beans
2 ounces chopped red onion
1 tablespoon chopped fresh parsley
2 teaspoons vegetable oil
2 teaspoons vinegar or lemon juice
⅛ teaspoon ground cumin
Salt and pepper to taste
Dash cayenne pepper

Rub individual salad bowl with cut clove of garlic. Arrange greens in bowl. Add a layer of beans, and a layer of onions. Sprinkle with parsley. Repeat layers. Combine remaining ingredients and stir gently into bean mixture in salad bowl. Makes 1 serving.

BANANA SOUFFLE PUDDING (Pudim de Banana)*

Very ripe bananas have their own natural sweetness, but if you wish, you may add artificial sweetener to the egg yolk-banana mixture.

4 medium eggs, separated
½ cup evaporated skimmed milk
1 tablespoon vanilla extract, divided
Artificial sweetener to equal 4 teaspoons sugar (optional)

Few drops yellow food coloring
2 very ripe medium bananas, sliced
¼ teaspoon cream of tartar
Dash of salt

Preheat oven to 350°F. In the top of a double boiler, combine yolks, milk, 1½ teaspoons vanilla, artificial sweetener and food coloring. Cook over boiling water, stirring constantly, until thick. Fold in bananas and pour into 8-inch round baking dish. Beat egg whites with cream of tartar and salt, until stiff but still shiny. Fold in remaining vanilla. Top banana-egg mixture with egg whites. Bake 15 to 20 minutes or until meringue is golden brown. Serve chilled. Makes 4 servings.

SPONGE CAKE ROLL (Brazo de Gitano)*

4 medium eggs, separated
Artificial sweetener to equal 8 teaspoons sugar, divided
½ teaspoon cream of tartar
1 teaspoon vanilla or almond extract

⅓ cup nonfat dry milk
2 slices enriched white bread, made into crumbs
Filling (recipe follows)
Whipped Topping (see page x)

Preheat oven to 350°F. With an electric mixer, beat egg yolks until lemony in color, about 5 minutes. Add artificial sweetener to equal 4 teaspoons sugar. Beat to mix about 30 seconds. Set aside. Wash beaters clean and dry well. Beat whites until foamy; combine cream of tartar with egg whites and beat until stiff but not dry. Fold in extract, nonfat dry milk and remaining sweetener. Fold yolks into whites until well blended. Fold in bread crumbs, a little at a time, until well blended. Pour mixture into a 10x15x1-inch nonstick baking pan† and bake

†If a nonstick pan is not available, line any 10x15x1-inch baking sheet with aluminum foil or wax paper. After baking, freeze until hard and then remove cake from pan. Peel off paper immediately. Let thaw completely before filling.

for 15 minutes or until a toothpick inserted in the center comes out dry. Use a long plastic pancake turner to help remove cake from pan. Loosen the bottom by forcing the pancake turner under the cake. Turn cake out onto a moist towel. Evenly trim away crisp edges. Place crisp edges in blender container and process to form crumbs. Combine crumbs with filling. Spread on cake, reserving ½ cup for decorating top, and roll cake from short end. Wrap in aluminum foil and refrigerate. Before serving, decorate with reserved filling. Serve with Whipped Topping. Makes 4 servings.

Filling for Sponge Cake Roll

1 envelope unflavored gelatin
¼ cup cold water
2 cups strawberries

Artificial sweetener to equal
4 teaspoons sugar or to taste

In a small saucepan, sprinkle gelatin over water. Place over low heat and stir until gelatin dissolves. In a medium mixing bowl, crush strawberries with a fork, add gelatin mixture and sweetener. Mix with electric mixer until well blended. Chill until almost set. Remove from refrigerator and remix with electric mixer to form a thick jam-like consistency. Spread on cake roll.

Scandinavia

Scandinavians—the people of Denmark, Finland, Iceland, Norway and Sweden—share with us a taste for fine food and plenty of it. We have a mutual predilection for "coffee and Danish." The traditional Danish pastry is baked with butter, flour and yeast, frequently enriched with nuts and many other fattening ingredients. Our version is not merely as rich, but you'll probably enjoy it more because you can have your portion as part of our Food Program. Fruit soups from Finland and Norway are less well known here than Danish pastry, but we think you'll like them, especially as a summertime treat. You'll also find vegetables and salads for your *smorgasbord* buffet—a word and a method of entertaining that we borrowed from Sweden. Iceland should not be omitted from the roll call of Scandinavian countries. It is noted for its codfish, and our recipe for using it is as distinctive as it is authentic.

HUCKLEBERRY SOUP

A popular Norwegian soup. Our version is a luncheon main course. The berries could be served in buttermilk or yogurt as an alternative to the "sour cream."

2 cups water
1 cup blueberries or huckleberries
½ teaspoon grated lemon rind
Dash salt

1⅓ cups cottage cheese
1 teaspoon lemon juice
¼ cup water

In saucepan combine water, berries, lemon rind and salt. Cook until berries are very soft. Serve cold in bowls with "sour cream" topping. To make "sour cream," combine remaining ingredients in blender container and process until smooth. Makes 2 servings.

VEGETABLE SOUP WITH MILK (Kesäkeitto)

A substantial everyday soup in Finland.

1 cup water
½ cup cauliflower florets, diced
½ cup shredded spinach,
   kale or cabbage
½ cup diced celery
¼ cup diced carrots

1 ounce green peas
½ teaspoon salt
¼ cup evaporated skimmed milk
1 teaspoon chopped fresh
   parsley

In saucepan combine water, cauliflower, spinach, celery, carrots, peas and salt. Bring to a boil. Cover and simmer until vegetables are tender, 10 to 15 minutes. Remove from heat. Stir in evaporated skimmed milk and parsley and serve hot. Makes 1 serving.

DANISH-LIKE BREAKFAST BUNS

2 slices whole wheat bread,
   made into crumbs
⅔ cup nonfat dry milk
2 teaspoons baking powder
Artificial sweetener to equal
   8 teaspoons sugar

2 tablespoons imitation (or
   diet) margarine
2 medium eggs, lightly beaten
1 medium apple, pared and
   finely chopped

Preheat oven to 375°F. Place bread crumbs, dry milk, baking powder and sweetener in a mixing bowl. Add margarine, mix well; fold in eggs and apple. Spoon into a 6-cup nonstick muffin pan and bake for 20 minutes. Makes 2 servings (3 muffins each).

SCANDINAVIAN FISH SALAD

Cod, flounder, halibut, herring, pike, sardines and whitefish are some of the typical fish of this part of the world.

3 ounces cooked potato,
 diced fine
1 ounce cooked beets, diced fine
½ medium dill pickle, diced fine
1 tart medium apple, diced fine
¼ cup cooked carrot, diced fine

1 teaspoon chopped chives
2 tablespoons vinegar
Dash of salt and pepper
6 ounces cooked fillet of fish,
 flaked or diced
Parsley

Combine potato, beets, pickle, apple, carrot and chives. Stir in vinegar, salt and pepper. Add flaked fish and mix gently to avoid mashing the vegetables or fish. Pack into small wet mold (such as large coffee cup). Chill for several hours. Unmold onto dinner plate. Garnish with parsley. Makes 1 serving.

POACHED COD WITH EGG SAUCE

½ cup clam juice
½ cup water
½ teaspoon imitation butter
 flavoring
2 hard-cooked medium eggs,
 finely chopped
1 medium tomato, peeled, seeded
 and chopped

2 tablespoons chopped fresh
 parsley
½ teaspoon salt
4 ounces poached cod
 (or other fish)

In saucepan, combine clam juice, water and imitation butter flavoring; cook over low heat for 2 minutes. Add eggs, tomato, parsley and salt. Continue cooking, gently, stirring frequently 5 minutes or until heated throughout. Place ½ of fish on each of 2 luncheon plates. Spoon ½ of egg mixture on each portion of fish. Makes 2 servings.

POACHED SALMON STEAKS WITH "CREAMED" MUSHROOMS
(Fiske med Champinjoner)

For a typical Scandinavian meal, serve poached salmon with "creamed" mushrooms and spinach.

¼ cup salt	Lemon slices to garnish
6 cups water	Dill sprigs to garnish
3 10-ounce salmon steaks	

Combine salt and water in roasting pan or fish poacher. Bring to a boil; reduce heat. Using a spatula, gently slide salmon steaks into water. Simmer fish 5 minutes or until fish flakes easily with fork. Remove fish with slotted spatula to paper towels; drain. Transfer to serving platter. Garnish with lemon slices and dill sprigs. Makes 3 servings.

"Creamed" Mushrooms

1½ cups mushrooms, cut thin	1 tablespoon dehydrated onion flakes
½ cup water	2 peppercorns
1 bay leaf	½ teaspoon salt
3 tablespoons chopped fresh parsley	½ cup evaporated skimmed milk

In saucepan combine mushrooms, water, bay leaf, parsley, dehydrated onion flakes, peppercorns and salt. Cover pan and cook until mushrooms are done, 8 to 10 minutes. Strain off liquid; remove bay leaf and peppercorns. Place liquid in blender container with half of the mushrooms. Puree. Heat with evaporated skimmed milk and remaining mushrooms. Serve over poached salmon. Makes 3 servings.

CELERY SALMON LOAF

4 ounces drained canned salmon, flaked	1 teaspoon chopped fresh parsley
⅓ cup finely chopped celery	1 teaspoon vinegar
1 ounce onion, diced	½ packet instant chicken broth and seasoning mix
¼ medium green pepper, diced	2 teaspoons unflavored gelatin
1 teaspoon chopped pimento	¾ cup water
1 tablespoon mayonnaise	Lettuce

Combine salmon, celery, onion, green pepper and pimento in a mixing bowl. Add mayonnaise, parsley and vinegar. Sprinkle in broth mix and mix well. In a saucepan, sprinkle gelatin over water to soften. Place over low heat, stirring until gelatin is dissolved. Add to salmon mixture. Turn mixture into a mold and chill in refrigerator until firm. Unmold on lettuce. Makes 1 serving.

SWEDISH MEAT PATTIES (Biff à la Lindström)

If you follow the old Scandinavian custom of grinding beef at home, you can put the capers and onion flakes into the grinder too.

2 tablespoons dehydrated onion flakes
¾ cup water
1½ pounds finely ground beef

2 tablespoons capers, rinsed and chopped
Salt and pepper to taste
3 ounces cooked beets, shredded

Reconstitute onion in water. Combine in mixing bowl with beef and capers. Mix well; season to taste. Shape into six patties and broil on rack or open grill 5 to 6 minutes each side, or until deep brown in color. Top with beets and serve. Makes 3 servings.

BEETS IN ASPIC

Make this in pretty individual molds that could go on a smorgasbord table.

4 ounces canned shoestring beets (reserve ½ cup liquid)
¼ cup celery, diced
Artificial sweetener to equal 1 teaspoon sugar
4 teaspoons lemon juice
⅓ cup chicken bouillon

¼ teaspoon dehydrated onion flakes
1½ teaspoons prepared horseradish
Dash celery salt
1 envelope unflavored gelatin
3 tablespoons water
White pepper to taste

Place beets (with liquid), celery, sweetener, lemon juice, bouillon and onion in a pint mold. Add horseradish and celery salt. Sprinkle gelatin over cold water in small saucepan to soften. Dissolve over low heat; stir into beets with a wooden spoon, mixing thoroughly. Season to taste with white pepper. Set in refrigerator, chill for several hours, or until gelatin molds. Makes 1 serving.

DILLED TUNA SALAD

Dill, an herb of biblical days, is a characteristic seasoning in Sweden.

1 tablespoon mayonnaise
1 teaspoon lemon juice
¼ teaspoon dill weed
⅛ teaspoon celery seed

Dash paprika
4 ounces drained, canned tuna, flaked
1 (1-ounce) enriched white roll

In small bowl, combine all ingredients except tuna and roll. Add tuna; mix and chill. Serve on roll. Makes 1 serving.

DANISH CUCUMBER SALAD

This is served as a first course or in little saucers as a relish for meat, chicken and fish. For a refreshing luncheon salad, yogurt could be served with the cucumbers.

2 medium cucumbers
1½ teaspoons salt
2 tablespoons water
2 tablespoons lemon juice

1 tablespoon chopped fresh parsley or dill
Freshly ground black pepper to taste

Peel and score cucumbers and cut into thin slices. Sprinkle with salt and let stand 2 hours. Drain and rinse thoroughly. In jar, combine remaining ingredients, shake well and pour over cucumbers. Let stand at least 30 minutes. Makes 2 to 4 servings.

PINEAPPLE BREAKFAST

¾ cup water
Dash salt
1 ounce uncooked, granulated rice cereal

¼ cup canned crushed pineapple, no sugar added
¼ teaspoon cinnamon
½ cup skim milk

In small saucepan bring water and salt to a boil. Sprinkle in cereal, stirring. Cook and stir over moderate heat 30 seconds. Remove from heat, cover and let stand for 30 seconds. Stir pineapple and cinnamon into cooked cereal. Serve with skim milk. Makes 1 serving.

NORWEGIAN CARDAMOM COOKIES*

Follow recipe for Almond Cookies (see page 96) but add ½ teaspoon ground or powdered cardamom to egg-milk-bread crumb mixture before beating. Makes 2 servings.

The South Pacific

Dreaming of an unspoiled South Sea island where enchanting natives wearing colorful sarongs dance a lively hula? Does Malaysia sound as remote and romantic as Paradise? Chances are good that the island of your dreams has a jetport, modern hotels and a few hundred thousand tourists visiting each year. But don't let that stop you from enjoying an exciting part of the world, where the Stone Age meets the twentieth century. Along with the natives, you'll find Americans on Samoa, British on Fiji and Cook's Island, French in Tahiti, and the Japanese in Guam. On the Philippines are the Malay, Chinese, Spanish, and Americans, too. Indonesia is Hindu-Buddhist as well as Colonial Dutch. So in our South Pacific chapter, a little sample of the dazzling variety of palate-tingling foods which you can find in this picturesque part of the world, prepared for you in our easy-on-the-waistline style, awaits you.

INDONESIAN THICK "CREAMY" VEGETABLE SOUP
(Sajur Lodeh)

Seasoning options include 1 chopped garlic clove and a dash of ground coriander.

3 cups chicken bouillon
1 tablespoon dehydrated bell pepper flakes
1 tablespoon dehydrated onion flakes
1 bay leaf
2 cups combined shredded cabbage, green beans and cauliflower (or bean sprouts)

1 cup shredded carrots
2 cups cooked fresh soybeans or lima beans (or cooked thin enriched egg noodles)
1 cup evaporated skimmed milk

In saucepan, bring to boil bouillon, bell pepper flakes, onion flakes and bay leaf. Add shredded cabbage, green beans, cauliflower and carrots, and simmer for 30 minutes. Stir in soybeans (lima beans or noodles). Cook for 3 minutes. Add milk and heat gently for 2 minutes more; do not boil. Remove bay leaf. Serve hot. Makes 4 servings.

FILIPINO FISH SOUP

2 medium tomatoes, sliced ½-inch thick
2 medium green peppers, cut into rings ¼-inch wide
4 ounces onion, cut in thin slices

1½ teaspoons salt
3 cups water
1½ pounds fish, cut into 1½-inch slices
⅓ cup watercress, chopped

In saucepan combine tomatoes, green peppers, onion, salt and water and bring to boil. Add fish and cook 5 to 8 minutes, or until fish is tender. Add watercress, heat 1 minute and serve at once. Makes 4 servings.

JAVANESE EGG AND POTATO IN RED PEPPER SAUCE*
(Sambal Goreng Telor)

3 ounces cooked potato, cut in julienne pieces
1 ounce chopped onion
1 small garlic clove, minced
¼ teaspoon crushed red pepper
¼ bay leaf
¼ medium tomato, diced
¼ cup beef bouillon
¼ cup skim milk
1 hard-cooked medium egg, cut in half

In nonstick skillet, brown potato, onion and garlic, turning on all sides. Add pepper, bay leaf, tomato and beef bouillon. Bring to boil, stirring often. Add skim milk and egg, and continue simmering, stirring gently, for 3 minutes. Makes 1 serving.

MULLET IN COCONUT MILK TAHITI

1½ pounds mullet (or whitefish) fillets, sliced
1 cup skim milk
1 teaspoon coconut extract
½ teaspoon salt
Watercress for garnish

Place fish slices in pan with milk. Simmer until fish flakes, turning once very carefully. Stir in coconut extract and salt. Garnish with watercress. Serve hot. Makes 3 servings.

FILIPINO DIP FOR LOBSTER

Float pieces of garlic in a small bowl of vinegar and serve as a dipping sauce for boiled lobster or other shellfish.

SHRIMP SALAD

⅓ cup cottage cheese
1 teaspoon water
¼ teaspoon lemon juice
2 ounces cooked shrimp, thinly sliced
¼ medium apple, peeled and finely diced
1 tablespoon mayonnaise
¼ teaspoon curry powder
Lettuce leaves

Place cottage cheese, water and lemon juice in blender container. Process until smooth. Combine remaining ingredients except lettuce in a mixing bowl; add cheese mixture. Toss lightly. Chill thoroughly. Serve on a bed of lettuce. Makes 1 serving.

FILIPINO BEAN, SHRIMP AND SPINACH

2½ cups water
1 medium tomato, sliced
4 ounces onion, finely diced
1 small garlic clove, minced
Salt and pepper or soy sauce to
taste

12 ounces cleaned shrimp
1 cup cooked fresh lima beans
1 cup cleaned spinach

In saucepan combine water, tomato, onion, garlic, salt and pepper. Bring to boil. Lower heat and simmer for 15 minutes. Add shrimp, beans and spinach and return to simmer for 5 to 8 minutes more or until shrimp are pink and firm. Makes 2 servings.

PHILIPPINE CHICKEN AND VEAL STEW (Adobo)

A typical stew which blends the Oriental and the Western cuisines. It is said that Philippine dishes require garlic and bay leaf from Spain, pepper from Malay, soy sauce from China, and vinegar to prove it's a native of the Philippines.

8 ounces skinned and boned
chicken breasts, cut into 1-inch
pieces
8 ounces veal, cut into 1-inch
pieces
3 tablespoons cider vinegar
2 tablespoons soy sauce
1½ garlic cloves, crushed

½ small bay leaf
4 crushed peppercorns
2 cups water
Pimento to garnish
1 cup cooked enriched rice,
sprinkled with chopped fresh
parsley

Broil chicken and veal on rack close to source of heat. Turn once to brown on all sides. Transfer to flameproof serving casserole with cider vinegar, soy sauce, garlic, bay leaf and peppercorns. Let stand at least 1 hour, turning meat pieces several times. Add water to cover meat. Cover casserole and let simmer very slowly for 1 to 1½ hours. At the end of the cooking process there should be very little sauce left in pan. If necessary, remove cover and let simmer until liquid reduces. Remove bay leaf. Garnish with pimento. Serve each portion over ½ cup rice. Makes 2 servings.

INDONESIAN CURRIED RICE WITH CHICKEN (Nasi Goreng)

Indonesia, that great chain of islands between Asia and Australia, is a blend of many religions and peoples—Buddhists, Hindus, Malays, Arabs, Chinese and Dutch—and its famous national dish salutes this diversity.

4 ounces cooked chicken, cut into thin strips
4 ounces cooked shrimp, cut into pieces
¾ cup chicken bouillon or homemade chicken stock, divided (see page ix)
2 garlic cloves, crushed
2½ teaspoons curry powder, divided

Salt to taste
Dash cayenne pepper
2 cups cooked enriched rice
4 ounces chopped scallions, divided
1 recipe Shredded Egg Pancakes (recipe follows)
1 medium cucumber or dill pickle, chilled, peeled and cut into strips

Marinate chicken and shrimp in separate bowls, each containing ¼ cup chicken bouillon, 1 garlic clove, ¼ teaspoon curry powder, salt and cayenne for at least 1 hour. Drain. Discard marinade. Pour remaining bouillon into a large preheated nonstick skillet or wok. Add chicken, shrimp, rice, 3 ounces scallions, remaining curry powder, salt and cayenne; stir frequently until all ingredients are heated through. Pour Nasi Goreng into warmed individual dishes. Sprinkle ½ ounce of scallions on each serving; add 1 serving of pancakes to each serving. Serve with cucumber or pickle strips. Makes 4 servings.

Shredded Egg Pancakes

4 medium eggs
1 tablespoon soy sauce

Freshly ground pepper to taste

Combine eggs, soy sauce and pepper, and beat well to make a thin batter; pour through a strainer to make the batter an even consistency. Pour ⅛ of the batter into heated nonstick skillet, swirling to coat pan. Cook until set on one side, turn and cook briefly on other side. Continue processing until all batter is used. (Makes 8 pancakes.) For each serving slice two pancakes into thin shreds. Serve with Nasi Goreng. Makes 4 servings.

BEEF AND PEPPERS, MANILA STYLE

Serve over a bed of fluffy rice. For Nasi Kuning (yellow rice) cook the rice with a bay leaf and ½ teaspoon turmeric.

1½ pounds lean beef round steak, cut ½-inch thick
1 tablespoon paprika
2 garlic cloves, crushed
1½ cups beef bouillon
4 ounces sliced scallions, including tops
2 medium green peppers, cut in strips
¼ cup soy sauce
2 medium tomatoes, cut in eighths

Pound steak to ¼-inch thickness. Cut into ¼-inch-wide strips. Sprinkle meat with paprika and let marinate while preparing other ingredients. Brown beef on rack under broiler, turning once. Combine meat in saucepan with garlic and bouillon. Cover and simmer 30 minutes. Stir in scallions and green peppers. Cover and cook 5 minutes more. Stir in soy sauce. Cook about 2 minutes. Add tomatoes and stir gently. Makes 4 servings.

SWEET AND SOUR PORK PHILIPPINE ISLAND

8 ounces lean boneless pork loin
½ cup chicken bouillon
¼ medium green pepper, diced
Dash garlic powder
½ cup canned crushed pineapple, no sugar added
Artificial sweetener to equal ½ teaspoon sugar
1 tablespoon vinegar
½ cup cooked enriched rice
1 medium tomato, cut into six wedges
Salt to taste
½ teaspoon chopped fresh parsley

Broil pork 4 inches from source of heat 5 minutes on each side. Remove; cool; cut into 1-inch cubes. Place in a nonstick skillet with bouillon, pepper and garlic. Simmer, stirring, until liquid has reduced to half its volume. Add pineapple, sweetener and vinegar. Fold in rice and tomato. Season to taste. Heat thoroughly over low flame, stirring gently, until liquid is absorbed. Sprinkle with parsley. Makes 1 serving.

CHICKEN LIVER SAMOA

1 pound chicken livers
1 medium green pepper, diced
½ cup canned crushed pineapple, no sugar added

⅓ cup soy sauce
1 tablespoon dehydrated onion flakes
1 tablespoon prepared mustard

In large nonstick skillet, cook chicken livers and green pepper; divide evenly into two small casseroles. Combine pineapple, soy sauce, onion flakes and mustard. Pour evenly over chicken livers. Bake in 350°F. oven for 20 minutes. Makes 2 servings.

BEAN SPROUT, CELERY AND APPLE SALAD

2 cups bean sprouts (see note)
1 cup chopped celery
1 medium red apple, diced
1 tablespoon chopped fresh chives
1 tablespoon chopped fresh parsley
2 lettuce leaves

1 tablespoon soy sauce
2 teaspoons lemon juice
Dash dry mustard
¼ teaspoon minced fresh ginger root
Artificial sweetener to equal 2 teaspoons sugar
Salt and pepper to taste

Combine bean sprouts, celery, apples, chives and parsley. Divide onto two lettuce leaves. Mix remaining ingredients and serve over salad. Makes 2 servings.

NOTE: If you use canned bean sprouts, rinse in colander under cold water and drain well; if fresh bean sprouts, parboil first by covering with boiling water and cooking for 2 to 3 minutes. Drain well.

PEPPERY HOT VEGETABLE DISH

2 ounces onion, chopped
6 ounces peeled potatoes, cut in 1-inch dice
2 cups peeled eggplant, cut in 1-inch dice
½ teaspoon salt
½ teaspoon dry mustard

⅛ teaspoon turmeric
⅛ teaspoon ginger
½ dried red chili pepper, seeds removed or ½ teaspoon cayenne pepper or to taste
1¼ cups water

Brown onions in nonstick pan. Add potatoes, eggplant, salt, mustard, turmeric, ginger and chili pepper or cayenne. Lightly brown on all sides, in hot skillet, turning constantly. Add water, cover pan, and cook until vegetables are tender and no liquid is left. Makes 2 servings.

VEGETABLE SALAD-STEW FIJI ISLANDS

You can drink it or eat it with a spoon. It's a warm-climate soupy salad, not unlike Spanish gazpacho, but this one shows the strong Hindu influence in Fiji, where more than 50 percent of the population originally came from India.

2 medium tomatoes, peeled and diced
4 ounces onion, minced
¼ cup fresh coriander leaves, or parsley
1 teaspoon freshly minced hot green chili pepper, or canned Mexican or Italian chili peppers to taste

¼ teaspoon dry mustard
¼ teaspoon ground cumin
Salt to taste
¾ cup buttermilk

Place first 7 ingredients in a large mixing bowl. Pour buttermilk over and stir to combine. Serve cold. Makes 2 servings.

SKEWERED BANANAS WITH DIPPING SAUCE

At your next barbecue, skewer peeled medium bananas on bamboo skewers and barbecue (or broil) on all sides, turning as necessary. Allow ½ banana per serving. Good with Dipping Sauce, below.

Dipping Sauce

2 small fresh hot red peppers, chopped fine or ½ dried hot red chili pepper (seeds removed) or ½ teaspoon cayenne pepper (or to taste)

¼ cup vinegar or lemon juice
1 teaspoon dehydrated bell pepper flakes

Chop peppers and mix with vinegar or lemon juice and pepper flakes. Serve as a dip with bananas, pineapples or other fruits.

BALINESE FRUIT SALAD

1 medium apple, peeled and shredded
1 small pear, shredded
1 medium cucumber, peeled, seeded and shredded
½ cup shredded carrot

1 tablespoon vinegar
1 teaspoon salt
1 teaspoon crushed red pepper
Dash of coconut or other nut extract

Combine apple, pear, cucumber and carrot in bowl. Mix remaining ingredients and pour over fruits and vegetables. Refrigerate for at least 2 hours. Serve cold. Makes 4 servings.

TAHITIAN PINEAPPLE-COCONUT MOUSSE

2 envelopes unflavored gelatin
1½ cups water, divided
1½ cups evaporated skimmed milk
½ teaspoon rum extract
½ teaspoon coconut extract

¼ teaspoon vanilla extract
Artificial sweetener to equal 4 teaspoons sugar
1½ cups canned crushed pineapple, no sugar added

In a medium saucepan sprinkle gelatin over 1 cup water; heat, stirring until gelatin is dissolved. Pour gelatin mixture into blender container; add remaining water, milk, extracts and sweetener. Process at low speed until smooth. Add pineapple; process at medium speed until smooth. Pour into a 1½-quart mold. Chill. Unmold. Makes 6 servings.

COFFEE GELATIN

1 envelope unflavored gelatin
2 cups cooled coffee

Artificial sweetener to equal 4 teaspoons sugar

Sprinkle gelatin over ½ cup coffee in small saucepan; stir over low heat until gelatin dissolves. Add remaining coffee and artificial sweetener. Pour into medium bowl; cover. Chill until firm. Makes 4 servings.

Spain

Sol y sombra—sunlight and shadow, simplicity and complexity—these are the elusive elements of Spanish culture. In the Gothic cathedrals and shaded Moorish mosques, the arched silent court-yards surrounding bubbling fountains, the romantic tracery of black iron against whitewashed stucco walls, lies the enchantment of Spain, a country where different forces of history, the European and the Arabic, met and fused in the eighth century.

Our Spanish chapter abounds with recipes from some of the fifty provinces encompassed in the country. Each recipe has a typical and traditional Spanish flavor but has been modified to fit our Food Program. Once you've sampled these dishes, you'll see why everyone is an *aficionado* of tantalizing Spanish cuisine.

GARLIC SOUP

2 quarts boiling water
16 garlic cloves, pressed
2 cloves
¼ teaspoon sage
¼ teaspoon thyme

Dash cayenne pepper
Salt and pepper to taste
6 slices stale enriched white bread,
   toasted and cubed
1 tablespoon minced fresh parsley

Place water, garlic, cloves, sage, thyme, cayenne, salt and pepper in Dutch oven. Carefully add toasted bread cubes, allowing them to become totally saturated, but remaining whole. Bring mixture to a boil, lower heat, cover and simmer for 1 hour. Remove cloves before serving. Divide evenly into 6 soup bowls. Garnish each portion with ½ teaspoon parsley. Makes 6 servings.

VARIATION: After simmering for 1 hour, add 6 beaten eggs, pouring slowly and stirring constantly. Continue simmering until eggs are just set. Makes 6 servings.

MALAGA GAZPACHO

3 ripe medium tomatoes, peeled
   and coarsely chopped
2 medium cucumbers, peeled and
   coarsely chopped
1 medium green pepper, seeded
   and coarsely chopped
½ cup water

¼ cup wine vinegar, or to taste
3 tablespoons vegetable oil
1 garlic clove, minced
Salt to taste
3 slices enriched white bread,
   cubed
Chopped fresh parsley or chives

Combine first 8 ingredients in blender container or food processor. Process at medium speed until smooth. Increase speed to high and add bread, a few cubes at a time, processing after each addition. Stir down with rubber spatula if necessary. Chill soup thoroughly. Garnish with parsley or chives before serving. Makes 6 servings.

SEVILLE GAZPACHO*

Omit bread from preceding recipe. Instead add 1 diced hard-cooked medium egg to each bowl before serving. Makes 6 servings.

HEARTY BEAN AND VEGETABLE SOUP (Caldo Gallego)

2 cups beef bouillon
12 ounces cooked dried white beans (canned white cannellini)
4 ounces cooked beef, cut in strips
3 ounces cooked ham, cut in strips
1 cup peeled and cubed turnips
1 medium tomato, peeled, seeded and quartered
2 cups cabbage, shredded
2 tablespoons dehydrated onion flakes
1 garlic clove, peeled and minced
Salt and freshly ground pepper to taste

Combine all ingredients in a 2-quart saucepan, and bring to a boil. Cover and simmer gently until turnips are tender, 15 to 20 minutes. Divide evenly and serve. Makes 4 servings.

COD STEWED WITH EGGPLANT (Merluza con Berenjenas)

2 cups eggplant, cut into cubes
1 medium green pepper, cut into small pieces
2 ounces onion, cut into small pieces
4 8-ounce codfish steaks
1 cup water
½ cup sliced celery
½ tablespoon vinegar
½ garlic clove
Salt, pepper, paprika to taste
1 tablespoon chopped capers, rinsed

Place eggplant, green pepper and onion in a preheated nonstick skillet, turning often until the water from the eggplant evaporates. Put in cod steaks. Add water, celery, vinegar, garlic, salt, pepper and paprika. Simmer until fish is done. Sprinkle with capers. Serve hot. Makes 4 servings.

BAKED RED SNAPPER WITH POTATOES

8 ounces red snapper fillets
Pinch of salt, cayenne pepper and paprika
3 ounces cooked potato, sliced
¼ cup chopped celery
1 medium tomato, chopped
2 ounces onion, chopped
½ cup chicken bouillon
½ teaspoon chopped fresh parsley

Season fish with salt, cayenne and paprika. Make a layer of potato slices and celery in a shallow casserole. Add fish. Top with tomato and onion. Pour in bouillon. Cover with aluminum foil. Bake in hot oven (400°F.) for 30 minutes. Garnish with parsley. Makes 1 serving.

EGGS WITH TOMATO TOPPING (Tortilla de Tomate)

4 ounces chopped onion
1 medium green pepper, chopped
Beef bouillon
¾ cup tomato puree
½ cup water

1 teaspoon salt, divided
1 teaspoon chili powder
8 medium eggs
½ cup skim milk
Dash pepper

To prepare topping, cook onion and green pepper in bouillon to cover until they are soft. Stir in tomato puree, water, ½ teaspoon salt and chili powder. Bring to a boil; then simmer, uncovered, about 10 to 15 minutes, stirring occasionally. Meanwhile, prepare omelet. Beat eggs, milk, remaining ½ teaspoon salt and pepper. Pour into preheated large nonstick skillet, and cook over low heat. As bottom of eggs set, loosen and lift edge with spatula, tilting pan to let uncooked portion run underneath. Continue lifting and tilting procedure until omelet is almost dry on top. Loosen omelet with spatula; fold or roll and tilt out onto warm serving plate. Serve immediately with hot topping. Makes 4 servings.

OCTOPUS STEW (Cazuela de Pulpo)

⅛ teaspoon saffron
½ cup boiling water
4 ounces onion, thinly sliced
1 medium green pepper, chopped
1 pound cleaned baby octopus,
  cut into bite-size pieces
2 medium tomatoes, sliced
1 tablespoon white wine vinegar
¼ cup chopped fresh parsley

1 garlic clove, minced
½ bay leaf
½ teaspoon paprika
¼ teaspoon thyme
Salt and freshly ground pepper to
  taste
1 pound peeled and deveined
  shrimp
2 cups cooked enriched rice

Place saffron in a small bowl and add water. Let stand for at least 1 hour. In a large nonstick saucepan, cook onion and green pepper, stirring frequently until onion starts to brown. Add octopus, tomatoes, vinegar, parsley, garlic, bay leaf, paprika, thyme, salt and pepper. Cook uncovered 10 minutes. Cover and cook 10 minutes longer. Add shrimp. Cook uncovered 5 minutes longer or until shrimp are cooked. Do not overcook. Divide evenly into 4 portions. Serve each over ½ cup rice. Makes 4 servings.

PERCH FILLETS BAY OF BISCAY

1 pound perch fillets
Salt and freshly ground pepper to
  taste
2 ounces onion, finely chopped
¼ cup chopped fresh parsley
1 garlic clove, minced
½ teaspoon thyme

1 medium tomato, peeled and
  chopped
1 bay leaf
½ cup clam juice
½ cup water
2 tablespoons tomato paste
3 slices lemon

Sprinkle fish with salt and pepper and place in a shallow nonstick baking dish. Combine onion, parsley, garlic and thyme in a large nonstick skillet. Cook, stirring occasionally, until onion becomes tender. Add tomato and bay leaf; continue to cook and stir until well blended. Mix in clam juice, water and tomato paste and simmer for 5 minutes. Remove from heat and pour over fish. Garnish with lemon slices and bake in moderate oven (350°F.) for 30 minutes, basting occasionally. Makes 2 servings.

BAKED FISH WITH MUSHROOMS, GALICIA
(Pescado con Champiñones)

2 ounces thinly sliced onions
1 tablespoon chopped pimentos
½ cup onion bouillon
1 pound bass fillets, cut in
  1-inch strips
½ teaspoon salt
Dash pepper

Dash hot pepper sauce
Dash nutmeg
1 medium tomato, peeled and
  sliced
1½ teaspoons snipped chives
1 cup thinly sliced mushrooms
2 tablespoons white vinegar

Layer onions evenly in baking dish. Sprinkle chopped pimentos over onions. Pour bouillon over onions and pimentos. Add fish strips. Combine salt, pepper, hot pepper sauce and nutmeg; sprinkle on fish. Add tomatoes; sprinkle with chives, and top with mushrooms. Pour vinegar over mushrooms. Cover dish tightly. Marinate 1 hour. Bake in hot oven (450°F.) 20 minutes or until fish flakes easily with fork. Makes 2 servings.

FISH VINAIGRETTE (Pescado a la Vinagreta)

24 ounces cooked fish fillets
(scrod, haddock or flounder),
cut in cubes
1 medium cucumber, seeded and
sliced into cubes
2 tablespoons chopped fresh
parsley
1 tablespoon dehydrated onion
flakes, reconstituted

1 tablespoon chopped capers
1 garlic clove, minced
2 tablespoons vegetable oil
2 tablespoons vinegar
Salt and pepper to taste
2 medium tomatoes, peeled,
seeded and diced

Arrange fish in large bowl; add cucumber, parsley, onion flakes,
capers and garlic. Sprinkle with oil and vinegar; season with salt and
pepper. Toss gently to avoid breaking fish. Cover bowl and marinate
in refrigerator about 2 hours. Gently toss in diced tomato. Serve
cold. Makes 4 servings.

SHRIMP WITH SAFFRON

2 pounds large peeled and
deveined shrimp
6 tablespoons lemon juice
1 teaspoon saffron
3 sprigs parsley, finely chopped
1 garlic clove, minced

1 teaspoon finely chopped fresh
thyme (or ½ teaspoon dried)
½ bay leaf, crumbled
Salt and freshly ground pepper to
taste
4 teaspoons margarine

Dry shrimp and place in a bowl. Add lemon juice and saffron. Combine chopped parsley, garlic, thyme, bay leaf, salt and pepper. Add to
shrimp and stir until they are well coated with the mixture. Remove
shrimp from marinade, reserving liquid. Place on a baking sheet and
broil about 4 inches from heat 4 to 5 minutes; turn once, continue
broiling 1 to 2 minutes or until shrimp are cooked through. Do not
overcook, as they will toughen. Heat marinade. Remove from heat
and stir in margarine until it melts. Divide shrimp evenly into 4 portions. Pour ¼ of the sauce over each portion. Makes 4 servings.

PAELLA

A paella that's better than most.

5 medium canned or fresh tomatoes, chopped
6 ounces onion, diced
1 medium green pepper, diced
3 ounces frozen artichoke hearts, slightly thawed
1 tablespoon chopped capers, rinsed
1 clove garlic, minced or pressed
¼ teaspoon paprika
¼ teaspoon thyme
⅛ teaspoon cinnamon
⅛ teaspoon saffron
Salt and freshly ground pepper to taste
1½ pounds skinned and boned chicken breast, cut into bite-size pieces
1½ pounds fresh peeled and deveined shrimp
3 cups cooked enriched rice, prepared in chicken bouillon
2 pimentos, chopped
Dash hot pepper sauce
3 ounces frozen peas

Combine tomatoes, onion, green pepper, artichoke hearts, capers, garlic, paprika, thyme, cinnamon, saffron, salt and pepper in paella pan or Dutch oven. Cover and simmer for 15 minutes or until vegetables are tender. Remove cover and add chicken. Simmer 10 minutes, add shrimp; cook 3 minutes longer. Stir in rice, pimentos and hot pepper sauce. Top with peas and cook only long enough to heat peas. Makes 6 servings.

CHICKEN VALENCIA STYLE (Arroz con Pollo a la Valenciana)

8 ounces diced, skinned and boned chicken breast
1 cup chicken bouillon or homemade chicken stock (see page ix)
1 medium canned or fresh tomato, cut in pieces
2 teaspoons dehydrated onion flakes
¼ teaspoon garlic powder or ½ garlic clove, mashed
¼ teaspoon chili powder or cayenne pepper to taste
2 threads saffron
2 ounces peas
½ cup cooked enriched rice

Combine first 7 ingredients in a saucepan and simmer, uncovered, approximately 20 minutes or until mixture is reduced by about one-half. Stir in peas and cook 5 minutes. Add rice. Heat well but do not boil. Makes 1 serving.

CHICKEN FLAMENCO

4 8-ounce skinned and boned
  chicken breasts
Salt and pepper to taste
4 ounces onion, chopped
2 ribs celery, diced
1 medium green pepper, seeded
  and diced

1 garlic clove, finely minced
1½ cups chicken bouillon
2 cups mushrooms, sliced
1 tablespoon pimento, cut in
  pieces

Season chicken with salt and pepper, and brown in nonstick skillet. Transfer to 1½-quart casserole. Add onion, celery, green pepper and garlic to skillet, and cook, stirring for about 5 minutes or until tender-crisp. Spoon over chicken. In a small saucepan, bring bouillon to boil and pour over chicken and vegetables. Cover casserole and bake in moderately slow oven (325°F.) 30 to 45 minutes or until chicken is tender. Meanwhile cook mushrooms in a hot nonstick skillet about 5 minutes. Shortly before chicken is done add mushrooms and pimento to casserole. Return casserole to oven to finish baking. Makes 4 servings.

SAFFRON BEEF

Roast bottom round of beef on a rack in moderate oven (325°F.) until done. Cut as directed, reserving natural juices extracted from meat during cutting.

1 pound onions, thinly sliced
1 garlic clove, minced
1½ pounds cooked bottom round
  of beef, cut into 1½-inch
  cubes
1 cup tomato puree plus beef
  juices (see above)
3½ medium tomatoes, peeled and
  diced

½ medium green pepper, cut into
  1-inch squares
1 tablespoon loosely packed
  saffron
½ teaspoon chopped fresh thyme
  (or ¼ teaspoon dried)
Salt and pepper to taste

In a large flameproof casserole at moderately high heat, cook onions and garlic, stirring constantly until onion is wilted, about 5 minutes. Add remaining ingredients. Bring to a boil, stirring to combine. Cover and bake in moderately slow oven (325°F.) for 2 hours or until meat is tender. Makes 4 servings.

SPANISH MEATBALLS (Albóndigas)

1½ pounds ground beef
1 tablespoon minced fresh
parsley
½ teaspoon salt
¼ teaspoon white pepper
⅛ teaspoon nutmeg
4 ounces chopped onions

1½ cups beef bouillon, divided
12 ounces tiny peas
2 medium tomatoes, chopped
4 pimentos, diced
2 teaspoons brandy extract
½ teaspoon garlic powder

Combine ground beef, parsley, salt, white pepper and nutmeg; mix well; shape into meatballs about 1½-inches in diameter. Bake on rack in pan at 350°F. for 15 minutes or until cooked throughout. Turn once during baking. In saucepan, cook onions in ½ cup of bouillon over low heat for 5 minutes or until onions are just tender. Add peas, tomatoes, pimentos, extract, remaining bouillon, garlic powder and baked meatballs. Stir to combine. Simmer 5 to 7 minutes or until peas are done. Makes 4 servings.

SPANISH SHREDDED BEEF

2¼ pounds cooked flank steak
1¼ cups peeled, cubed turnip
1 cup scraped carrot, sliced
3 ounces leeks, washed well and
chopped
Water
6 ounces onion, chopped
1 medium green pepper, seeded
and chopped
½ fresh hot chili, seeded and
chopped, or to taste

1 garlic clove, minced or pressed
2 medium tomatoes, peeled and
chopped
1 bay leaf
⅛ teaspoon cinnamon
⅛ teaspoon ground cloves
Salt and freshly ground pepper to
taste
2 pimentos, chopped
1 tablespoon chopped capers
(optional)

In a 5-quart pot or Dutch oven, bring to boil beef, turnips, carrots and leeks in water to cover. Lower heat, cover pot and simmer gently until tender, about 1½ hours. Allow to cool sufficiently to handle. Remove meat from liquid; reserve liquid. Shred meat with fingers. Return meat to liquid, reserving ¼ cup for later use. In a covered saucepan, cook onion, green pepper, chili and garlic in ¼ cup reserved liquid until tender. Remove cover; add tomatoes, bay leaf, cinnamon, cloves, salt and pepper. Cook, stirring occasionally, until sauce is thickened and flavors are well blended. Remove bay leaf. Combine with remaining liquid and meat. Add pimentos and simmer 5 minutes longer. Add capers, if desired, and stir to blend. Makes 6 servings.

SPANISH STEW (Cocido Madrileño)

1 pound stew beef, cut in cubes	¼ cup diced celery
3 cups water	2 packets instant beef broth and seasoning mix
1 medium green pepper, diced	
1 cup diced peeled turnips	½ garlic clove, minced
1 cup cored cabbage, cut in two wedges	1 cup cooked fresh cowpeas or lima beans
4 ounces onion, diced	Salt and pepper to taste
½ cup sliced mushrooms	

Cover beef with water, bring to boil and cook until beef is tender, about 1 hour. Remove beef and refrigerate stock and beef separately. When fat congeals on stock, skim to remove and discard fat. Transfer 1½ cups fat-free stock to saucepan. Add green pepper, turnips, cabbage, onion, mushrooms and celery. Add broth mix and garlic and simmer over low heat until vegetables are tender, 40 minutes or so. Add beef and cowpeas or lima beans, and season to taste. Reheat an additional 10 minutes. Makes 2 servings.

LAMB KABOBS LA MANCHA

The Moors invaded Spain from the South more than a thousand years ago, so, Arabic culinary traditions have strong roots here; hence, kabobs.

2 tablespoons lemon juice	1 pound boneless, lean lamb cubes
2 teaspoons orange extract	1 cup mushrooms
½ teaspoon salt	½ medium green pepper, sliced
¼ teaspoon cumin	½ medium tomato, sliced
Dash oregano	

Combine lemon juice, orange extract, salt, cumin and oregano. Pour over lamb in bowl; toss lightly until well mixed. Let stand at room temperature 1 hour. On each of 2 skewers spear ½ of lamb, mushrooms, pepper and tomato in that order. Broil on a rack about 4 inches from source of heat 10 minutes or until lamb is grilled to taste. Turn once during broiling. Makes 2 servings.

MARINATED PORK WITH PIMENTO

In Spain the midday siesta, which precedes the long and late dinner, provides plenty of time for marinating the pork.

2 large or 3 small garlic cloves, finely chopped
1 teaspoon salt, preferably coarse salt
½ teaspoon freshly ground black pepper
1½ pounds cooked boneless pork loin, cut in ¼-inch thick slices
1½ cups canned pimento (or 4 fresh seeded medium red peppers), cut in ½-inch strips
1½ cups chicken bouillon
1 lemon, cut into 6 wedges

With a mortar and pestle or back of a large spoon, mash garlic, salt and pepper together to form a smooth paste. Lightly spread pork slices with the paste, place them in a bowl, cover tightly and marinate for several hours or overnight in refrigerator. In a large nonstick skillet brown pork slices, a few at a time, and transfer to a plate. Add the pimentos to pan, stirring frequently; cook for 5 minutes or until most of the moisture is evaporated. Transfer pork to pan; add bouillon; cover tightly; reduce heat to low and simmer for 45 minutes or until pork is tender and shows no resistance when pierced with a fork. Remove pork and pimentos from pan, reserving liquid. Divide evenly onto 4 individual plates. Liquid can be poured over each serving, if desired. Garnish with lemon wedges. Makes 4 servings.

PORK ESPANOL

1½ pounds cooked pork, cut in strips ½-inch wide
2 tablespoons cider vinegar
1 garlic clove, minced
1 tablespoon dehydrated onion flakes
½ teaspoon freshly ground pepper
½ bay leaf
Salt to taste
2 medium canned tomatoes, chopped
2 cups cooked enriched rice

In a large mixing bowl, combine pork, vinegar, garlic, onion flakes, pepper, bay leaf and salt. Mix well to coat pork. Let stand 1 hour or even longer. Combine meat and marinade with tomato and rice. Spoon into a 2-quart casserole. Bake covered in moderate oven (350°F.) until heated through, about 30 minutes. Remove bay leaf. Makes 4 servings.

GARLIC-MARINATED CARROTS

2 tablespoons wine or cider vinegar
1 tablespoon vegetable oil
1 garlic clove, minced
Freshly ground black pepper to taste
Oregano to taste
2 cups finely sliced boiled carrots

Combine first 5 ingredients to form a marinade. Add carrots; stir to coat with mixture. Let stand in refrigerator at least one day. Makes 2 servings.

LIMA BEANS WITH CHEESE

2 ounces chopped onion
1 medium green pepper, chopped
½ cup beef bouillon
½ cup tomato puree
½ teaspoon Worcestershire
¼ teaspoon salt
⅛ teaspoon cayenne pepper
1 cup cooked fresh lima beans
4 ounces shredded American cheese

Cook onion and green pepper in bouillon over low heat 5 minutes or until onion is just tender. Add tomato puree; simmer 5 minutes. Stir in Worcestershire, salt and cayenne pepper. Spoon ½ of cooked lima beans in an even layer in baking dish. Spoon ½ of shredded cheese in an even layer over lima beans. Spoon ½ of vegetable-tomato puree mixture over cheese. Repeat layers with remaining beans, cheese and tomato puree mixture. Bake at 350°F. for 15 minutes. Makes 2 servings.

CUCUMBERS WITH ORANGE SAUCE
(Cohombros con Salsa de Naranja)

4 medium cucumbers
2 cups orange juice
2 tablespoons grated orange rind
¼ teaspoon salt
⅛ teaspoon freshly ground black pepper
8 teaspoons margarine

Peel cucumbers. Take a thin slice off both sides. Score lengthwise with a fork on all sides and cut cucumbers in ½-inch slices. Cover slices with water and cook covered for 15 minutes. Drain cucumbers and set aside. Combine orange juice and rind, salt and pepper; heat, and add to cooked cucumber slices. Stir in margarine. Serve as a vegetable. Makes 8 servings.

[319]

POTATOES WITH STRING BEANS (Patatas con Judías Verdes)

1 ounce onion, finely chopped
1 cup chicken bouillon
¼ bay leaf
¼ garlic clove
Dash of ground cloves
3 ounces cooked potatoes,
thinly sliced

1 cup cooked string beans
Salt and pepper to taste
Garnish: 2 strips pimento and
parsley sprigs

Lightly brown onion in nonstick skillet. Add chicken bouillon, bay leaf, garlic and cloves. Simmer 10 minutes. Discard bay leaf and garlic. Layer potatoes over beans in pan with bouillon and simmer covered until well heated. Season to taste. Garnish with pimento and parsley. Makes 1 serving.

PEPPERY MUSHROOMS (Champiñones Picante)

Or bake the seasoned mushrooms in the oven until they are crisp and crackly.

4 cups (about 1 pound)
mushrooms
3 small dried chili peppers,
minced, or ½ teaspoon ground
red pepper

⅓ cup chicken bouillon
Salt to taste

Wipe mushrooms clean. Slice them through stems and caps. In nonstick skillet brown over moderate heat; add minced chili peppers and cook with mushrooms, stirring often. Pour in chicken bouillon and salt to taste. Simmer uncovered, 3 to 4 minutes, and serve hot. Makes 8 appetizer servings.

VALENCIAN RICE (Arroz con Legumbres)

2 medium tomatoes, peeled and
cubed
1 cup zucchini, cut in small cubes
2 cups cooked enriched rice,
prepared in onion bouillon

Salt and freshly ground pepper
to taste
4 ounces cooked fresh green peas
2 tablespoons chopped pimentos
Dash hot pepper sauce

Cook tomatoes and zucchini in nonstick pan on top of the stove, stirring, until most of the liquid evaporates. Transfer mixture to a 2-quart casserole. Combine with rice and season with salt and pepper. Cover casserole and bake at 350°F. for about 20 minutes or until heated through. Remove from oven, add peas, pimento and hot pepper sauce, tossing to mix thoroughly. Makes 4 servings.

VARIATION: Omit tomatoes; combine rice with 2 cups tomato juice in casserole.

WIDOW'S RICE (Arroz Viudo)

It's a dish that lives without meat, hence alone or widowed.

2 ounces onions, chopped
¼ cup onion bouillon
1 cup cooked enriched rice
⅔ cup tomato puree
1½ teaspoons chopped pimentos

1 teaspoon dehydrated bell pepper flakes
½ teaspoon Worcestershire
½ teaspoon seasoned salt
Dash pepper and garlic powder

Cook onions in bouillon over low heat in skillet 4 minutes or until just tender. Add rice, puree, pimentos, dehydrated pepper flakes, Worcestershire, salt, pepper and garlic powder; mix well. Cook over low heat 5 minutes or until heated throughout. Makes 2 servings.

RICE SALAD (Ensalada de Arroz a la Valenciana)

2 cups cooked enriched rice, steaming hot
1 teaspoon sherry extract
2 medium green peppers, seeded and cut in quarters
1 tablespoon dry mustard

1 teaspoon water
¼ cup vegetable oil
¼ cup vinegar
¼ teaspoon pepper
Salt to taste

Combine rice and sherry extract, and let rice cool. Prepare peppers as directed in Ensalada a la Andaluza (see page 322). In a large bowl, moisten mustard with water to make a paste, add oil and vinegar, pepper and salt. Mix to combine for a dressing. Stir in diced peppers and cooled rice. Marinate, refrigerated, at least 30 minutes. Makes 4 servings.

TUNA FISH AND BEAN SALAD BASQUE STYLE

4 ounces drained, canned tuna fish
½ cup cooked fresh red beans
½ cup cooked wax beans
1 small rib celery, diced

2 tablespoons vinegar
1 tablespoon vegetable oil
½ garlic clove, minced
Dash each cumin, cloves, salt and pepper

Combine ingredients in salad bowl and chill before serving. Makes 1 serving.

BLACK BEAN SALAD

4 ounces diced onion
4 medium green peppers, chopped
2 garlic cloves, mashed
1½ pounds cooked dried black beans (see note)
1 cup beef bouillon
Dash oregano

Dash brandy extract
¼ cup vegetable oil
¼ cup wine vinegar
¾ teaspoon prepared mustard
Salt and freshly ground pepper to taste

In preheated nonstick saucepan, lightly brown onion, green pepper and garlic. Add the beans, bouillon, oregano and brandy extract. Simmer for 45 minutes. Let cool. Combine oil, wine vinegar, mustard, salt and pepper. Pour over beans. Chill until ready to serve. Makes 4 servings.

NOTE: To cook dried beans: Cover 1½ cups dried black beans with 4½ cups water. Let soak overnight. Cook about 2 to 2½ hours or until beans are soft. Weigh serving.

MIXED VEGETABLE SALAD (Ensalada a la Andaluza)

¼ cup vegetable oil
¼ cup vinegar
¼ teaspoon pepper
2 medium cucumbers, peeled, seeded and diced
Salt to taste
6 medium green peppers, seeded and cut in quarters

2 medium tomatoes, peeled, seeded and diced
½ clove garlic (optional)
1 tablespoon dehydrated onion flakes, reconstituted

Mix oil, vinegar and pepper for a dressing; set aside. Place diced cucumber in bowl; sprinkle with salt and let stand 20 minutes. Liquid will accumulate. Drain and dry on paper towels. Remove to small bowl and toss with ½ the dressing. Broil peppers 4 inches from source of heat until skin browns and puckers, about 15 minutes. Watch carefully. Skin will look burnt when peppers are ready. Peel skin and dice peppers. Place in small bowl; sprinkle with salt and let stand 15 minutes. Place tomatoes in a separate bowl, sprinkle with salt and let stand for 15 minutes also. Drain peppers and toss with remaining dressing. Drain tomatoes. Rub salad bowl with garlic if desired. Add cucumbers to green peppers and their dressing. Add tomatoes and onion flakes; toss lightly and chill. Makes 8 servings.

BANANA CUSTARD (Flan de Plátano)*

1 fully ripe medium banana,
 peeled, diced
Dash cinnamon
1½ teaspoons brown sugar
 replacement

2 medium eggs, beaten
1 cup skim milk

Spoon banana into two custard cups or a small baking dish. Sprinkle each with cinnamon. In a mixing bowl combine sugar replacement and eggs. Heat milk in a saucepan (*do not boil*). Pour a little into eggs to temper them. Add egg mixture to remaining milk in saucepan, stirring constantly. Dividing evenly, pour over banana. Place cups or baking dish in a pan of hot water and bake in moderately hot oven (375°F.) 20 to 25 minutes or until set. Refrigerate. Serve cold. Makes 2 servings.

ALMOND-FLAVORED FRUIT MOLD

½ small pear
½ medium apple
2 slices canned pineapple, with
 2 tablespoons juice, no sugar
 added
1 envelope unflavored gelatin

¼ cup plus 2 tablespoons
 water
1 cup orange juice
Artificial sweetener to equal
 2 teaspoons sugar
¼ teaspoon almond extract

Core, peel and cut fruit into small cubes and place in a mold. In a small saucepan soften gelatin in water, juices and sweetener. Heat to dissolve gelatin; remove from stove and add almond flavoring. Mix well. Pour liquid over fruit in mold and refrigerate. Makes 4 servings.

"SANGRIA"

½ cup chilled orange juice
¾ cup chilled grape-flavored
 dietetic soda

½ teaspoon rum extract
Lemon or lime slice (to garnish)

Combine orange juice, dietetic soda and rum extract in glass. Garnish with lemon slice. Makes 1 serving.

Switzerland

Swiss cuisine is a hybrid, a blend of varied cultures that makes one delightful and unified whole. In three cantons—French, German and Italian—foods appropriate to their separate origins are served. Of course, in this health-conscious country the dairy products and the greens are very popular, and most Swiss restaurants feature salads and vegetables, raw as well as cooked. So do we.

The Swiss love desserts. So do we. We've satisfied everybody's craving for an authentic sweet to end the Swiss meal by including recipes for plum tarts and a rhubarb meringue pie. Or why not serve a tray of the famous Emmentaler cheese (called Swiss in the United States and Gruyère in France) and ripe fresh fruits, just as they do in Switzerland?

BEAN SOUP BASEL STYLE

½ cup cooked fresh lima beans
(with liquid)
2 cups chicken bouillon
½ cup finely chopped carrots
¼ cup chopped celery
¼ medium green pepper,
finely chopped

1 ounce chopped onion
Dash basil
Dash thyme
¼ cup evaporated skimmed milk
Salt and pepper to taste

Place beans (with liquid) and bouillon in blender container. Process until smooth. Pour into saucepan; add carrots, celery, pepper, onion and herbs. Simmer 20 minutes or until vegetables are tender. Add milk; reheat (do not boil). Season to taste and serve. Makes 1 serving.

CHEESE SOUFFLE LUCERNE

For mittagessen *(lunch) try a cheese soufflé like this, with a platter of raw vegetables.*

½ cup skim milk
1 medium egg, separated
1 ounce Swiss (Emmentaler or
Gruyère) cheese, grated

1 slice enriched white bread,
made into crumbs
⅛ teaspoon salt
Dash paprika, nutmeg

Combine milk, egg yolk, cheese and bread crumbs in a saucepan. Season with salt, paprika and nutmeg. Place over low heat. Cook and stir until mixture is slightly thickened. Set aside. Cool. Beat egg white with rotary beater until peaks form; fold into mixture. Pour into custard cup or small dish. Bake in moderately hot (375°F.) oven for 25 to 30 minutes. Makes 1 serving.

CARAWAY BREAD STIX

2 tablespoons margarine
4 slices whole wheat bread

1 teaspoon coarse salt
½ teaspoon caraway seeds

Spread 1½ teaspoons margarine on one side of each bread slice. Sprinkle with seasonings. Place on nonstick baking sheet margarine-side up. Bake in hot oven (400°F.) for 10 minutes or until toasted. Cut toast slices in thirds. Makes 4 servings.

VEAL AND CABBAGE BAKE ZURICH

1 cup cabbage leaves
Water
¾ cup tomato juice
½ teaspoon nutmeg

½ teaspoon dry mustard
¼ teaspoon salt
6 ounces cooked ground veal,
  crumbled

Cover cabbage leaves with water and bring to a boil. Cook until leaves become limp, but do not shred. In a small bowl combine tomato juice, nutmeg, dry mustard and salt. Set aside. In an individual heatproof casserole or serving dish, layer ½ the cabbage leaves, veal and tomato juice mixture. Repeat layers. Bake in moderate oven (350°F.) about 15 minutes or until heated through. Makes 1 serving.

SWISS STEAK LUGANO

You'll find this kind of meat dish in the Italian canton, served with cooked enriched pasta.

6 ounces shoulder steak
  (½-inch thick)
1 cup tomato juice
1 cup beef bouillon
1 medium tomato, sliced

¼ cup diced celery
2 ounces onion, sliced
½ bay leaf
Dash garlic powder
Salt and pepper to taste

Preheat broiler. Place steak on rack under broiler 4 inches from heat. Cook 3 to 4 minutes on each side until brown. Transfer to small saucepan. Add remaining ingredients; season to taste. Simmer over low heat for 30 minutes or until vegetables are cooked and sauce thickens. Makes 1 serving.

PAN-BROWN POTATOES

⅓ cup water
1 packet instant onion broth and
  seasoning mix
¼ teaspoon dehydrated onion
  flakes

¼ teaspoon caraway seeds
⅛ teaspoon tarragon
⅛ teaspoon salt
Dash paprika
6 ounces cooked potato, sliced

In nonstick skillet, heat water to boiling; add remaining ingredients except potatoes; cover and cook 2 minutes. Add potatoes, cook over medium heat until liquid is evaporated. Makes 2 servings.

DILL BOILED POTATOES

2¼ pounds new potatoes   1 tablespoon chopped fresh dill
1 teaspoon salt

Place potatoes, water to cover, and salt in a large saucepan; cover
and boil slowly about 30 minutes or until tender. Drain and peel.
Sprinkle with dill. Serve hot. Makes 12 servings.

SPRING SALAD BOWL WITH BUTTERMILK DRESSING

1 head iceberg lettuce, shredded   12 sprigs parsley or watercress
1 bunch watercress   6 leaves of escarole
8 radishes, sliced thin   Buttermilk Dressing (recipe
3 ribs celery, diced   follows)

In a large salad bowl toss together all the ingredients, except the
escarole. Arrange the escarole leaves around the mixture. Serve with
Buttermilk Dressing. Makes 6 servings.

Buttermilk Dressing

¾ cup buttermilk   ¼ teaspoon dill seed
3 tablespoons mayonnaise   1 teaspoon chopped fresh
1 teaspoon lemon juice   parsley
½ teaspoon dehydrated onion   Salt and pepper to taste
  flakes

Combine all ingredients except salt and pepper in a mixing bowl. Mix
well with hand whisk or fork until smooth. Season to taste. Divide
equally into 6 portions and serve with Spring Salad Bowl. Makes 6
servings.

STUFFED TOMATOES

6 medium tomatoes   ½ teaspoon salt
3 tart medium apples, peeled   3 tablespoons vegetable oil
  and shredded   1 tablespoon chives or watercress,
3 cups diced celery   minced
¼ cup lemon juice

Cut a thin slice off top of each tomato; peel and remove seeds and
pulp (reserve pulp) leaving a thick shell. Turn tomatoes upside down

to drain. Combine apples, celery, lemon juice and salt with drained tomato pulp. Let stand 20 to 30 minutes. Add oil; mix well. Use filling for tomatoes. Top with chives or watercress. Makes 6 servings.

RHUBARB MERINGUE PIE*

2 cups rhubarb, sliced
2 medium egg yolks, beaten
2 slices enriched white bread, made into crumbs

Artificial sweetener to equal ½ cup sugar
½ teaspoon grated lemon rind
Meringue (recipe follows)

In a bowl mix rhubarb, egg yolks, bread crumbs, sweetener and lemon rind. Pour into 8- or 9-inch pie pan. Bake in preheated moderately slow oven (325°F.) for 40 minutes or until rhubarb is very tender. Remove from oven and top with meringue. Bake an additional 15 to 20 minutes or until meringue browns. Cool. Makes 2 servings.

Meringue

2 medium egg whites
Artificial sweetener to equal ¼ cup sugar

¼ teaspoon vanilla extract
Dash salt

Beat egg whites until stiff but not dry. Add remaining ingredients. Beat to combine. Use with Rhubarb Meringue Pie. Makes 2 servings.

PLUM CRUMB TART (Pflaumentorte)

1 ounce uncooked farina, prepared according to package directions
2 tablespoons brown sugar replacement

2 medium plums, pared, pitted and sliced
½ teaspoon lemon juice
1 tablespoon imitation (or diet) margarine

Prepare farina according to package directions. Stir in brown sugar replacement. Layer plum slices in bottom of a small casserole. Sprinkle with lemon juice. Spoon farina mixture evenly over plum slices. Dot with margarine. Bake in moderately hot oven (375°F.) for 30 to 40 minutes or until plums are tender. Makes 1 serving.

NOTE: Serve with ½ cup skim milk.

The United States

Navy Bean Soup and Philadelphia Pepper Pot. Chowders from New England, New York and Florida. Indian Corn Pudding. Granola. Catfish and Key Lime Fish Medley. Shrimp de Jonghe from Chicago and Shrimp Rémoulade from New Orleans. Ham and Grits with Red-Eye Gravy. Sweet-Soul Pork Blade Steak. Oyster Jambalaya. New England Baked Lima Beans and California Caesar Salad. Brown Betty and Banana Nut Brownie. We've gone from one coast of the United States to the other, from Yankee North to Deep Deep South, to prove that America does indeed have a unique regional cuisine of its own. We've also included recipes for dishes born in this country but of foreign parentage: Cioppino, Hexel, Deviled Chicken Legs, soufflés, because they are American, too. Israel Zangwill said it best more than 75 years ago, when, in his play about immigration, he first called the United States a "melting pot." We dedicate this chapter to the melting pot, home of many different ethnic groups, cultures, and cuisines: to America, with love.

SOYBEAN VEGETABLE SOUP

½ cup cooked fresh soybeans, divided
2 cups chicken bouillon, divided
⅔ cup diced carrots
½ cup diced celery
½ teaspoon dehydrated onion flakes

¼ medium green pepper, diced
Dash basil
Dash thyme
¼ cup evaporated skimmed milk
Salt and pepper to taste

Place half the soybeans and bouillon in blender container; process until mixture is liquefied. Pour into a saucepan; add carrots, celery, onion flakes, green pepper and remaining bouillon. Bring to a boil; add basil and thyme. Simmer for 20 minutes or until carrots are tender. Add milk and remaining soybeans; reheat. Season to taste. Makes 1 serving.

CHICKEN OKRA SOUP WITH RICE

To spike up the flavor, add ½ teaspoon finely chopped fresh hot chili or hot pepper sauce to taste. In the South ½ teaspoon or so of gumbo filé, the powder made from sassafras leaves, is sometimes added.

8 ounces frozen okra, sliced and thawed
2 cups cooked enriched rice
2 medium tomatoes, peeled, seeded and chopped

4 cups chicken bouillon
¼ teaspoon allspice
Salt and pepper to taste

Cook okra following package directions. Transfer to colander and rinse well with cold water. (If you are using fresh okra, wash it well with a brush to remove surface fuzz, slice and cook in boiling water until just tender. Rinse in colander and continue as directed.) In saucepan, combine cooked okra, rice, tomatoes, bouillon, allspice, salt and pepper. Simmer, covered, 10 to 15 minutes; stir well and serve hot. Makes 4 servings.

PHILADELPHIA PEPPER POT

John Adams wrote about dining in Philadelphia: "A most sinful feast again, everything that would delight the eye or allure the taste . . ." We've prepared this specialty for feasting without sinning.

1½ pounds precooked honeycomb tripe, cut into ¼-inch pieces
2 tablespoons dehydrated onion flakes
3 cups chicken bouillon
2 cups diced celery
1½ cups sliced carrots
3 tablespoons chopped fresh parsley

2 teaspoons mixed dry herbs: marjoram, basil, summer savory, thyme
Dash hot pepper sauce or cayenne pepper
2 cloves
4 3-ounce cooked and peeled potatoes

Wash and scrub tripe thoroughly. Cover generously with cold salted water, using about 1 teaspoon salt. Bring to boil and let cook at simmer until tripe is tender (about 1½ to 2 hours). Add more water if necessary as tripe must be immersed as it cooks. Drain tripe. In saucepan, combine tripe with remaining ingredients. Cover and cook for 45 minutes. Serve hot. Makes 4 servings.

PHILADELPHIA PEPPER POT WITH VEAL

Use only 12 ounces of the tripe. Cook as directed above. To saucepan, add 12 ounces cooked diced veal left from a roast or inexpensive cut and follow preceding recipe. Makes 4 servings.

NAVY BEAN SOUP

A hearty soup, a favorite in the United States Senate restaurant.

4 ounces cooked, dried navy beans, drained, reserving liquid
Water
¼ cup diced celery
¼ cup diced cooked carrots

1 ounce chopped onion
¼ teaspoon garlic powder
¼ small bay leaf
2 ounces cooked ham, finely diced
Salt, pepper and ground cloves to taste

In a medium saucepan combine liquid from cooked beans and enough water to make 1½ cups. Add celery, carrots, onions, garlic and bay leaf. Simmer 15 minutes or until vegetables are tender. Remove bay leaf. Add beans and ham. Heat through. Season with salt, pepper and cloves to taste. Makes 1 serving.

MANHATTAN FISH CHOWDER

Chowder is from the French chaudière, *the pot in which fish soup is made.*

1 pound cod or haddock fillets
(or combination), fresh or
frozen and defrosted
3 cups boiling water
6 ounces peeled potatoes, diced
⅓ cup diced carrots
½ cup chopped celery
2 ounces chopped onion

2 medium tomatoes
¼ cup tomato puree
2 teaspoons Worcestershire
¾ teaspoon salt
¼ teaspoon pepper
¼ teaspoon thyme
Chopped fresh parsley for garnish

Cut fish into 1-inch pieces and refrigerate. In saucepan, combine water, potatoes, carrots, celery, onion, tomatoes, tomato puree and seasonings (except parsley). Cover and simmer for 40 to 45 minutes or until vegetables are tender. Add fish. Cover and simmer about 10 minutes longer or until fish is done. Sprinkle with parsley. Serve hot. Makes 2 servings.

RED SNAPPER CHOWDER, FLORIDA STYLE

2½ pound red snapper, cut in
4 large pieces
4 ounces onion, sliced
1½ cups tomato puree
¼ cup tomato paste
2 medium green peppers,
finely diced

1 cup chopped celery
1 garlic clove, crushed
Few drops hot pepper sauce or
small hot pepper pod

Cover fish with water; cook until it is tender. Remove skin and bones from fish and flake. Return 1½ pounds of flaked fish to water in which it was boiled. Add everything but the hot pepper sauce. Cook until vegetables are tender. Stir in hot pepper sauce. Serve in bowls. Makes 4 servings.

FISH GUMBO

Make chowder above, adding these Creole seasonings: ½ teaspoon thyme and a bay leaf; just before serving, add 2 teaspoons gumbo filé to taste. Other fish could replace the red snapper. Makes 4 servings.

GLOUCESTER CLAM CHOWDER

A mighty fine chowder from a picturesque Massachusetts fishing port.

2 cups water
12 ounces peeled potatoes, cubed
2 cups clam juice
2 cups diced celery
2 tablespoons dehydrated onion flakes
1 garlic clove
1 bay leaf
1 teaspoon chopped fresh parsley
1 pound drained, canned minced clams
1 cup evaporated skimmed milk
Salt, freshly ground pepper and paprika to taste

In saucepan, combine 2 cups water, potatoes, clam juice, celery, onion flakes, garlic, bay leaf and parsley. Bring to boil, then simmer until potatoes are tender. Remove bay leaf. Put through strainer (or puree in blender in two batches), making certain to press everything through. Put back into saucepan with clams; add evaporated skimmed milk and heat well without boiling. Add salt, pepper and dusting of paprika. Makes 4 servings.

QUICK CRAB CIOPPINO FISHERMAN'S WHARF

4 ounces onion, chopped
2 garlic cloves, minced
1½ cups tomato puree
1 cup clam juice
4 medium tomatoes, sliced
3 tablespoons chopped fresh parsley
2 tablespoons chopped fresh basil or 1 teaspoon dried
12 ounces shelled and deveined raw shrimp
12 ounces flaked canned crab meat
4 ounces canned drained clams
Salt and freshly ground pepper to taste
1 tablespoon sherry or sauterne extract
Chopped fresh parsley for garnish

In nonstick pan, cook onions and garlic for a few minutes or until onions are tender-crisp, stirring occasionally to prevent sticking. Add tomato puree, clam juice, tomatoes, parsley and basil. Cover and simmer briskly for 30 minutes. Add shrimp and cook 5 minutes or until they are pink. Add crab meat and clams, salt and freshly ground pepper. Heat but do not boil. Stir in wine extract. Divide into 4 bowls, sprinkling each portion with parsley. Makes 4 servings.

PENNSYLVANIA DUTCH PICKLED EGGS AND BEETS*

2 cups vinegar
Beet liquid and water to equal
  ½ cup
2½ tablespoons brown sugar
  replacement
Small piece cinnamon stick

2 cloves
Dash of allspice
2 hard-cooked medium eggs,
  shelled
4 ounces cooked diced beets
  (reserve liquid)

In saucepan combine vinegar, beet liquid and water, brown sugar replacement, cinnamon, cloves and allspice. Bring to boil, then simmer for 10 minutes. Pour into wide jar. Add eggs and beets. Refrigerate two days before use. Serve on bed of lettuce. Makes 2 servings.

EGGPLANT AND CORNMEAL SOUFFLE

1 cup skim milk
1 ounce enriched dry cornmeal
¾ cup cooked eggplant, pureed
¼ cup tomato puree
½ teaspoon salt

¼ teaspoon oregano
¼ teaspoon basil
Dash pepper or to taste
2 medium eggs, separated

Pour milk into saucepan; sprinkle in cornmeal, stirring with wooden spoon. Simmer 10 minutes or until mixture thickens. Remove from heat; add eggplant, tomato puree, salt, oregano, basil and pepper; cool. Add egg yolks and mix well. Beat egg whites until stiff peaks form; fold into mixture. Pour mixture into nonstick baking dish and bake at 400°F. for 15 minutes, then lower temperature to 325°F. and bake an additional 20 minutes or until top crust is golden brown. Serve immediately. Makes 1 serving.

HOMINY GRITS SOUFFLE, PLANTATION STYLE*

Preheat oven to 375°F. Into 1½ cups cooked hominy grits (prepared according to package directions), stir 2 medium egg yolks, 1 cup skim milk and 1 tablespoon imitation (or diet) margarine. Mix well. Beat egg whites separately. Fold into grits mixture. Bake in 1-quart baking dish for about 30 minutes or until top begins to brown. Makes 2 servings.

CHEESE STRATA

1 slice enriched white bread	¼ teaspoon prepared mustard
1 ounce sliced American cheese	¼ teaspoon salt
½ cup evaporated skimmed milk	Dash Worcestershire
1 medium egg	Dash hot pepper sauce
¼ teaspoon dehydrated onion flakes	

Cut bread into two slices by slicing in half, horizontally. Place one slice of halved bread on the bottom of a 6- or 7-inch heatproof shallow baking dish; place cheese on bread; top with remaining bread slice. Beat together remaining ingredients; pour over layers of bread and cheese. Bake 40 to 50 minutes at 325°F. or until puffy and golden brown. Makes 1 serving.

CORN PONES

Think corn pones when the main dish is fish. Serve them piping hot from the oven, along with icy cold buttermilk straight from the fridge.

4 ounces enriched dry cornmeal	4 teaspoons margarine
¼ teaspoon salt	½ cup boiling water
2 teaspoons baking powder	

In medium bowl combine cornmeal, salt and baking powder. Add margarine and boiling water. Stir until margarine melts. Cool just enough to handle. Divide mixture into four equal portions. Shape each portion into an oval by patting between your hands. Bake on nonstick pan in 350°F. oven for 1 hour. Makes 4 servings.

INDIAN CORN PUDDING WITH "CREAM" TOPPING*

1 cup skim milk	Dash cloves
1 ounce enriched dry cornmeal	1 medium egg, well beaten
Artificial sweetener to equal 6 teaspoons sugar	¼ cup chilled evaporated skimmed milk
Dash cinnamon	Artificial sweetener to taste
Dash nutmeg	½ teaspoon grated lemon rind (optional)
Dash allspice	
Dash ginger	

In a small saucepan bring milk to a boil; add cornmeal gradually, beating with wire whisk. When mixture starts to thicken, set aside to cool. When mixture is almost cool, stir in spices and egg. Pour into a small nonstick baking dish and bake at 325°F. for 1 hour. Make topping: Combine evaporated milk, sweetener and lemon rind, if desired. Whip with rotary beater until peaks form. Serve immediately on top of hot pudding. Makes 1 serving.

LOST BREAD*
Pain Perdu (French Toast, Creole Style)

Many New Orleanians prefer it this way—serve it with a wedge of lemon to be squeezed onto the toast at table. One serving can be easily baked in a toaster-oven, or the recipe can be multiplied for family service. To make this a classically Creole breakfast, serve it with café au lait. For one serving combine ½ cup each of steaming hot coffee and scalded skim milk.

¼ cup skim milk	1 slice enriched white bread
⅛ teaspoon vanilla or brandy extract	1 medium egg, separated
	Dash grated lemon rind

In a shallow plate or pie pan, combine milk and extract. Soak bread in mixture, turning once, until bread absorbs all of the liquid. In a small mixing bowl, lightly beat egg yolk with lemon rind. In a separate mixing bowl, beat egg white until stiff. Fold into yolk mixture. Place soaked bread on a nonstick baking sheet. Cover bread with egg mixture. Bake at 350°F. for 25 to 30 minutes or until egg becomes golden brown. Makes 1 serving.

CATFISH POORBOY

4 6-ounce catfish fillets	2 dashes hot pepper sauce
Salt and pepper to taste	4 slices enriched white bread, toasted
½ cup tomato puree	1 medium dill pickle, thinly sliced
1 teaspoon prepared mustard	
½ teaspoon dehydrated onion flakes	

Place fish fillets in a broiling pan; season with salt and pepper. Broil about 4 inches from heat until fish flakes easily with touch of fork; set aside. Combine tomato puree, mustard, onion flakes and hot pepper sauce in a saucepan; simmer for about 10 minutes until thickened. Spread over toast; cover each slice toast with a fillet and top each with ¼ sliced pickle. Makes 4 servings.

BAKED MACKEREL

1 10-ounce mackerel, dressed and split
¾ cup chicken bouillon
1 lemon slice
2 ounces onion, thinly sliced

Salt and pepper to taste
Paprika
Dash hot pepper sauce
1 tablespoon margarine

Place fish in small baking dish. Add bouillon and lemon. Place onion slices on top of fish. Then sprinkle with salt, pepper, paprika and hot pepper sauce. Cover with aluminum foil. Bake in hot oven (400°F.) for about 15 minutes or until fish flakes easily with touch of fork. Remove fish and onions with slotted spatula; place onions on serving plate. Drain excess liquid from baking dish and return fish to dish. Pierce fish lightly; spread with margarine and return to oven for 30 seconds until margarine melts. Makes 1 serving.

NATIVE GRANOLA

4 ounces uncooked oatmeal
2 teaspoons poppy seeds
¼ teaspoon cinnamon
⅛ teaspoon allspice
⅛ teaspoon nutmeg
⅛ teaspoon salt
1 medium apple, pared, cored, finely chopped

1⅓ cups nonfat dry milk
2 envelopes unflavored gelatin
½ cup boiling water
4 teaspoons margarine
¼ teaspoon vanilla extract
¼ teaspoon coconut extract

Combine and evenly spread oatmeal, poppy seeds, cinnamon, allspice, nutmeg, salt and apple on a rectangular nonstick shallow baking pan. Bake in 250°F. oven for 45 minutes. Remove from oven; broil 2 inches from heat source until golden brown. Remove from broiler; mix in milk and gelatin. In a measuring cup combine water, margarine and extracts; stir until margarine melts. Pour over oatmeal mixture, stirring quickly with a fork to combine. Mixture will be lumpy. Cool. Makes 4 servings.

NOTE: May be served in cereal bowl with additional boiling water.

KEY LIME FISH MEDLEY (Dinner in a Dish)

Vegetable Bed

4 cups cooked vegetables
(asparagus, bean sprouts,
broccoli, cauliflower, eggplant,
kale, mushrooms, well-drained
spinach or zucchini), see note
2 teaspoons dehydrated onion
flakes
2 teaspoons dehydrated bell
pepper flakes

2 pounds skinless fish fillets, fresh
or frozen and thawed (use
flounder, mullet, sole, etc.)
1 teaspoon salt
Dash pepper
¼ cup lime juice
4 medium tomatoes, sliced thick

Topping

¼ cup margarine
1 tablespoon chopped fresh
parsley

½ teaspoon salt
¼ teaspoon pepper
2 cups cooked enriched rice

Use a large shallow baking dish, oven-to-table type for easy cleanup. Make a bed of the vegetables (which should be cut into fairly uniform pieces; they can also be pureed in blender or food processor). Sprinkle flakes on top. Cut fish into 2-inch squares and arrange on the vegetable bed. Season with salt, pepper and lime juice and refrigerate for at least 30 minutes. When ready to use, put slices of tomato on top of fish, mash together the ingredients for topping, and dot tomatoes and fish. Bake in moderately hot oven (375°F.) for about ¾ hour or until fish flakes and tomatoes are tender. Serve each portion of fish with sauce over ½ cup fluffed cooked rice. Makes 4 servings.

NOTE: Don't put the liquid left from cooking vegetables down the drain! Leftover liquid can be cooked down to about half a cup and poured over fish before it is baked. Or use the liquid for reheating cold rice. Or combine leftover liquid with chicken bouillon for a first-course soup.

FISH GRILLED IN FOIL WITH VEGETABLES

You can bake these bundles on a baking sheet in a hot oven, allowing same timing. Other vegetables could be substituted.

For each serving:

1 8-ounce fish fillet, fresh preferred (thawed if frozen)
1 14-inch square heavy duty aluminum foil
1 3-ounce potato, partially cooked (about 10 minutes), sliced
2 ounces frozen small onions, defrosted
½ cup celery, cut in julienne strips and partly cooked (about 5 minutes)

1 medium tomato in 3 slices
Salt, pepper and paprika to taste
Optional seasonings: Ground ginger, garlic, Worcestershire, lemon juice and hot pepper sauce

Cut fish into 1-inch chunks and place on aluminum foil sheet. Add potato, onion, celery and tomato slices. Sprinkle with salt, pepper and paprika and add optional seasonings to taste. Wrap package with a double fold on top and at the ends, making the package as flat as possible. Be sure coals are ash gray, then put packet on grill and cook 20 to 25 minutes, turning at least once. Makes 1 serving.

Prepare Ahead Note: For serving a larger quantity, prepare the packets several hours ahead, refrigerate until ready to use.

HEXEL

Hash in the Pennsylvania Dutch dialect.

4 ounces diced onion
1 small garlic clove, cut
1½ pounds cold cooked fish, in large flakes
12 ounces cooked potatoes, diced

4 ounces cooked diced beets
¼ cup vinegar
½ teaspoon salt
¼ teaspoon pepper or to taste
2 medium dill pickles

Brown onions and garlic in large nonstick pan. Press garlic with fork as it browns to release its juices, then discard the clove. Add remaining ingredients (except pickles). Mix well; cover and let cook slowly to heat thoroughly and blend flavors, stirring as needed. Serve hot and well browned with sliced pickles. Makes 4 servings.

BAKED STUFFED RED SNAPPER

2 8-ounce red snapper fillets
1 teaspoon lemon juice

Salt and pepper to taste
Stuffing (recipe follows)

Place one fillet on nonstick baking dish. Pile stuffing on fillet. Top with remaining fillet. Sprinkle fish with lemon juice, salt and pepper. Bake in preheated moderately hot oven (375°F.) for 30 minutes or until fish flakes. Makes 2 servings.

Stuffing

½ cup finely chopped celery
1 tablespoon dehydrated onion flakes
1 cup mushrooms, minced
½ cup chicken bouillon
1 tablespoon chopped fresh parsley

½ teaspoon rubbed sage
½ teaspoon imitation butter flavoring
2 slices enriched fresh white bread, made into crumbs
Salt and pepper to taste

Cover celery and onion flakes with water in a saucepan, and cook until celery is tender. Drain and combine celery and onion flakes with remaining ingredients; season to taste and mix well. Fill red snapper fillets. Makes 2 servings.

TUNA AND POTATO CASSEROLE

12 ounces cooked potatoes, sliced (see note)
1 pound drained canned tuna, flaked
½ cup potato liquid

½ cup chicken bouillon
½ cup tomato puree
½ cup evaporated skimmed milk
2 teaspoons chopped fresh parsley

Place 3 ounces of potato slices in each of 4 individual heatproof casseroles. Top each with 4 ounces tuna. In a medium saucepan, combine potato liquid and bouillon. Stir in tomato puree. Bring to a boil. Simmer for 15 minutes. Stir in milk. With a wire whisk, beat the sauce smooth, or pour into blender container and process. Divide evenly and pour into casseroles. Sprinkle with parsley and bake at 400°F. for 20 minutes. Makes 4 servings.

NOTE: To prepare potatoes, place them in a medium saucepan with 2 cups water, 2 teaspoons dehydrated onion flakes, 1 teaspoon salt and 1 clove minced or pressed garlic; bring to a boil and cook until potatoes are tender. Remove potato from liquid and weigh portions for use in recipe. Reserve ½ cup potato liquid.

SARASOTA KEDGEREE

¾ cup chicken bouillon
½ cup cooked enriched rice
1 hard-cooked medium egg, sliced

2 ounces cooked cold, flaked fish
1 teaspoon margarine (optional)

Heat bouillon in small saucepan; add rice, egg slices and fish. Bring to boil; transfer to serving bowl and stir in margarine, if desired. Makes 1 serving.

SHRIMP DE JONGHE

Developed by a Chicago-American restaurateur and still served in homes and restaurants throughout the United States.

¼ cup vegetable oil
2 slices enriched white bread, made into fine dry bread crumbs
3 tablespoons chopped fresh parsley
1 tablespoon minced garlic
¾ teaspoon salt

¼ teaspoon paprika
Dash cayenne pepper or a few drops of hot pepper sauce
2 teaspoons coconut extract
2 pounds shelled and cleaned raw shrimp

Combine oil, bread crumbs (reserve 2 tablespoons), chopped parsley, minced garlic, salt, paprika, cayenne and coconut extract. Toss shrimp lightly in mixture until shrimp are well coated. Mix well. Turn into shallow pan. Sprinkle reserved bread crumbs on top. Bake uncovered, in moderately hot oven (375°F.) until shrimp are tender, about 40 minutes. Makes 4 servings.

OYSTER JAMBALAYA

¼ cup chopped celery
2 ounces finely chopped onion
1 medium tomato, diced
½ cup clam juice
⅛ teaspoon salt
½ small garlic clove, minced

Dash cayenne or black pepper or hot pepper sauce
Dash each, thyme and ginger
Dash ground coriander and fennel
6 ounces canned drained oysters
½ cup cooked enriched rice

Cook celery and onion in nonstick pan. When softened, add tomato, clam juice, salt, garlic, cayenne and other seasonings. Cook for 20 minutes. Add oysters and rice. Let simmer gently uncovered until fairly dry. Mix well and serve hot. Makes 1 serving.

BAYOU SHRIMP-STUFFED PEPPERS

2 medium green peppers
½ cup cooked enriched rice
6 ounces cooked tiny shrimp
¼ cup tomato puree
1 teaspoon prepared white
  horseradish

Dash hot pepper sauce
⅛ teaspoon lemon juice
Salt and pepper to taste

Remove stem end and seeds from green peppers. Dip in boiling water; let stand for a few minutes; drain. In a mixing bowl combine rice, shrimp, tomato puree, horseradish, hot pepper sauce and lemon juice. Mix well; season to taste. Stuff peppers with the mixture and bake at 425°F. for 25 minutes or until thoroughly heated and peppers are tender. Makes 1 serving.

SHRIMP REMOULADE (or Arnaud)

As served in New Orleans, Atlanta and many other cosmopolitan cities.

12 ounces cooked, shelled shrimp

Rémoulade Sauce

2 tablespoons finely diced celery
1 tablespoon vegetable oil
1 tablespoon vinegar
¼ teaspoon salt
¼ teaspoon prepared Creole or
  spicy mustard
¼ teaspoon prepared horseradish

¼ teaspoon minced chives
¼ teaspoon washed, minced
  capers
Dash paprika and hot pepper sauce
  or cayenne pepper
Dash garlic powder
Black pepper to taste

In serving bowl, marinate shrimp in Rémoulade Sauce made by combining all remaining ingredients. Refrigerate for at least 30 minutes before use, turning shrimp frequently in the sauce. Serve with sauce. Makes 2 servings.

SEAFOOD NEWBURG

½ cup chicken bouillon
¼ cup cooked cauliflower
¼ cup tomato juice
¼ cup evaporated skimmed milk
½ teaspoon lemon juice
½ teaspoon brandy extract
¼ teaspoon dehydrated onion
  flakes

⅛ teaspoon paprika
6 ounces cooked crabmeat, shrimp
  or lobster
Salt and pepper to taste
½ teaspoon chopped fresh
  parsley

Place bouillon, cauliflower, tomato juice, milk, lemon juice, extract, onion flakes and paprika in a blender container and process until smooth. Pour into saucepan; add fish. Heat thoroughly. Season with salt and pepper; sprinkle with parsley. Makes 1 serving.

CALIFORNIA ORANGE-TUNA SALAD

8 ounces drained, flaked canned
  tuna
1 small navel orange, peeled and
  cut in bite-size pieces
  (reserve rind)
1 teaspoon freshly grated
  orange rind

½ cup chopped celery
2 tablespoons diced pimento
2 tablespoons mayonnaise
Lettuce

Combine tuna, orange pieces, rind, celery and pimento; mix well. Stir in mayonnaise. Serve on lettuce. Makes 2 servings.

CHICKEN SALAD STATEN ISLAND

Just a trace of pleasant Italian accent here . . . as there is in the speech of some old-time Staten Islanders.

½ cup tomato juice
½ teaspoon celery seed
¼ teaspoon lemon juice
¼ teaspoon tarragon
Dash onion powder
4 ounces cooked and boned
  chicken, diced

3 ounces boiled potato, cubed
2 ounces cooked artichoke
  hearts, quartered
½ cup sliced celery
Shredded lettuce

In small saucepan heat first 5 ingredients to boiling; reduce heat. Cover and simmer 5 minutes. Combine remaining ingredients except lettuce in medium bowl; stir in hot marinade. Cover and chill. Serve on shredded lettuce, using marinade as dressing. Makes 1 serving.

BAR-B-QUE CHICKEN TEXAS STYLE

The basting sauce adds the smoky sweet flavor.

1 cup dietetic cola
¼ cup tomato paste
1 tablespoon dehydrated onion
  flakes
1 teaspoon Worcestershire

1 teaspoon lemon juice
1 teaspoon salt
1 garlic clove, minced
1¼ pounds skinned chicken
  parts

In medium saucepan add cola to tomato paste, stirring to combine, Add remaining ingredients except chicken; heat to boiling. Reduce heat and simmer 5 minutes. Pour barbecue sauce over chicken in shallow casserole. Marinate at room temperature, 30 minutes, turning once. Remove chicken; return sauce to saucepan; keep warm. Grill chicken for 20 minutes 5 to 6 inches from charcoal that has turned ash-gray, brushing occasionally with sauce. Turn chicken; grill 15 to 20 minutes longer. Serve with remaining sauce. Makes 2 servings.

PICNIC CHICKEN

½ teaspoon garlic powder
¼ teaspoon paprika
⅓ cup lemon juice
⅓ cup wine vinegar
⅓ cup water

¼ teaspoon allspice
¼ teaspoon salt
⅛ teaspoon dry mustard
1¼ pounds skinned chicken
  pieces

Combine garlic powder and paprika in a small foil packet; reserve. In a small saucepan heat remaining ingredients, except chicken, to boiling. Place chicken in a heatproof dish, with a cover, which can be transported. Marinate chicken uncovered, in refrigerator, at least one hour. Cover and transport. At picnic site, remove chicken from marinade; sprinkle with garlic powder and paprika. Grill, 4 inches from heat source, turning once, 40 minutes or until chicken is tender. Brush occasionally with marinade. Makes 2 servings.

DEVILED CHICKEN LEGS

1 garlic clove, cut
2 to 2½ pounds chicken legs, skin removed
1 teaspoon salt

¾ teaspoon pepper
¾ cup tomato puree
¾ cup prepared yellow mustard

Rub garlic over chicken; sprinkle with salt and pepper. Place in shallow 2-quart casserole with cover. Mix tomato puree and mustard. Pour over chicken in pan. Bake covered at 350°F. (moderate oven) 45 minutes or until chicken is done. Makes 4 servings.

ROAST TURKEY WITH ONION SAGE STUFFING

To New Englanders, Thanksgiving without sage stuffing and cranberry sauce would be as unthinkable as celebrating the day minus turkey and pumpkin.

1 ready-to-roast turkey (6-8 pounds)

Salt
2 cups chicken bouillon

Place turkey, breast side up, on rack in shallow pan. Season and roast at 325°F. for 2 to 2½ hours. Baste every 20 minutes with bouillon until done. Weigh portions and serve with stuffing. Makes 8 to 10 servings.

Onion Sage Stuffing

8 ounces onion, chopped
¼ cup finely diced celery
1½ teaspoons sage
½ cup chicken bouillon
2 slices enriched white bread, cut into ½-inch cubes

8 teaspoons imitation (or diet) margarine
2 teaspoons chopped fresh parsley
Dash salt

Lightly brown onions, celery and sage in nonstick skillet. Remove; add bouillon and remaining ingredients. Transfer to a casserole and bake 30 minutes (same oven as turkey). Divide into 4 equal portions and serve with turkey. Makes 4 servings.

ROAST CORNISH HEN WITH CHERRY SAUCE

1 1¼-pound oven-ready
  Cornish hen
1 cup chicken bouillon
2 tablespoons chopped celery

Salt and pepper to taste
1 cup cooked enriched rice
Cherry Sauce (recipe follows)

Place hen on a rack in small baking pan. Combine bouillon, celery and seasonings. Place in blender container; process until smooth. Bake hen at 400°F. about 40 minutes, or until tender. Baste occasionally with bouillon mixture. Remove skin. Serve on bed of rice with Cherry Sauce. Makes 2 servings.

Cherry Sauce

1 cup canned sweet pitted
  cherries, no sugar added

1 cup water
2 teaspoons lemon juice

Put all but 10 cherries in blender with water and lemon juice. Blend until smooth. Pour into small saucepan and simmer for a few minutes until thick. Add remainder of cherries and heat. If sauce becomes too thick, add a little more water. Makes 2 servings.

GREEN PEPPER STUFFED WITH VEAL AND SOYBEAN

1 medium green pepper, seeded
  and cut in half
Water
3 ounces cooked, dried soybeans
2 ounces cooked veal, diced
2 tablespoons chopped celery
¼ cup finely grated carrots
½ teaspoon dehydrated onion
  flakes, reconstituted in
  1 tablespoon water and drained

½ cup tomato puree
Salt and freshly ground pepper
  to taste
½ slice enriched white bread,
  made into crumbs

In a medium saucepan, boil green pepper in water for 3 minutes. Remove from water and drain. Combine soybeans, veal, celery, carrots and onion flakes in a medium mixing bowl. Add tomato puree and stir to combine. Season with salt and pepper. Fill pepper halves with as much of the mixture as will fit. Spoon the rest over the bottom of an individual heatproof casserole. Arrange filled peppers over soybean mixture. Sprinkle ½ the bread crumbs over each green pepper half. Bake for 5 to 7 minutes at 425°F. until bread crumbs begin to brown. Lower heat to 375°F. and continue baking for 15 minutes or until pepper is tender. Serve hot in casserole dish. Makes 1 serving.

NEW ORLEANS HAMBURGER "BORDELAISE"

1 teaspoon minced chives
1 teaspoon vegetable oil
¼ teaspoon garlic salt
⅛ teaspoon burgundy extract
   or bitters

Pepper to taste
4 to 6 ounces broiled boneless
   steak or ground beef patty

Combine first 5 ingredients and pour onto steak or patty just before serving. Makes 1 serving.

HEART STEW

1 pound, 2 ounces cooked beef
   heart, cut into thin slices,
   (see note)
1½ cups water
1 cup sliced celery

6 ounces onion, sliced
½ teaspoon chopped fresh
   parsley
1 garlic clove, minced or pressed
Salt and pepper to taste

Combine heart, water, celery, onions, parsley, garlic, salt and pepper; bring to boil; lower heat; cover and simmer 15 to 20 minutes or until meat is tender and vegetables are cooked. Makes 3 servings.

NOTE: Beef heart is best prepared by slow cooking. Wash well, remove fat, cut in half lengthwise to remove arteries, veins and blood. Place in deep pot, add salted water to cover (1 teaspoon salt for each quart of water). Cover and simmer until tender, about 3 to 4 hours.

KIDNEY STEW

2 ounces onion, finely chopped
1 garlic clove, minced or pressed
2 medium tomatoes, peeled
   and chopped
1 fresh hot chili pepper,
   seeded and chopped

1 tablespoon cider vinegar
Salt and freshly ground pepper
   to taste
12 ounces cooked lamb kidneys,
   thinly sliced

Cook onion and garlic in a nonstick skillet, stirring constantly until onion is tender, but not browned. Add tomatoes, chili pepper, vinegar, salt and pepper. Stir to combine and cook 5 minutes or until sauce is thickened and well blended. Add kidneys to sauce and heat through. Do not overcook as kidneys toughen very quickly. Divide evenly into 2 portions. Makes 2 servings.

MARYLAND SPICED HAM

Often served with cooked kale, collards or mustard greens.

1 pound cooked boneless ham, cut into 4 equal slices
3 strips lemon rind (2 inches long)
½ cup water

½ cup brown sugar replacement
2 tablespoons lemon juice
1 teaspoon grated lemon rind
¼ teaspoon cloves
¼ teaspoon mace or ginger

Bake ham on rack at 325°F. (slow oven) for ½ hour. Remove from stove and put lemon strips on top. Return to oven and continue baking for ½ hour longer. Meanwhile, combine water, brown sugar replacement, lemon juice, lemon rind, cloves and mace or ginger; simmer 5 minutes. When ham has been baked for a total of 1 hour, increase oven temperature to 400°F. (hot oven). Spoon sauce over ham every 10 minutes for ½ hour. Serve hot or cold. Makes 4 servings.

PLANTATION HAM LOAF

2 envelopes unflavored gelatin
¼ cup cold water
1 cup tomato juice
1 tablespoon lemon juice (or vinegar)
¾ teaspoon paprika

¼ teaspoon onion salt
¼ cup mayonnaise
2 medium green peppers, chopped
1 pound cooked boneless ham, finely diced

In top of double boiler, sprinkle gelatin over cold water. Add tomato juice, lemon juice, paprika and onion salt. Cook over boiling water until gelatin is dissolved. Set mixture aside to cool and thicken. Fold in mayonnaise, green pepper and ham. Transfer to 1-quart mold and refrigerate until firm. Makes 4 servings.

HAM AND GRITS WITH RED-EYE GRAVY

3 ounces cooked ham
½ cup brewed coffee

¾ cup fresh-cooked enriched hominy grits

Brown ham in preheated nonstick skillet, turning once. Pour brewed coffee over ham; bring to boil and serve with hot hominy grits. Makes 1 serving.

NEW ENGLAND BOILED DINNER

3 to 4 pounds lean beef roast (any inexpensive cut)
1 garlic clove, crushed
1 tablespoon pickling spice
5 to 6 peppercorns
4 cups (1 small head) cabbage, cut into 8 wedges

1½ pounds peeled small potatoes
2 cups diced turnips
8 ounces small white onions, parboiled
8 medium carrots
Parsley sprigs and chopped fresh parsley to garnish

Roast the beef on a rack in a 375°F. oven until done. Transfer to Dutch oven and cover with water. Bring rapidly to a boil. Add garlic, pickling spice and peppercorns. Cover and simmer for 3 hours or until beef is very tender. Remove meat from pot and keep warm. Add remaining ingredients, except garnish, to pot. Cover and cook briskly until tender, about 25 to 30 minutes. Drain vegetables and arrange around weighed, sliced meat. Makes 8 servings.

CHICKEN LIVER TURNOVERS

1½ cups chicken bouillon
2 cups sliced celery
2 tablespoons dehydrated onion flakes
1 pound chicken livers, cut into halves

2 ounces onion, chopped
1 teaspoon prepared mustard
½ teaspoon curry powder
2 slices enriched white bread, sliced in half horizontally

In medium saucepan combine bouillon, celery and onion flakes. Simmer until celery is tender. Process celery mixture in blender container until smooth; return to saucepan. In nonstick skillet, cook chicken livers, onion, mustard and curry powder, mashing livers, until thoroughly cooked. Stir 2 tablespoons celery sauce into chicken livers. Roll bread flat. Place ¼ of chicken liver filling on one half of each slice of bread. Moisten edge of bread with water; fold from corner so edges come together to form triangles. Place on nonstick baking sheet and seal edges with a wet fork. Bake at 400°F. for 15 to 20 minutes. Heat remaining celery sauce and serve over turnovers. Makes 2 servings.

SWEET-SOUR PORK BLADE STEAK

½ cup wine vinegar
1 tablespoon chopped chives
1 tablespoon diced pimento
1 teaspoon dehydrated onion
  flakes
½ teaspoon thyme

½ teaspoon salt
Artificial sweetener to equal
  6 teaspoons sugar
2 pork blade steaks (8 to 10
  ounces each), cut ¾-inch thick

Combine all ingredients except pork steaks in a shallow dish; place pork steaks in marinade. Cover; marinate in refrigerator 3 hours, turning occasionally. Place pork steaks on rack in broiler pan. Broil about 4 inches from heat source, basting with marinade; turn steak; baste. Pork must be served without any trace of pink either in the meat or in the juice. Makes 2 servings.

ORANGE BAKED PORK CHOPS

2 trimmed center-cut pork chops,
  4 to 5 ounces each
Salt and pepper to taste
2 ounces onion, sliced
¼ cup tomato juice
½ teaspoon grated lemon rind

½ cup orange sections, no
  sugar added, drained
  (reserve juice)
Dash marjoram
1 teaspoon chopped fresh
  parsley

Season chops and broil on a rack 4 inches from source of heat, 4 to 5 minutes on each side until brown. Turn off broiler and place chops in a small baking dish. Add onions, tomato juice and lemon rind to pork chops. Arrange orange sections on top; add juice. Sprinkle on marjoram. Bake covered at 400°F. for 15 to 20 minutes, or until onions are tender. Place pork chops on serving dish and top with sauce. Garnish with parsley. Makes 1 serving.

BAKED LAMB PATTIES WITH GREENLINGS

½ cup water
2 medium green apples,
  cored and sliced
¼ teaspoon cinnamon
⅛ teaspoon nutmeg

1 pound ground lamb
1 teaspoon grated lemon rind
1 teaspoon black pepper
1 teaspoon salt

In nonstick skillet combine water, apples, cinnamon and nutmeg. Cook over low heat, stirring frequently, 8 minutes or until apples are tender. Keep warm over boiling water or very low heat. Combine lamb, lemon rind, pepper and salt; mix well. Shape meat into an even number of patties, about 2½ x 1-inch each. Broil on rack about 4 inches from source of heat for 6 minutes, or until cooked throughout. Serve each portion of meat with ½ of apple mixture. Makes 2 servings.

SOYBEANS

This excellent bean is grown extensively in the U.S. An almost perfect food—unadulterated, highly nourishing, easy to digest, easy to grow and inexpensive—we added it to our Food Program several years ago. Soybeans are quite bland and take on the flavor of the other ingredients you serve with them.

In China, soybeans are known as the "food of the ancients" but in America, it's the young people who are "into" them. How about getting some soybeans into you?

SOYBEAN CUTLETS WITH TOMATO SAUCE

8 ounces cooked dried soybeans	¼ garlic clove, crushed
¼ cup cooked, finely chopped mushrooms	1 teaspoon Worcestershire
¼ cup finely chopped celery	1 teaspoon chopped fresh parsley
½ packet instant chicken broth and seasoning mix	½ cup tomato puree
1 teaspoon dehydrated onion flakes	Salt and pepper to taste
	¼ bay leaf

Puree beans in blender container, pushing down with rubber spatula as needed. Transfer to mixing bowl. Add mushrooms, celery, broth mix, onion flakes, garlic, Worcestershire, parsley and sufficient tomato puree to moisten. Season to taste. Shape into 2 patties. Bake at 375°F. 20 minutes in nonstick baking pan. Place bay leaf and remaining tomato puree in saucepan and simmer to blend flavors; season and serve over Cutlets. Makes 1 serving.

SOY SPINACH LOAF

8 ounces cooked, dried soybeans
¼ cup water
1 packet instant chicken broth and seasoning mix
1 teaspoon dehydrated onion flakes, reconstituted
Dash garlic powder
Dash thyme

Dash basil
½ cup cooked spinach, finely chopped
¼ cup cooked diced celery
1 slice whole wheat bread, made into crumbs
Salt and pepper to taste

Combine beans, water, chicken broth mix, onion flakes, garlic powder, thyme and basil in blender container. Process until smooth. Transfer to mixing bowl. Fold in spinach, celery, bread crumbs and season to taste. Turn into a small nonstick loaf pan and bake at 400°F. for 35 minutes. Makes 1 serving.

BUTTERNUT SQUASH-CHEESE SOUFFLE

8 ounces cooked, mashed butternut or other winter squash
¼ cup evaporated skimmed milk
2 ounces grated cheddar cheese

2 tablespoons margarine
Salt and pepper to taste
2 medium eggs, separated

Preheat oven to 350°F. In baking dish, combine squash with milk, cheese, margarine, salt and pepper. Add the well-beaten egg yolks. Beat egg whites until stiff but not dry and fold into the squash mixture. Set baking dish in pan of hot water in oven for 30 to 40 minutes. Makes 2 servings.

CAPE COD LUNCHEON SOUFFLE

6 ounces cooked and peeled potatoes
1 teaspoon dehydrated onion flakes
½ cup water

1 cup grated carrots
4 ounces cold, cooked fish, flaked
Salt and pepper to taste
2 medium eggs, separated

Preheat oven to 350°F. Process potatoes, onion flakes and water in blender container until thick and smooth. Remove to bowl; stir in carrots, fish, salt and pepper. Fold in slightly beaten yolks. Beat egg whites until stiff. Fold egg whites into fish mixture. Place in baking dish and set dish in larger pan with 1 inch warm water. Bake for 30 to 40 minutes. Makes 2 servings.

NEW ENGLAND BAKED LIMA BEANS

Mark Twain loved 'em.

4 cups fresh cooked lima beans or cowpeas
¾ cup tomato puree
3 tablespoons brown sugar replacement

1 tablespoon Worcestershire
½ teaspoon ginger
½ teaspoon dry mustard

Combine ingredients in baking dish or casserole. Bake at 375°F. (moderate oven) until lightly browned on top, about 1 hour. Makes 8 servings.

BAKED BEANS WITH FRUIT

To ingredients above, add 2 sliced medium apples, 4 fresh medium apricot halves, and ½ cup canned crushed pineapple, no sugar added. Arrange in layers, alternating with the seasoned beans. Bake as directed above. Makes 8 servings.

LANCASTER COUNTY CABBAGE*

Skim milk is sometimes substituted for the water.

4 cups shredded cabbage
½ cup boiling salted water
⅔ cup cottage cheese

¼ teaspoon celery seed
Salt and pepper to taste

In saucepan combine cabbage and boiling salted water. Cover and cook 5 minutes, until cabbage is barely tender. Do not drain. Stir in remaining ingredients and serve when cheese is melted. Makes 2 servings.

RHODE ISLAND APPLE-CARROT CASSEROLE

2 medium apples, pared, cored and sliced
½ cup cold water

2 cups cooked sliced carrots
4 teaspoons margarine
⅛ teaspoon cinnamon

Combine apples and water in a small saucepan; cover and cook until apples are tender. Drain and combine with remaining ingredients in a 1-quart casserole. Mix well. Bake at 350°F. for about 15 minutes. Makes 4 servings.

CAULIFLOWER-ORANGE RELISH

To serve with roast chicken or beef.

Boiling water
2 tablespoons fresh-squeezed lemon juice
4 cups cauliflower, broken into small florets
8 ounces onion, sliced and separated into rings
1 medium green pepper, seeded and cut into strips

1 cup white vinegar
¾ cup water
¾ teaspoon salt
8 peppercorns, crushed
½ teaspoon celery seed
½ teaspoon tarragon leaves
2 teaspoons fresh grated orange rind
4 small oranges

Pour boiling water and lemon juice over florets, onion rings and green pepper strips to cover; let stand while preparing vinegar mixture. Combine vinegar, water, salt and spices in saucepan. Grate rind from one of the 4 oranges to measure 2 teaspoons; add to vinegar mixture. Bring to boil; reduce heat and simmer 5 minutes. Peel oranges and cut into bite-size pieces; set aside. Drain water from cauliflower; add orange pieces. Toss lightly. Pour hot vinegar mixture over cauliflower mixture. Cool; cover and chill several hours or overnight. Stir occasionally to allow flavors to blend. Makes 8 servings.

KALE GREENS

You will need an enamel, stainless steel or ceramic pan. Do not use aluminum or iron for cooking kale as these metals darken the vegetable and make it bitter. Before measuring, separate stalks of kale, discard bruised tough leaves and heavy stems and ribs. Wash well.

2 cups kale
Boiling salted water
½ garlic clove, pressed
Imitation bacon-flavored salt to taste

Freshly ground pepper to taste
2 teaspoons margarine

In saucepan cover leaves with boiling salted water. Add garlic and cook until leaves are tender (5 to 10 minutes). Drain; chop coarsely. Season with bacon salt and pepper and stir in margarine. Mix and serve hot. Makes 2 servings.

LONG ISLAND PEAS AND POTATO STEW

12 ounces new potatoes, scrubbed
  clean
8 ounces frozen or fresh peas
1 cup boiling water
2 teaspoons dehydrated onion
  flakes

¾ teaspoon salt
¼ teaspoon pepper
2 teaspoons minced fresh
  parsley

In saucepan, combine ingredients except parsley. Bring to a boil, cover and simmer quickly until peas and potatoes are tender. Serve in soup bowls with pot "liquor." Sprinkle with parsley. Makes 4 servings.

YANKEE SKILLET SCALLOPED POTATOES

¾ cup water
Dash garlic powder
2 ounces onion, chopped
2 packets chicken broth and
  seasoning mix
1 tablespoon chopped pimento

2 teaspoons chopped fresh
  parsley
Salt and pepper to taste
3 ounces boiled potato, thinly
  sliced

In small skillet, heat water, garlic powder and onions until onions are tender. Stir in remaining ingredients except potatoes. Layer potatoes over onion mixture. Cover and simmer until potatoes are heated. Remove cover and continue cooking until liquid is reduced. Makes 1 serving.

BAKED POTATO CHIPS WITH PEELS

For fish and chips . . .

12 ounces potatoes, with skin
Salt or barbecue salt, pepper
  and paprika to taste

Wash potatoes, but do not peel. Wipe dry. Cut potatoes into slices about ¼-inch thick and arrange one layer deep on shallow nonstick baking sheet. Sprinkle with salt, pepper and paprika (or other seasonings to taste). Bake in hot oven (400°F. to 425°F.) until potatoes are browned, about 10 minutes each side. Makes 4 servings.

MAINE PUMPKIN PUDDING

¼ cup water
1 envelope unflavored gelatin
¼ cup boiling water
4 ounces cooked or canned
  pumpkin (see note)
⅔ cup nonfat dry milk

¼ teaspoon pumpkin pie spice
  or to taste
¼ teaspoon maple extract
Artificial sweetener to equal
  6 teaspoons sugar
6 to 8 ice cubes

Pour water into blender container. Sprinkle gelatin over water to soften. Add boiling water. Process about 30 seconds. Add remaining ingredients except ice cubes and process until smooth. Add ice cubes one at a time processing after each addition, until all the cubes are used. Pour into dessert glasses. Serve immediately or chill, if desired. Makes 4 servings.

NOTE: To cook raw pumpkin, cut it in half, remove seeds and stringy parts, and cut off rind. Cut pumpkin into pieces and steam over low heat for 25 to 30 minutes. Pumpkin has its own water, and in a heavy pot, over a low flame, no added water should be required. (If necessary, add just enough water to keep it from burning.) Drain the cooked pumpkin well, then puree it in a food mill or processor. Cooked pumpkin can be frozen for future use. Weigh it in 4-ounce portions and defrost as needed.

PUREE OF SORREL

To serve with fish.

4 cups cleaned and stemmed
  sorrel (sour grass)
Chicken bouillon

4 teaspoons margarine
¼ cup evaporated skimmed milk

Steam sorrel in steamer basket placed in pot so sorrel does not touch water. When very tender, drain thoroughly and puree (through food mill, in blender or in food processor) until very smooth. Put into saucepan with just enough chicken bouillon to keep it from burning; heat through; remove from heat and stir in margarine and evaporated skimmed milk. Makes 4 servings.

SUCCOTASH

American Indian origin.

1 cup cooked whole-kernel corn
1 cup cooked fresh lima beans
2 tablespoons margarine
2 teaspoons dehydrated onion flakes

½ teaspoon salt
⅛ teaspoon pepper
¼ cup evaporated skimmed milk
Chopped pimento

Combine all ingredients, except pimento, in a double boiler. Heat over, not in, boiling water. Garnish with pimento. Makes 4 servings.

TOMATO SCALLOP*

4 medium tomatoes
2 medium green peppers, cut into long strips, ½-inch wide
4 ounces sharp cheddar cheese, grated

2 slices enriched white bread, made into crumbs
Salt, paprika to taste
4 teaspoons imitation (or diet) margarine

Peel tomatoes and cut into thick slices (about 4 per tomato). In casserole arrange layers of half of the tomatoes, pepper strips, cheese, bread crumbs, salt and paprika. Dot evenly with margarine. Repeat layers. Bake at 425°F. until crumbs are brown, about 30 minutes. Makes 4 servings.

HOLIDAY WILD RICE DRESSING

To serve as a side dish with roast chicken, turkey or wild game.

1 cup uncooked wild rice
3½ cups chicken stock (see page ix)
1 cup diced celery
1 cup sliced mushrooms
4 ounces diced onion or shallots

2 cups cooked brown or enriched white rice
¼ teaspoon sage
2 teaspoons sherry or wine extract (optional)

Rinse wild rice in water several times. Bring chicken stock to a boil. Add wild rice. Cover tightly and cook over low heat, about 30 minutes. Drain. Measure 3 cups cooked wild rice, reserving liquid. (Remaining rice may be frozen.) Brown celery, mushrooms and onions in nonstick skillet. Combine with wild rice and brown or white rice, sage and optional wine extract. Mix well, adding reserved liquid to desired moistness. Bake in casserole in oven with roasting chicken or at 350°F. for about 30 minutes. Makes 10 servings.

ZIPPY ZUCCHINI

4 cups sliced zucchini, cut in
  ½-inch slices
1 teaspoon salt
¾ cup water
3 tablespoons chopped fresh
  parsley
1 tablespoon dehydrated onion
  flakes

1 tablespoon freshly squeezed
  lemon juice
¼ teaspoon freshly grated
  lemon rind
4 teaspoons margarine

In covered skillet, cook zucchini with salt in water until just tender (8 to 10 minutes). Drain. Add parsley, onion flakes, lemon juice and lemon rind. Heat quickly, turning zucchini slices. Transfer to 4 individual vegetable plates and stir 1 teaspoon margarine into each serving of vegetable. Serve at once. Makes 4 servings.

USING NATIVE GREENS

You can pick these from your garden or sometimes find them in New England or New York markets.

1. Fiddleheads. Ostrich, regal, royal or cinnamon fern are some of the names by which they are known. In very early spring, you can see them in the woods, curled tips unfolding as they mature. Pick them in the wild only if you are certain that state conservation laws do not forbid it. Of course in your garden this restriction does not apply. Break off about 5 inches of the tender top (don't pull up roots). Remove the wooly coating. Wash 1 cup of the ferns, bunch them together and steam until tender in steaming basket set above water (so water does not touch greens). While vegetable is still hot, stir into it salt, fresh pepper, 2 teaspoons margarine and ½ teaspoon lemon juice. Makes 1 serving.

2. Watercress. In spring, you can find fresh bunches of the "water weed" in the market. Wash very well and crisp in cold water. Shake dry and serve with salt and pepper, to be eaten out of hand. Maybe

with a bowl of hot bouillon if there's a chill in the air, or with chilled tomato juice.

3. Dandelions. Cut away the tough roots and any coarse leaves. Soak 1 cup leaves in salt water for several hours, changing water at least once. Steam until leaves are wilted. Season. Makes 1 serving.

CALIFORNIA CAESAR SALAD

A popular West Coast salad, modified to the Food Program requirements. The lettuce should be washed, dried, wrapped in towel and kept crisp in refrigerator. If watercress droops, crisp it in ice-cold water and keep in water bath until ready to serve. Then dry and use.

1 tablespoon vegetable oil
½ garlic clove, crushed
1 teaspoon Worcestershire
1 teaspoon lemon juice
Dash each of salt, pepper and dry mustard
Assorted salad greens (romaine, escarole, Boston or Bibb, and watercress)

1 ounce freshly grated Parmesan cheese
1 slice enriched white bread, toasted, cut into cubes and dried
1 medium egg, coddled for 1 minute

In jar with cover, combine oil, garlic, Worcestershire, lemon juice, salt, pepper and mustard; shake well. Tear greens into individual salad or soup bowl. Sprinkle with Parmesan cheese, bread cubes and contents of jar. Add egg and toss lightly to mix well. Serve immediately. Makes 1 serving.

HEARTS OF LETTUCE WITH RUSSIAN DRESSING

The salad served in restaurants all over America.

1 tablespoon mayonnaise
1 tablespoon tomato paste
1½ teaspoons hot pepper sauce
1 teaspoon chopped chives

1 teaspoon finely chopped pimento
¼ head lettuce, cut in wedge (remove wilted outer leaves)

Combine all ingredients except lettuce; mix well. Serve over lettuce. Makes 2 servings.

TOSSED GREEN SALAD WITH MOHAWK DRESSING

Lots of delicious greens are on the American market throughout the year. Vary the greens and use what the greengrocer offers (otherwise, he'll stop buying anything but iceberg). Try colorful peppery watercress. Curly endive with its tangy taste and crunchy texture. Delicate light leaf lettuce. Firm flavorful romaine. And, of course, soft and velvety Boston and Bibb.

1 head Boston lettuce
½ head romaine lettuce

1 bunch or bag radishes, sliced
Mohawk Dressing (recipe follows)

Rinse lettuce, wrap loosely in a clean damp towel and chill. Just before serving break lettuce into bite-size pieces. Add radish slices. Toss. Place on a chilled salad plate and serve with Mohawk Dressing. Makes 4 servings.

Mohawk Dressing

¼ cup wine vinegar
2 tablespoons tomato paste
2 tablespoons vegetable oil
1 garlic clove

1 teaspoon chopped chives
¼ teaspoon paprika
Freshly ground pepper to taste

Combine all ingredients in blender container. Process about 3 minutes. Serve over Tossed Green Salad. Makes 4 servings.

SPICED TOMATO ASPIC

3 cups tomato juice, divided
2 envelopes unflavored gelatin
1 tablespoon lemon juice or
vinegar
1 teaspoon prepared horseradish
1 teaspoon celery seed

1 teaspoon Worcestershire
½ teaspoon onion powder
Dash cayenne pepper
Lettuce leaves
Parsley sprigs (optional)

Pour 1 cup tomato juice into medium saucepan; sprinkle with gelatin; heat slowly until gelatin dissolves. Remove from heat; add seasonings and remaining tomato juice. Pour into 6 individual salad molds. Chill until set. Unmold on lettuce leaves. Garnish with parsley, if desired. Makes 6 servings.

DRIED APPLE SLICES (Schnitz)

A Pennsylvania Dutch schnitzing party was as much a community event as the quilting bee. Like other crafts of an earlier America, quilting is back, and now you can bring back schnitzing. To rehydrate apple, cover with water and let stand several hours. Use the water in which the apple soaked.

8 medium apples, peeled and
   cored

2 quarts water
2 tablespoons lemon juice

Cut each apple into 8 thin wedges. As apples are sliced, dip them into a large bowl containing water and lemon juice. (This prevents discoloration.) Let stand 1 minute. Drain, discard liquid, and dry slices immediately. Place apple slices on baking racks or sheets and place in oven set at 200°F. Let bake until fruit is dry, 4 to 5 hours. Cool and store in cool dry place, or pack in freezer paper (8 wedges = 1 apple) and seal tightly; store in tightly closed tin can. Makes 8 servings.

APRICOT BROWN BETTY

16 canned apricot halves, no
   sugar added, or 8 fresh ripe
   medium apricots, sliced
½ cup apricot liquid (or use
   half lemon juice, half water)
2 slices enriched white bread,
   cut into small cubes
4 teaspoons margarine, melted

3 tablespoons brown sugar
   replacement
1 teaspoon cinnamon
¼ teaspoon allspice
¼ teaspoon salt
1 teaspoon grated lemon rind or
   vanilla extract

Combine all ingredients and mix well. Bake in covered pudding dish in moderate (350°F.) oven for 50 to 60 minutes. Makes 4 servings.

PLUM BROWN BETTY

Substitute 8 medium plums for the apricot halves and use 3 tablespoons lemon juice and 3 tablespoons water. Follow recipe above. Makes 4 servings.

APPLE STRAWBERRY CHIFFON

¼ cup cold water
1 envelope unflavored gelatin
⅓ cup boiling water
½ cup whole strawberries
  (reserve 2 strawberries)
¼ teaspoon strawberry extract

⅔ cup nonfat dry milk
Artificial sweetener to equal
  8 teaspoons sugar
8 to 10 ice cubes
½ medium apple, pared and diced

In blender container, sprinkle gelatin over cold water to soften. Add boiling water; process until gelatin dissolves. Add strawberries, extract, milk and sweetener. Process until smooth. Add ice cubes, one at a time, processing after each addition. Pour into medium mixing bowl. Immediately fold apple into mixture and spoon into 2 dessert glasses. Top each with a whole strawberry and chill. Makes 2 servings.

BANANA PEACH PUDDING*

1 slice enriched white bread, diced
½ medium banana, peeled and
  diced
1 medium peach, peeled and diced
2 medium eggs

¼ cup evaporated skimmed milk
½ teaspoon vanilla extract
Artificial sweetener to equal
  8 teaspoons sugar
1 cup skim milk

Place bread, banana and peach in a 1-quart ovenproof dish. Combine eggs, evaporated skimmed milk, extract and sweetener in a mixing bowl and beat well. Heat skim milk over low heat, but *do not boil,* and gradually add to egg mixture. Pour over bread and fruit mixture. Set ovenproof dish in a pan of hot water and bake at 350°F. for 25 minutes or until set. May be served hot or cold. Makes 2 servings.

CRANBERRY SHERBET PARFAIT

3 cups cranberries
1½ cups water
2 teaspoons unflavored gelatin
⅓ cup water

Artificial sweetener to equal
  ½ cup sugar or to taste
Whipped Topping (see page x)

Reserve 6 berries. Heat cranberries and water in medium saucepan just until cranberry skins pop open. Using a wooden spoon or food mill, strain cranberries into shallow pan, discarding skins. Soften gelatin in the ⅓ cup water. Stir into hot cranberry puree; add sweetener; cool ½ hour. Place in freezer; freeze until firm. Put into a chilled bowl. Using an electric mixer, beat until thick and mushy. Spoon into parfait or dessert dishes alternating with Whipped Topping (end with Whipped Topping). Cover; return to freezer. Remove from freezer 10 to 15 minutes before serving. Garnish each parfait with reserved berry. Makes 6 servings.

PINEAPPLE ON PINEAPPLE STRAWBERRY COMPOTE

You can't improve on fresh pineapple picked truly ripe and sweet and served in its natural state, but if the pineapple you bought is immature, here's one way to conceal it.

1 cup strawberries
2 tablespoons water
½ teaspoon vanilla extract

½ cup canned crushed pineapple,
    no sugar added
1 fresh medium pineapple, cored,
    pared, cubed

Process strawberries, water and vanilla in blender container until smooth; combine with crushed pineapple in large bowl. Stir in fresh pineapple. Chill and divide equally. Makes 6 servings.

BANANA NUT BROWNIES*

4 medium eggs, separated
⅓ cup nonfat dry milk
2 tablespoons chocolate extract
2 teaspoons almond extract
Artificial sweetener to equal
    ½ cup sugar

4 ripe medium bananas, quartered
4 slices enriched white bread,
    made into crumbs

Place egg yolks, milk, extracts and sweetener in blender container. Process at medium speed to combine. Gradually add banana pieces and continue to process until very smooth. Transfer mixture to large bowl. Fold in bread crumbs until uniformly combined. Beat egg whites until stiff but not dry. Fold into batter. Pour into 8-inch square nonstick baking pan. Bake at 375°F. for 1 hour and 15 minutes. Makes 4 servings.

CHOCOLATE LAYER CAKE WITH VANILLA FILLING*

4 medium eggs, separated
¼ cup water
7 teaspoons chocolate extract
Artificial sweetener to equal
   10 teaspoons sugar

4 slices enriched white bread,
   made into fine crumbs
⅓ cup nonfat dry milk
Vanilla Filling (recipe follows)

Place yolks in mixing bowl. Add water, extract and sweetener. Whip until frothy. Add bread crumbs and milk; mix. Beat egg whites until stiff peaks form. Carefully fold egg whites into yolk mixture. Prepare an 8x8x2-inch baking pan by spraying it with release agent. Pour batter into pan and bake at 350°F. for 1 hour or until a toothpick inserted in the center comes out dry. Remove from pan and place on rack to cool. Slice in half horizontally. Spread one layer with Vanilla Filling. Replace top layer. Makes 4 servings.

Vanilla Filling

¼ cup unsalted margarine
⅓ cup nonfat dry milk
Artificial sweetener to equal
   6 teaspoons sugar

1 teaspoon vanilla extract

In a small bowl cream margarine. Add milk and sweetener and beat until fluffy. Add extract slowly and contine beating to blend. Spread evenly between cake layers. Makes 4 servings.

MOCHA CHEESE CAKE*

1 envelope unflavored gelatin
¾ cup water
⅔ cup cottage cheese
⅓ cup nonfat dry milk

1 teaspoon chocolate extract
½ teaspoon instant coffee
Artificial sweetener to equal
   6 teaspoons sugar

Sprinkle gelatin over ¼ cup cold water in blender container. Heat remaining water to boiling; add to softened gelatin; process at low speed until gelatin dissolves. Add remaining ingredients; process at medium speed and then high speed until smooth. Pour, dividing evenly, into 2 individual 1-cup serving dishes; chill. Makes 2 servings.

'TIS—'TAINT FRUIT CAKE

⅓ cup nonfat dry milk
¼ cup chilled orange juice
½ medium apple, cored and
  chopped
¾ cup red currants
2 teaspoons lemon juice
¼ teaspoon cinnamon

⅛ teaspoon maple extract
⅛ teaspoon vanilla extract
Artificial sweetener to equal
  6 teaspoons sugar
2 slices enriched white bread,
  toasted and grated

Combine milk and orange juice in a large bowl and whip until stiff, using a hand or electric mixer. Fold in remaining ingredients. Line a small loaf pan with wax paper. Transfer all ingredients to pan and bake at 350°F. for 1 hour. Remove and cool thoroughly. Divide in half. Makes 2 servings.

BLACK BOTTOM CHEESECAKE*

⅓ cup unflavored gelatin, divided
1 cup cold water, divided
2 cups boiling water, divided
4 cups canned pineapple chunks,
  no sugar added, divided
2⅔ cups nonfat dry milk, divided
Artificial sweetener to equal
  ½ cup sugar, divided
1 tablespoon grated lemon rind,
  divided

2 teaspoons vanilla extract,
  divided
2 tablespoons unsweetened cocoa
Few drops brown food coloring
  (if desired)
2⅔ cups skim milk ricotta cheese,
  divided

In blender container, soften 8 teaspoons gelatin in ½ cup cold water. Add 1 cup boiling water; process until gelatin dissolves. Add half the pineapple, milk, sweetener, lemon rind, vanilla and all of the cocoa and food coloring. Process until smooth. Transfer to a large mixing bowl; beat in half the cheese with a wire whisk or rotary mixer. Pour into 9x3-inch spring form pan, reserving ½ cup for decoration. Place pan in refrigerator until almost firm. Repeat above procedure with remaining ingredients but do not reserve any mixture. Pour over chocolate layer; refrigerate until slightly firm. Place reserved chocolate mixture in a pastry bag with a plain tip. Draw 3 circles, one inside the other. With the tip of a knife, from the outside to the center, drag the knife through the circles to make pointed designs. Refrigerate until firm. Makes 8 servings.

COUNTRY SPONGE CAKE*

4 medium eggs, separated
4 slices enriched white bread,
  made into fine crumbs
⅔ cup nonfat dry milk
Artificial sweetener to equal
  20 teaspoons sugar

1 teaspoon vanilla extract
½ teaspoon lemon extract
½ teaspoon orange extract

Preheat oven to 350°F. In a small bowl, beat egg whites until stiff but not dry. In medium bowl, beat egg yolks until thick and lemon colored; stir in remaining ingredients except whites. Fold egg whites into yolk mixture. Pour into a 10-inch nonstick tube pan. Bake for 30 to 35 minutes. Makes 4 servings.

CHERRY YOGURT POPS

1 cup plain yogurt
20 large or 30 small frozen
  pitted cherries

1 teaspoon fresh lemon juice
Artificial sweetener to equal
  6 teaspoons sugar

Combine all ingredients in blender container and process until smooth. Divide evenly into 4 plastic freezer containers. Freeze until crystals form. Insert wooden skewer in center of each. Freeze until firm. Remove from containers. Makes 4 servings.

COLD COFFEE "SOUFFLE"

2 envelopes unflavored gelatin
½ cup water
2¼ cups skim milk
3 medium eggs, separated
Artificial sweetener to equal
  ½ cup sugar

4 teaspoons instant coffee
1 teaspoon salt
1 teaspoon vanilla extract
¼ teaspoon cream of tartar

In top of double boiler, sprinkle gelatin over water to soften. Add milk, egg yolks, sweetener, coffee, salt and vanilla. Place over boiling water; cook, stirring constantly, until mixture thickens slightly. Chill until the consistency of unbeaten egg white. Beat egg whites until frothy; add cream of tartar. Continue beating until stiff peaks form. Fold egg whites into coffee mixture. Pour into a pretty soufflé dish. Chill until firm. Unmold. Makes 3 servings.

CHOCOLATE FROTH

1 cup water
2 teaspoons unsweetened cocoa
⅓ cup nonfat dry milk
½ cup evaporated skimmed milk

Artificial sweetener to equal
  8 teaspoons sugar
4 ice cubes

Bring water to a boil; stir in cocoa until dissolved. Place in blender container or food processor fitted with steel blade; add remaining ingredients, except ice cubes; process. Add ice cubes, one at a time, processing after each addition until crushed. Chill. Divide evenly. Makes 2 servings.

LEMON MERINGUE PUDDING*

1 medium egg, separated
1 cup lemon-lime flavored
  dietetic soda
2 tablespoons lemon juice

1 envelope unflavored gelatin
Artificial sweetener to equal
  2 teaspoons sugar

In small saucepan, combine egg yolk, dietetic soda, lemon juice and gelatin. Cook over low heat, stirring, until gelatin dissolves and lemon mixture thickens slightly (do not boil). Pour into an individual soufflé dish; cool. Beat egg white and artificial sweetener until stiff but not dry. Place mounds of egg white on lemon mixture; spread to edge of dish. With back of spoon, pull up points on meringue. Bake in preheated oven, at 425°F. 3 to 4 minutes or until slightly browned. Makes 1 serving.

Metric Conversion Table

WEIGHT . . . .

To Change	*to*	*Multiply by*
Ounces	Grams	30.0
Pounds	Kilograms	0.45
Grams	Ounces	0.035
Kilograms	Pounds	2.2

VOLUME . . . .

To Change	*to*	*Multiply by*
Teaspoons	Milliliters	5.0
Tablespoons	Milliliters	15.0
Fluid Ounces	Milliliters	30.0
Cups	Liters	0.24
Pints	Liters	0.47
Quarts	Liters	0.95
Gallons	Liters	3.8
Milliliters	Fluid Ounces	0.03
Liters	Pints	2.1
Liters	Quarts	1.06
Liters	Gallons	0.26

Index

[380]

Mulligatawny, 167
Mushroom, Sizzling, 73
Navy Bean, 334-335
Oyster, 74
Pasta and Potato, 189
Pea Quebec Style, 55
Pepper Pot, Philadelphia, 334
Potato and Kale, 279
Potato and Radish Puree, 102
Pumpkin, 63
Scotch Broth, 41
Soybean Vegetable, 333
Split Pea, 167-168
Spring Vegetable, 104
Turnip–Top, "Creamy" Green, 273
Vegetable, 157
Vegetable with Milk, 291
Vegetable, Thick "Creamy," 299
Vermicelli and Zucchini, 191
Watercress, 103-104
Winter Melon, 74
Yogurt, Sweet, 259
see also Chowders; Consommés
Soups, Cold
Jellied Beef Bouillon, 41
Jellied "Wine" Consommé, 102
Malaga Gazpacho, 309
Seville Gazpacho, 309
Soybeans, 354
Cutlets with Tomato Sauce, 354
Salad, 26
and Spinach Loaf, 355
and Veal Stuffed Green Pepper, 349-350
Vegetable Soup, 333
Soy Sauce
Anise Beef, 85
–Mustard, 84
with Radish, 239-240
Spaghetti
Celery, 222
Celery and Fettucini, 214
Chicken Livers, 211
with Meatballs, 207-208
Twists with Tuna, 197
Spanakopita, 158
Spiced Fruit Sauce, 15
Spiced Grapes, 254
Spiced Grilled Beef, 47
Spiced Oyster Plant Salad, 170
Spiced Tomato Aspic, 363
Spicy Banana Sauce, 172
Spinach
and Bean and Shrimp, 301
and Cheese Pie, 158
and Cheese Ring, 57
Consommé, 102
"Creamed," Garlic, 264
and Egg and Cheese Soup, 190
and Egg Salad, 50
and Lentil Soup, 259
and Mushroom Salad with Poppy Seed
Dressing, 27
Pancakes, 178

with Peppery Sauce, Peking Style, 95
Pudding, 193
Salad with Mustard Dressing, 225
and Soy Loaf, 355
and Tuna Loaf, 196-197
–Tuna Omelet, 192
Split Pea Soup, 167-168
Sponge Cakes
Country, 369
Roll, 286-287
Steamed, 98
Tangerine, 27
Spring Salad Bowl with Buttermilk Dressing, 329
Spring Vegetable Soup, 104
Sprouting Beans, 89-90
Squash
–Cheese Soufflé, 355
Maple, Stuffed with Frankfurters, 55
Tsimiss, 180
Squashed Radishes, 239
Staten Island Chicken Salad, 346-347
Steak
Charcoal–Boiled Szechuan, 86
with Peppercorns, 124-125
Steamed Cucumbers, 91-92
Steamed Eggplant, 93
Steamed Egg Pudding, 236-237
Steamed Eggs with Fish, 78
Steamed Eggs with Vegetables, 78
Steamed Fish with Ginger Topping, 79-80
Steamed Sponge Cake, 98
Stews
Black Bean and Rice, 251
Calaloo, 63
Chicken and Veal, 301
Couscous, 5
Finnan Haddie, 43
Fish, Brittany Style, 109
Fish, Ligurian, 194
Five–Fragrant Beef, 82
Green Beans Beira, 284
Heart, 350
Hunter's, 275
Kidney, 350
Lamb, 127
Lamb with Okra, 161
Lamb and Vegetable, 262
Lentil and Tomato, 171
Mackerel, Brittany Style, 112
Octopus, 311
Peas and Potato, Long Island, 356
Salmon and Green Bean, 195
Scotia, 56
Spanish, 317
Split Pea, 167-168
Tomato, 284
Tripe, 4-5
Vegetable Hotch Potch, 50
see also Gulyas; Ragout
Stew–Salad, Vegetable, 305
Stir–Cooked Chicken Livers with Bamboo Shoots and Water Chestnuts, 89